# TRANSPACIFIC ANTIRACISM

# TRANSPACIFIC ANTIRACISM

*Afro-Asian Solidarity in Twentieth-Century*
*Black America, Japan, and Okinawa*

Yuichiro Onishi

NEW YORK UNIVERSITY PRESS
*New York and London*

NEW YORK UNIVERSITY PRESS
New York and London
www.nyupress.org

References to Internet websites (URLs) were accurate at the time of writing.
Neither the author nor New York University Press is responsible for URLs
that may have expired or changed since the manuscript was prepared.

Library of Congress Cataloging-in-Publication Data
Onishi, Yuichiro.
Transpacific antiracism : Afro-Asian solidarity in twentieth-century
Black America, Japan, and Okinawa / Yuichiro Onishi.
pages   cm
Includes bibliographical references and index.
ISBN 978-0-8147-6264-6 (cl : alk. paper)
1. African Americans—Race identity—History—20th century.
2. African Americans—Relations with Japanese—History—20th century.
3. African Americans—Foreign public opinion, Japanese.  4. Du Bois, W. E. B.
(William Edward Burghardt), 1868–1963—Political and social views.
5.  Anti-racism—United States—History—20th century.  6. Anti-racism—
Japan—History—20th century.  7. African Americans—Study and teaching—
Japan—History—20th century.  8. Okinawa-shi (Japan)—Race relations—
History—20th century.    I. Title.
E185.625.O55 2013
305.896'073052—dc23            2012038064

New York University Press books are printed on acid-free paper,
and their binding materials are chosen for strength and durability.
We strive to use environmentally responsible suppliers and materials
to the greatest extent possible in publishing our books.

Manufactured in the United States of America

c  10 9 8 7 6 5 4 3 2 1
p  10 9 8 7 6 5 4 3 2 1

# CONTENTS

## ACKNOWLEDGMENTS

I consider myself a fortunate one to have both Peter Rachleff and David Roediger, great historians of race and labor, as my mentors. This fortuitousness, I have come to appreciate, has much to do with the community of thinkers, writers, and activists from which both Peter and Dave came that I found nearly two decades ago. Upon entry, I latched onto the ways of studying and writing U.S. history tightly bound up with "history making." I am deeply indebted to them for their visions, advice, close reading, utmost sensitivity toward the writer's craft, and above all unwavering solidarity. Equally pivotal to my intellectual development were Jeani O'Brien, Erika Lee, and Ted Farmer. Their enthusiasm kept me above water while I completed my dissertation at the University of Minnesota, and their feedback on my work came without missing a beat to help me achieve analytical sharpness.

Through the years, funding for research came from multiple sources at the University of Minnesota: the Interdisciplinary Center for the Study of Global Change; the Race, Ethnicity, and Migration Seminar; the Department of History; the Program in Asian American Studies; the Office of Equity and Diversity; and the College of Liberal Arts. Also vital were the research award from the Professional Staff Congress at The City University of New York and participation in the Network Summer Faculty Enrichment Program at New York University, specifically the seminar titled Modern Jazz and the Political Imagination convened by Robin D. G. Kelley. Furthermore, comments and research assistance from Shinoda Toru, Paul Barclay, David Tucker, Furukawa Hiromi, Furukawa Tetsushi, Takamine Tomokazu, John Russell, and staff at the Center for the Study of Cooperative Human Relations at Saitama University and the Okinawa City Hall opened up a new horizon of possibilities. My dear friend Toru-san continues to be my interlocutor in all aspects of a study in transpacific racial formation and transformation, and I remain, above all, indebted to Professor Furukawa Hiromi (1927–2012), who pioneered the transpacific approach to the study of African American history when others paid little attention.

My first two years as a graduate student in history at the University of Minnesota were foundational. I took seminars taught by Angela Dillard, David W. Noble, the late Rudolph J. Vecoli, Rose Brewer, and David Roediger, through which I not only matured intellectually but also found a group of fellow graduate students who exhibited commitment to keep race studies in the folds of social movements. With much respect, I am thinking fondly of Jennifer Guglielmo, Alex Lubin, May Fu, Adrian Gaskins, Tom Sabatini, Todd Michney, Marjorie Bryer, Jay Wendelberger, Ben Maegi, Mark Soderstrom, Robert Frame, Matt Basso, and Deborah Henry. I also met along the way a number of wonderful peers and friends. My thanks extend to Kazuyo Kubo, Taku Suzuki, the late Albert Matongo, the late Josie Fowler, Joel Helfrich, Seulky and Michael McInneshin, Michael Lansing, Brad Jarvis, David LaVigne, Mike Sizer, Andy Carhart, Matt Carhart, Jason Eden, and Lisong Liu.

My first academic appointment was in the Center for Ethnic Studies at Borough of Manhattan Community College of The City University of New York. I met fantastic colleagues who mentored me, offered first-rate support, and extended kindness. I want to especially thank Segundo Pantoja, Ana Daniels, Michelle Rief, Ron Doviak, Chris Stamos, Hsing-Lih Chou, Rebecca Hill, Khalil Koromantee, Peter Nguyen, James Blake, John Montanez, and Michael Gillespie. I am also very thankful to my students. Their passion for learning challenged me and made me want to become a better teacher. Returning to the University of Minnesota, I entered the new and old networks of support. I thank my colleagues in the Department of African American & African Studies and the Asian American Studies Program: Walt Jacobs, Charlene Hayes, Adrienne Todd-Walden, Rose Brewer, John Wright, Keletso Atkins, Vicki Coifman, Keith Mayes, Alexs Pate, Njeri Githire, Tade Okediji, Angaluki Muaka, Scott Redd, Jigna Desai, Erika Lee, Josephine Lee, Karen Ho, Rich Lee, Lisa Park, Teresa Swartz, Mai Na Lee, Kale Fajardo, and Saengmany Ratsabout. Encouragement and support also came from Hy Berman, David Pellow, Catherine Squires, and Zenzele Isoke. I particularly want to extend my thanks to Rose, Jigna, and David for mentorship.

During the past four years, David Roediger, Peter Rachleff, Scott Kurashige, Sophia Kim, and anonymous reviewers at NYU Press and the University of Minnesota Press read the entire manuscript closely, offering criticisms and suggestions to help me achieve clarity and coherence, both conceptually and analytically. For this, my book is stronger. I also want to express my gratitude to Ben Maegi, David LaVigne, Paul Barclay, George Lipsitz, Gerald Horne, Nikhil Pal Singh, V. P. Franklin, Ernest Allen Jr., Jeffrey Perry, Shinoda Toru, Furukawa Tetsushi, David Haekwon Kim, Mark Nowak, John Wright, Jigna Desai, Josephine Lee, Teresa Swartz, Kale Fajardo, Kelly Quinn, and the fellow participants of The Graduate Center/CUNY's Faculty Fellowship Publications Program convened by Virginia Sanchez-Korrol. At different stages, each one of them read or heard a portion of my work and offered comments and encouragement. Finally, working with NYU Press, I found much-needed guidance. Eric Zinner, Ciara McLaughlin, and Alicia Kirin Nadkarni have helped elevate my work to a whole new dimension. I am also grateful for Andrew Katz's copyediting and Robert Swanson's indexing in the final stage of manuscript preparation.

Throughout, my father, Onishi Hiroshi, and my sister, Hoshiai Mamiko, in Japan never cast doubt. Steadfast support also came from Onishi Keiko, Hoshiai Hiroshi, Takeshi and Hana, Yumiko *obachama*, my grandmother Ichikawa Michiko, Yamaguchi Kazuko and Hiroichi, and above all the late Onishi Kiichi and Tomiko, my paternal grandparents, who lived a very long life. The entire Mase family has been generous with me, and Mase Shinobu and Takeshi will be my lifelong friends. So will Yohji Shionoya, who is, like me, a transplant in Minnesota. Finally, I have known the Kim family—Janice, Dan, Greg, and *omonim*, now my mother-in-law—for a long time, nearly half my life. Your kindness means so much to me.

My wife, Sophia, from the very beginning, when we first met at Macalester, has been integral to my journey. A superb writer who pays as much attention to all-too-often-overlooked details as tone and texture in both life and writing, especially how they are all layered, the markings of her influence in my thinking have acquired gravity over the years. I owe my personal and intellectual formations to her. Now with our son we continue to widen the path we have always traveled with much anticipation. This book is in loving memory of my mother,

Onishi Chieko (1946–1990), and dedicated, with great love, to Epony and Romare, my wellspring of happiness.

Some portions from individual chapters have appeared previously in different versions. I would like to thank the following publishers and individuals for granting me permission to reprint: "The New Negro of the Pacific: How African Americans Forged Cross-Racial Solidarity with Japan, 1917–1922," *Journal of African American History* 92:2 (2007): 191–213, © 2007 Association for the Study of African American Life and History (ASALH), reprinted with the permission of ASALH and V. P. Franklin; "The Presence of (Black) Liberation in Okinawan Freedom: Transnational Moments, 1968–1972," in *Extending the Diaspora: New Histories of Black People*, edited by Dawne Y. Curry, Eric D. Duke, and Marshanda Smith, 178–202 (Urbana: University of Illinois Press, 2009), © 2009 by the Board of Trustees of the University of Illinois, reprinted with permission of the University of Illinois Press; "Afro-Asian Solidarities and the 'Circle of Culture,'" *XCP: Cross-Cultural Poetics* 20 (2008): 97–101, © 2008 *XCP: Cross-Cultural Poetics*, reprinted with the permission of the journal and Mark Nowak.

In Japan, the surname precedes the given name. Thus, in both the text and the notes, I have used this order for people residing in Japan and publishing their work in Japanese. I am responsible for all translations in the text unless otherwise noted.

# Introduction

## *Du Bois's Challenge*

As the culture of liberation, the tradition crossed the famil-
iar bounds of social and historical narrative.
—Cedric J. Robinson, *Black Marxism: The Making of the
Black Radical Tradition* (2000)

In late 1936, W. E. B. Du Bois toured the library of Tokyo Imperial University during his brief sojourn in Japan. He must have walked through
rows of bookshelves, casting his eyes for any evidence of race contact
between the African diaspora and Japan. With the help of an inter-
preter, he probably located some of his own books, most likely *The
Souls of Black Folk* and *The Negro*. He also saw a collection of Japanese
art, including the prints of Commodore Matthew Perry's expedition to
Japan in 1854. The significance of this event in Japanese history was well
established; the story had been retold many times to mark Japan's opening to the West. This event ushered in a new era called Meiji and introduced a new polity, economy, technology, and culture to an emergent
modern nation-state. Du Bois, however, derived a different meaning of
this event in history when he saw one of the prints. "I . . . saw a print of
Perry's expedition with Negro sailors," he later wrote in his column for
the *Pittsburgh Courier*.[1]

According to Du Bois, this event in Japanese history was not simply the beginning of modern Japan. Bearing in mind how the nexus
of race and empire transformed the world since the intensification of
European colonization in Africa in the nineteenth century, Du Bois,
three years later, reflected on the significance of this seemingly trivial
evidence of transpacific race contact. In *Dusk of Dawn*, a book conceived as "an autobiography of a  race concept," he presented a framing
strategy of transpacific strivings. His contention was that this evidence
of race contact across the Pacific communicated the global dynamics of
racial struggles that were animated by anti-imperialist and nationalist
currents, and he argued that such strivings appeared most explicitly at
the intersection of Japan's emergence on the world stage and European
imperial reach and colonial exploitation in Africa. Writing in the late
1930s, he explained,

> Japan was rising to national status and through the Chinese War and the
> Russian War, despite rivalry with Germany, Russia and Great Britain,
> she achieved a new and nearly equal status in the world, which only the
> United States refused to recognize. But all this, I began to realize was but
> a result of the expansion of Europe into Africa where a fierce fight was
> precipitated for the labor, gold, and diamonds of South Africa; for domi-
> nation of the Nile Valley; for the gold, cocoa, raw materials, and labor
> of West Africa; and for the exploitation of the Belgian Congo. Europe
> was determined to dominate China and all but succeeded in dividing it
> between the chief white nations when Japan stopped the process.[2]

For quite some time, at least since the turn of the twentieth century,
Du Bois had been exploring his interest in transpacific race contact and
groping toward a new global theory of racial struggles. In the wake of
Japan's victory over Russia in 1905, he interpreted this event as a crisis in what Howard Winant calls "the globality of race," arguing that
Japan had broken the "foolish modern magic of the word 'white'" and
demonstrated the "loftiest and most unselfish striving" of the nonwhite
world to shake off the burden of the racial past.[3] Throughout, he stood
resolute in defending his pro-Japan position, valorizing Japan's pan-
Asianism as a force of anti-imperialist nationalism against the underlying white supremacy of imperialism and colonialism, although by

the winter of 1936, during which he toured Manchukuo (Japan's puppet state in Manchuria), China, and Japan, the realities of atrocities
and violence resulting from Japanese imperialism, aggressive militarism, and colonial rule throughout Asia had become widely known. Du
Bois reiterated his position in the columns he wrote, first, for the *Pittsburgh Courier* during the late 1930s and, later, for the *Amsterdam News*,
thereby sharply diverging from the opinions critical of the conduct of
Japan's foreign policy that were coming out of both the left and right
sides of the political spectrum.

For instance, when leading Black communists spoke from soap-
boxes and in their writings, they often dismissed a pro-Japan orientation among Black Americans as a case of "sycophantic adoration"
and ridiculed Black Japanophiles as "Black Hitlers," "crackpots," or
"fanatics." The publication of a propagandist pamphlet titled *Is Japan
the Champion of the Colored Races?* (1938), coauthored by Harry Haywood, Theodore Bassett, Abner W. Berry, Cyril Briggs, and James Ford,
clearly demonstrated Black communists' preoccupation with their
efforts to discourage the Black working class from expressing its opposition to Western imperialism purely on the grounds of race. From a
different political vantage point, Henry L. Stimson, soon to be secretary of war under Franklin D. Roosevelt and a man with already a long
public-service career as secretary of war under William Howard Taft,
governor-general of the Philippines, and secretary of state under Herbert Hoover, was deeply concerned with the reach of Japan's aggressive
foreign policy. In fact, convinced of Japan's espionage campaign already
under way in the Black community, he "agonized over the 'explosive'
and seemingly insoluble race problem," as historian John W. Dower
writes. Stimson's letter to Du Bois, written in January 1940, persuad-
ing him, albeit without success, to publicly oppose Japanese militarism
and expansionism in Asia and rally behind China to protect America's
interests in the region, illustrated Stimson's apprehension over expanding race consciousness that threatened white polities globally and on
the home front.[4]

When juxtaposed against this unity of the diametrically opposite
political position, as far as their opposition to Japan was concerned, Du
Bois's pro-Japan politics certainly presented itself as a case of an epistemic impasse. During the same period, however, taking a position that

echoed the tone of Du Bois's political conviction was C. L. R. James, one of the foremost important Afrodiasporic revolutionary thinkers of the twentieth century, then enmeshed in Trotskyist activity and embarking on a new political and intellectual journey in the United States in search of seeds of world revolution. Analyzing the significance of the growing strength of the pro-Japan tendency in race-pride and religious organizations within the Black community in the late 1930s and early 1940s, James concluded that working-class Blacks' "desire for the success of Japan is in reality a desire for the destruction of the apparently unbreakable power of their own oppressor, American imperialism, and the humbling of its pride." Inside their strivings, he observed the dynamic ways in which the Black freedom struggle gained strength to "intervene with terrific force upon the general social and political life of the nation, despite the fact that" it gave expression to the pro-Japan tendency devoid a Marxist class analysis. He wrote, "That these [pro-Japan] sentiments can be exploited by fanatical idiots, Negro anti-Semites, or self-seeking Negro businessmen, does not alter their fundamentally progressive basis."[5]

For James, the work of unmasking Black Japanophiles entailed the recognition of this logic of race consciousness to move toward categorical unity, or understanding that racial struggles buoyed by the pulsating ontological and epistemological imperatives could invigorate independent political action. In other words, a deep desire on the part of working-class Black Americans to articulate, on their own terms, capacities for self-fashioning and self-emancipation was not "some diversion from the class struggle." As Robin D. G. Kelley explains, an outstanding feature of James's political outlook was his "claim that revolutionary movements take forms that are often cultural and religious rather than explicitly political." The tradition of the historical Black struggle "had a vitality and validity of its own," James explained, and could "exercise a powerful influence upon the revolutionary proletariat." What James found in cultural and social milieus from which working-class Black Americans asserted themselves as a single people with strong cultural conviction was the "instinctive striving of the people towards internationalism." Like Du Bois, James was aware of the revolutionary potential of the challenge of independent Black political thought and action, how it could exceed political expectations, even when its direction was guided by the pro-Japan Black nationalist orientation. Both of them were cognizant of the power of race not just to move the masses through the realms of the local and the global but also to fundamentally alter all existing categories of radicalism. Engaging with the politics of culture in a society where daily reminders of racial subordination crippled one's self-worth, they took seriously the utopian appeal that the image of a defiant Japan had on and could have in Black America.[6]

This exercise in counterfactual history—that is, putting C. L. R. James and W. E. B. Du Bois in conversation with each other—brings to bear what is at the core of the essential work of theorizing transpacific race contact, which I call Du Bois's challenge. However much the persistence of Du Bois's pro-Japan orientation represented a stupendous failure in judgment, it nonetheless illustrated how Du Bois, a leading Black intellectual concerned with civil and human rights, pan-Africanism, and decolonization, grappled with the pedagogy of human liberation to present a paradigm through which darker nations and people would take giant steps. He held promise that Japan could become the nation that could alter the politics of race and power and challenge the global system of racialized inequality and exploitation that Western imperialism and colonialism created and perpetuated. Linking Japan's entry into modernity with the histories of Africa and its diaspora, he sought to make visible the contours of transpacific strivings. Thus, contained in how he ascribed meanings to the significance of the print of Perry's expedition was a call to imagine a new form of political alliance across the Pacific to mobilize racial struggles against the world structured by white polities, interests, and mores. Rather than altogether dismissing Du Bois's woefully inadequate grasp of Asian affairs, not to mention his uncritical position on Japanese imperialism and colonialism, this book approaches instances of transpacific race contact such as this and others as objects of knowledge that demand a closer analysis. The aim is to make known the drama of racial struggles, especially how universal appeal, contradiction, and irony were brought to the fore when attempting to transcend colonial and capitalist modernity and its corrupting feature called race. The narration of that drama in variations across time and space occupies a central place in this book.

Taking Du Bois's cue to look at race contact between Black America and Japan as a theoretical, epistemic, and political challenge, *Trans-*

*pacific Antiracism* introduces, in two parts, four cases of transpacific strivings drawn from intellectual and radical political activities in Black America, Japan, and Okinawa in the twentieth century. Part 1 is concerned with the function of pro-Japan provocation in organizing the Black "counterpublic sphere" in the United States and how this cross-racial alliance through political imagination helped articulate the discourse of Black radicalism and internationalism during the first half of the twentieth century. Specifically, during the First World War era, among the leading Black intellectual-activists of New Negro radicalism, such as Hubert Harrison, Cyril Briggs, Andrea Razafinkeriefo, A. Philip Randolph, and Marcus Garvey, despite sharp differences in their politics of race and class, the anti-imperialist, anticolonial, and nationalist currents within Black American political life acquired critical purchase in the form of an "unlikely alliance" with imperialist Japan in social struggles and political thought. Chapter 1 chronicles how these intellectual-activists with varying and competing political orientations constructed the iconography of Japan's race-conscious defiance against the global white polity in their poems and prose to nurture the Black internationalist ethos of self-determination in opposition to the Wilsonian project of liberal internationalism.[7]

Chapter 2 turns to Du Bois's response to the growing strength of the imperialist Japanese state within the global white polity in the 1930s and 1940s. The purpose of this analysis is to show just how his persistent pro-Japan defense, albeit laden with fundamental and serious errors, influenced his transformation as a theorist of Black radicalism and internationalism. At best, his analysis of Japan's place in the world of race and empires allowed him to intervene in the prevailing discourses about race, anti-imperialism, and world revolution. Through this intellectual engagement, he developed the new racial philosophy of human emancipation, or what I call the Afro-Asian philosophy of world history. In his pro-Japan provocation, one finds his preoccupation with giving the categories of race and nation political and moral authority to transform the Black counterpublic sphere and to incite race-based collective action on a global scale against racism, imperialism, and colonialism.

However, the arena of pro-Japan provocation that Du Bois carved out could not generate a discourse of Black radicalism and internationalism that was capable of responding to the demand of criticism at a particular historical conjunction marked by the rising influence of pan-Asian orientations in Japanese foreign policy. Du Bois was essentially unable to produce an effective strategy of criticism to bring race and empire together to mount a rigorous critique of white supremacy. He did not forthrightly acknowledge that what actually helped underwrite the Japanese imperialist state's path to territorial expansion and colonial aggression throughout Asia was the state propaganda of creating a pan-anti-imperialist, Asian-nationalist front against white supremacy, as well as the bureaucracy of the state itself, not just Anglo-American racial and imperial arrogance. He became a captive of this bureaucracy of the Japanese imperialist state because, in this overdetermined instance, he thought of anti-imperialism solely in terms of race rather than working through the dialectics of race and nation. Revealed were his ideological predispositions to assign this imperialist state historical destiny. Ultimately, his pro-Japan appeals caused an epistemic short-circuit within his discourse of Black radicalism and internationalism.

During the second half of the twentieth century, the same currents of resistance, now exceeding beyond the Black counterpublic sphere in the United States and gaining strength in the African diaspora and the Third World, offered Japanese scholars, Okinawan intellectual-activists, antiwar Black and white GIs, and peace activists from mainland Japan and the United States essential intellectual resources and creative energies to help organize political projects at the grassroots. As this book shifts from part 1 to part 2, what becomes evident is that the central objective of Black intellectual-activists' strategy of pro-Japan provocation during the first half of the twentieth century found support in two places rarely seen as the centers of the African diaspora: postwar Japan and occupied Okinawa. Although Du Bois's pro-Japan challenge encountered theoretical and conceptual limits to achieving legitimacy in the 1930s and 1940s, he nonetheless exhibited a tremendous foresight to argue—just a couple of weeks after two atomic bombs were dropped in Hiroshima and Nagasaki in August 1945—that critical agency emanating out of the practice of pro-Japan provocation was far from weakening but was gaining ground worldwide. Du Bois's challenge resonated with thinkers and activists in Japan and Okinawa who were devising a global theory of racial struggles against white supremacy in the second half of the twentieth century.[8]

Carrying this key analytical thrust of Du Bois's challenge into part 2, chapter 3 introduces the eclectic intellectual orientation of Japanese scholars associated with *Kokujin Kenkyu no Kai* (Association of Negro Studies). These scholars entered the new horizon of political possibilities opened up by Du Bois's challenge. While pursuing their interests in the Marxist position on the "Negro Question," the Esperanto movement, antebellum utopianism and abolitionism, and postwar Japanese Popular Front activism, they began considering what it would take to respond to this challenge of creating a more just, humane, and egalitarian society. This chapter argues that these curious groundings helped the discourse of Black radicalism to become relevant in postsurrender Japan. Particularly important to this project of making the echo of Black radicalism heard in Japan was the practice of translation. By reproducing the idioms and texts of Black radicalism in Japanese, at times with great consistency and at other times unevenly, this collective linked up with the political world of Robert F. Williams, a contemporary of both Martin Luther King Jr., and Malcolm X, and developed a movement of their own by way of inventing the new discourse that they called "colored-internationalism."

Likewise, chapter 4 delineates the political visions that animated diverse constituents of radical social movements in occupied Okinawa to pursue the promise of transpacific strivings, a promise that was made concrete and tangible by the outburst of international solidarity projects across the world. This spirit of insurgency was guided by, as George Katsiaficas describes the revolutionary character of the New Left activism of the late 1960s, "the massive awakening of the instinctual human need for justice and for freedom." The dynamic of the freedom struggle during the period in which the politics of Okinawa reversion and the escalation of the Vietnam War coincided in the late 1960s and early 1970s was such that the vision of Black and white GIs' antiracism and anti-imperialism at times overlapped with Okinawan and white American peace activists' struggles against the occupation authority and aggressive militarism, and this convergence of multiracial organizing activity engendered a movement culture that was capable of articulating the radical possibility of creative coalition building. These movement participants understood that their collective search for racial belonging had everything to do with crossing over into "the right side of the world revolution," as King said in his declaration against the Vietnam War in April 1967, to become a part of something other than what was set by the terms of white supremacy, namely, the property interests of the political and economic elite class, military bases, wars, and other machineries of mass destruction, violence, and state repression.[9]

Together, these four chapters bring to the surface "the culture of liberation," to borrow Cedric Robinson's phrase, from which the participants of Afro-Asian solidarity projects communicated their deep desires to enter the circle of common humanity to inhabit this reality of emancipation.[10] What made this culture of liberation productive for political alliances in Black America, Japan, and Okinawa in the twentieth century were anti-imperialist, anticolonial, and antiracist currents within each community of solidarity that consistently challenged and rejected the dominant political idioms and conceptions, such as freedom and democracy, that purported to be universalistic. These currents were the raw materials out of which the racial appellation *Afro-Asian* in the collectivity that this book refers to as *Afro-Asian solidarity* has acquired meaning and exercised shaping power in thought and social practice.[11]

Although transpacific striving to forge Afro-Asian solidarity was episodic, each case cropped up during a key moment of change and transition in the twentieth century. Throughout the first half of the twentieth century, the participants of Afro-Asian solidarity in Black America called into question the legitimacy of the dominant discourse of international democracy trumpeted by the United States, as the path toward a "race war" with Japan widened and the struggle for Black freedom encountered definite limits to social mobility and political and economic empowerment. People in postwar Japan and occupied Okinawa also learned to unmask the face of American exceptionalism during the early Cold War years and at the height of the Vietnam War, connecting the line between the American idea of democracy and the global influence and reach of American hegemony as they found alternative realities in movements toward Black and Third World liberation, peace, and social justice. The important dynamic linking these two parts of the book across time and space is the process through which these activists and intellectuals enmeshed in transpacific strivings carved out a space for the rearticulation of Black radicalism and internationalism to recall and renew the political commitment to fulfill the promise of human liberation.

The case of Yoriko Nakajima's emergence as the key interlocutor within Japan's Black studies movement in postwar Japan (detailed in chapter 3), for instance, best captures how the transpacific culture of liberation helped constitute Afro-Asian solidarity. At once repulsed by widespread social miseries and hypocrisies of American democracy and invigorated by postwar insurgencies and the beginning of the end of white domination buttressed by colonialism, imperialism, and Jim Crow in the Black worlds across Africa and the African diaspora, Nakajima, then a young scholar of political science, first as a graduate student at the University of Michigan and later as a researcher and a professor in Japan, drifted toward the domain of resistance. Occupying this space, she seized on the politics of fulfillment that Robert F. Williams and local African Americans in the Jim Crow South fashioned out of the struggle for Black equality, a struggle that "operat[ed] at scales that [were] both smaller and larger than the nation-state." Just as such leading Black radical intellectual-activists as Hubert Harrison, Andrea Razafinkeriefo, and W. E. B. Du Bois helped constitute Afro-Asian solidarity through pro-Japan provocation a few decades earlier, Nakajima activated, from Japan and through the work of building *Kokujin Kenkyu no Kai*, the discursive logic of race immanent in an effort to manifest the aim of transpacific strivings.[12]

Thus, this book argues that the dynamism of the culture of liberation was such that by stepping into this space, the participants of Afro-Asian solidarity projects began moving in a "racial groove," as Du Bois so aptly put it, and changing the groove itself, they made connections across multiple efforts to revise the blueprint of Black radicalism to present a meaning of human liberation that exceeded the boundaries of nations and modern political thought. An outcome of this movement in a racial groove was that these participants, fashioning themselves as agents of social change, generated "many different cognitive maps of the future, of the world not yet born," as Robin D. G. Kelley writes, and in the process presented the category of race less as a matter of personal identity and injury than as the politics of identification. Race emerged as a political category of struggle with a distinct and necessary moral and ethical quality and vitality to "go on living in the present."[13]

Indeed, central to the analysis of the culture of liberation in Black America, Japan, and Okinawa is that what made short-lived, small-scale, and localized solidarity projects *racial* had little to do with the color of participants and everything to do with the fact that imagined and real political alliances were products of resistance to and consequences of historical and global processes—namely, imperial ascent and expansion, nationalism, wars, aggressive militarism, and colonial projects—that made and remade the modern world and race within it. As a product and property of modernity, race—much like such systems of beliefs as liberalism, nationalism, and Marxism—unleashed rationalizing power that decisively shaped and transformed the social identities and collective consciousness of diverse participants of solidarity projects on both sides of the Pacific.

Moreover, as Du Bois understood the imperative of defining the experience of race in terms of musical quality, this book takes seriously the generative capacities of the power of music, particularly, as Paul Gilroy highlights, "communicating information, organizing consciousness, and testing out or deploying the forms of subjectivity which are required by political agency, whether individual or collective, defensive or transformational."[14] The main concern of this book, in other words, is the analysis of this power emanating from the movement in a "racial groove" that aided the transpacific formations of the culture of liberation and sprouted collective consciousness that gave this culture necessary categorical unity to make the social and political struggles anew. At best, thus, race entered the communities of solidarities in Black America, Japan, and Okinawa as political theory, providing not fixed and biologically determined ideas about human difference but rather a mode of explanation to repudiate what Du Bois called the "social heritage of slavery," or the assumption that white people and nations, as the bearers of moral authority and scientific truth, had the right to shape and enjoy political and economic processes that would make the world's majority, people of color, their slaves. What came out of this experience was a strong urge to constitute independently of the grammar and vocabulary of Western political thought. This urge cleared the way for the participants of Afro-Asian solidarities to cultivate their own insights into human emancipation and to develop counterdiscourses and overarching theories that were capable of revising and enlarging ostensibly universal liberal democratic political ideals. The essence of the movement in a racial groove was that it garnered, borrowing Gilroy's insight into the counterculture of modernity, a certain kind of "theodicy but move[d] beyond it because the profane dimensions of that racial terror made theodicy impossible."[15]

But in such bold acts of racial transcendence and transformation, the ironies, contradictions, and problems inherent in the very concept and corruption of race abounded. Ever present were the epistemology and logic of heteronormativity that structured anti-imperialist, anticolonial, and nationalist currents in solidarity projects. As chapters 1 and 2 show, leading Black intellectual-activists participated in the global politics of race and power via imagined solidarity with Japan without interrogating the operations of gender and sexual normativity that reified diplomacy and international affairs as spheres of male activity. Particularly salient in Du Bois's opinions about the future of Pan-Asia, moreover, was his reliance on gender and sexual politics to communicate the coming unities between pan-Africa and pan-Asia in terms of the constitution and reproduction of colored world manhood. Likewise, the male participants of the freedom struggle in occupied Okinawa that mounted opposition to racism, militarism, and imperialism were unable to imagine beyond the social conditions of their own existence, although a small group of women of color and male supporters were organizing at the intersection of race, gender, and sexuality and engendering an alternative political tradition. Indeed, when one frames the articulation of transpacific strivings as a category of critique, the politics of race and power "that organize[d] critical agency around heterosexual gender and sexual normativity" becomes visible, as Roderick Ferguson writes.[16]

Capturing the supple workings of race in the constitution of solidarity is certainly not an easy task, for an effort to explain this process of collectivity and identification in narrative writing and analysis so often ends up stiffening this very category. Yet this book takes up this challenge not only to constitute "the epistemological and historical archive" of Afro-Asian solidarity, as such scholars as Vijay Prashad, Bill Mullen, and Fred Ho have done, but also to do so without veering away from the imperative of granting race a categorical autonomy, just as Du Bois and James did.[17] Such an intellectual challenge entails making known the dynamism of the culture of liberation, how those participating in transpacific strivings in Black America, Japan, and Okinawa "under the force of the present conjunction" in a particular moment of change in the twentieth century responded to a call to "rework" the tradition of the historical Black struggle to transform the very concept of race into grounds for resistance to racism, imperialism, and colonialism.[18]

For instance, not at all tightly bound up with the vision of the struggle for Black self-determination, although that was one of the key currents that made the transpacific culture of liberation enabling, the diverse participants of Afro-Asian solidarities took up numerous positions ranging from opposition to imperialism and colonialism to movements toward disarmament, peace, and Esperanto. Moreover, Black intellectuals and activists who were developing the argument against the theory and practice of white supremacy were learning from the significance of Japan's revolt against the West and Okinawan resistance to the U.S. occupation authority to revise the discourse of Black radicalism and internationalism. Animating human subjects to move in a racial groove, the culture of liberation aided the process of creating the communities of solidarity and helped give the political category of struggle called "Blackness" new meanings, functions, and possibilities.

Perhaps Paul Robeson's emergence as the most important theorist of Afro-Asian radicalism in the twentieth century serves as an exemplar of an outcome of this call to "rework" the culture of liberation. Robeson's process of "reworking" involved, borrowing the cultural critic and theorist Stuart Hall's necessarily layered explication, "organiz[ing] these huge, randomly varied, and diverse things we call human subjects into positions where they can recognize one another for long enough to act together, and thus to take up a position that one of these days they might live out and act through as an identity." Such a concentrated, intricate, self-conscious, and antiphonal process of identification and pursuit of singular universalism had an "almost musical" quality, Hall acknowledges, for it moved "through the contingent, antagonistic, and conflicting sentiments of which human beings are made up."[19] The great historian of race Sterling Stuckey has explored at great length the mainspring of Paul Robeson's aesthetic and politics, and that was indeed how Robeson's process of "reworking" unfolded as an artist, a scholar, and an activist in the late 1920s and throughout the 1930s, during which he lived, worked, and studied in England and entered the anticolonial network of Afro-Asian nationalists.[20]

Robeson achieved intellectual clarity and maturity as a theorist of Black radicalism and internationalism as a student of linguistics and several African languages at the London School of Oriental Languages. His academic pursuit to enrich the understanding of African heritage was always punctuated by not only his diasporic and comparative considerations but also his immersion into the communities of solidarity in Europe, where he made deep connections with anticolonial nationalists from Africa and Asia and European artists and intellectuals interested in African culture and art. As an artist thoroughly aware of the power of expressive culture rooted in the human struggle, he always drew similarities between the melodies and forms of Black music and those of other world folk music from places other than Africa and the African diaspora.

In 1933, speaking to a reporter, Robeson shared "some of the results of his explorations of other cultures" in this way:

> I know the wail of Hebrew and the plaint of the Russian. I understand both, as I do the philosophy of the Chinese, and I feel that both have much in common with the traditions of my race. And because I have been frequently asked to present something other than Negro art I may succeed in finding either a great Russian opera or play, or some great Hebrew or Chinese work, which I feel I shall be able to render [with the] necessary degree of understanding.[21]

As Robeson learned to listen to the wails of people worldwide who were struggling to find ways to inhabit alternative futures, while studying world languages and translating myriad traditions of human struggles in music, often in languages other than his own and in the context of the Afro-Asian anticolonial milieu in London, he entered the culture of liberation shaped by diverse currents of resistance. As an artist, this process of identification set him on the path, according to Stuckey, "to move closer to being African—all the while developing a new, more spacious conception of what being African could mean." Robeson's ecumenical pursuit of Africanity, in other words, was far from essentializing. What guided him was a collective ethos to stay human and to forge a new form of life that was universal in its appeal and reach. Stuckey has characterized this creative process that Robeson initiated as "darkly beautiful renderings of inner joy and pain of many peoples," in which the quality of his art was at once natural and "elemental . . . as the movement of wind on an open plain."[22]

What this book suggests is that, like Robeson, the ethos emanating from the creative process of identification made it possible for the participants of Afro-Asian solidarities in Black America, Japan, and Okinawa to develop the paradigm of a movement in a racial groove. What precipitated from this labor of "reworking," ultimately, was the "transfiguration" of the tradition of the historical Black struggle or, as Gilroy explains, "the emergence of qualitatively new desires, social relations, and modes of association within the racial community of interpretation and resistance *and* between that group and its erstwhile oppressors."[23] Imagining the different shapes of freedom while engaging in social struggles to expand the circle of common humanity, diverse groups of activists, writers, and intellectuals on both sides of the Pacific responded to a call to "rework" and concomitantly moved in a racial groove toward the new epistemology so central to the objective of moving toward human liberation. One of the outcomes of such transpacific strivings, albeit challenging and often contradictory, was that their pursuit produced a discourse of Black radicalism and internationalism that transgressed and stretched the boundaries of nation and modern political thought. How far these groups were able to stretch these boundaries by digging deep into the tradition of the historical Black struggle is the focal point of this book. Sometimes they overextended the epistemic limits and stunted the work of constituting a committed human life. But they also found solidarities, moving closer to finding a way to come together, "to inhabit . . . a site clear of racist detritus; a place where race both matters and is rendered impotent," writes Toni Morrison, all in hopes of marking the inauguration of a truly human society, a life after "the abolition of whiteness."[24] This book is a tale of such a collective search for a new political reality.

PART I

Discourses

The trouble with all Peace Conferences has been that they
have always talked "pieces" instead of Peace.
—Andrea Razaf[in]keriefo, "Just Thinking," *Crusader*,
January–February 1922

1

New Negro Radicalism and Pro-Japan Provocation

During the First World War, Harry Haywood, who later emerged as one of the leading theoreticians for the Communist Party of the United States of America (CPUSA), served in the 370th Infantry of the U.S. Army and fought in France. While in the trenches, Haywood and his fellow Black soldiers in the segregated unit often talked about their life back home. Writing in his autobiography *Black Bolshevik*, he recounted one of the conversations:

> The guys started reminiscing about what they were going to do when they got home. The news from home was bad. Discrimination and Jim Crow were rampant, worse than before. Blacks were being lynched everywhere. "Now, they want us to go to war with Japan," observed one of the fellows. . . .
> "Well," someone said, "they won't get me to fight their yellow peril. If it comes to that, I'll join the Japs [*sic*]. They are colored." There was unanimous agreement on that point.[1]

Haywood described fellow Black soldiers' disenchantment with the persistence of racism, a disenchantment that appeared in the form of an imagined political alliance with Japan. He was in agreement and ready to declare that he was through with white supremacy. Ultimately, the 1919 Chicago race riot was what made him feel "totally disillusioned about being able to find any solution to the racial problem through the help of the government," for as he explained, "official agencies of the country were among the most racist and most dangerous to me and my people."[2]

The snapshots of Haywood's family's and his own encounters with white terror must have flit by as he came to this self-realization. Perhaps he recalled the story of his grandfather's act of armed self-defense, shooting a Klansman "point blank" in Tennessee during the Reconstruction era, a story that he heard regularly growing up, or his father's "frightened, hunted look" after being brutally beaten by a mob of white workers in Omaha, Nebraska, or how he walked into an all-white eighth-grade classroom on his first day upon moving to Minneapolis, Minnesota, where students were "singing old darkie plantation songs ... [in a] mocking, derisive tone ... emphasizing the Negro dialect ... and really having a ball." All of this came to the fore in the midst of the Chicago race riot as he and his fellow veterans took arms to defend their neighborhood and people from the wrath of white mob violence. Soon after, Haywood was on his way to discovering Black nationalism and revolutionary Marxism via Nevis-born intellectual Cyril V. Briggs's militant organization, established in late 1919, called the African Blood Brotherhood (an outgrowth of the Hamitic League of the World), which eventually became one of the pipelines that brought Black activists to the CPUSA. Fashioning himself as a Black Bolshevik, he began his long career in the "struggle against whatever it was that made racism possible." As historian Chad L. Williams writes, "the Chicago race riot indelibly transformed Haywood's racial and political consciousness."[3]

Far from being marginal to First World War political mobilization around the concept of the New Negro, during which young Black intellectual-activists categorically repudiated "the political accommodationism of the 'Old Negro,'" Haywood's articulation of solidarity with Japan had resonance in the Black public sphere. Like Haywood, Hubert

Harrison, Andrea Razafinkeriefo (commonly known as Andy Razaf), Cyril V. Briggs, A. Philip Randolph, Chandler Owen, and Marcus Garvey also expressed solidarity with Japan. Particularly striking was how their discovery of the political efficacy of the symbolic significance of Japan's fight for racial equality on the international stage actually made the culture of liberation productive for coalition work at the local level among these intellectual-activists of diverse and conflicting ideological orientations. Converging at a critical juncture, Randolph and Garvey, for instance, moved to the same beat. Although the Garveyites, looking at the world in purely racial terms, generally failed to acknowledge Japan's imperialist aims and ambitions, they occupied the same lot with left-leaning New Negro activist-intellectuals, including the leading Black socialist, Randolph. Tapping into the capacity of the symbolic significance of Japan as a nonwhite world power to bring the vision and aim of New Negro radicalism into sharper focus, together they articulated in their political activity and thought the iconography of Japan's race-conscious defiance against the global white polity. Such a work of political imagination, which I call pro-Japan provocation, proved effective in nurturing the distinct ethos of Black self-determination.[4]

The outstanding feature of the practice of pro-Japan provocation among New Negro intellectual-activists with competing ideological and political orientations was that forging solidarity with Japan was all about politics; it had nothing to do with Japan as "a biologically determined racial group." Buoyed by militancy and urgency within the New Negro movement, they projected the image of Japan as "a racialized political group." This distinction was crucial, as historian Minkah Makalani emphasizes in his brilliant study of the pan-Africanist politics of race among the members of the African Blood Brotherhood. Approaching race as simultaneously grounds for resistance and a forum to make known the "political voice of the militant 'New Negro' " through the local and internationalist frames of insurgency, the participants of the New Negro movement marked the transpacific culture of liberation to push forward their agenda.[5] Even as New Negro radical-intellectuals disagreed with each other on whether to place the primacy of race over class or class over race, to shape this new agenda, the political category of struggle called the "New Negro" found flexibility in an unlikely alliance with Japan.

## The Articulation of a "Fifteenth Point"

In late 1918, William Monroe Trotter, finding President Woodrow Wilson's outline of war aims and blueprint for a postwar world order, called "Fourteen Points," to be Jim Crow writ large, called for the inclusion of a "Fifteenth Point"—the abolition of race-based policies in all nations. He was determined to make white supremacy a global issue at the upcoming Paris Peace Conference. Throughout Wilson's presidency, as the founder of the all-Black Niagara Movement and the National Equal Rights League, Trotter denounced the administration's refusal and resistance to resolve racial injustices against Black Americans and fought hard for Black equality. In his mind, as long as Jim Crow remained at the core of the American polity, there was no hope for postwar democracy and internationalism, especially since both were used as principles with which to create the new structure of world governance called the League of Nations. At the time, while the unspeakable scale of violence and savagery carried out by whites in the East St. Louis race riots in July 1917 still horrified and enraged many Black Americans, Trotter insisted that peace and justice would never materialize for Blacks and colonized people all over the world if the white-supremacist conceptions of Wilsonian liberal democracy and internationalism were legitimated.[6]

Trotter's political acquaintance and collaborator, St. Croix–born Hubert Harrison, had been making such a connection between the ascent of liberal democracy and internationalism and the persistence of white supremacy "as far back as 1915," as Harrison's biographer Jeffrey B. Perry writes, to highlight "the racial aspect of the war in Europe" and to impart this knowledge to participants in the Black public sphere.[7] In fact, Trotter and Harrison were central figures behind the organizing drive of the Liberty Congress that brought together 115 delegates from across the United States in June 1918 to present militant Black political demands in the midst of the First World War. The Liberty Congress confronted the underlying white supremacy of the First World War by sharply denouncing the absence of democracy at home for Black Americans while Wilson issued a call "to make the world safe for democracy." The delegates were resolved to mount opposition to white supremacy in America and the world dominated by European nations that were eyeing consolidation of their colonial powers over darker nations and

peoples in Africa, Asia, and Latin America. They called for the enforce-
ment of the Thirteen, Fourteenth, and Fifteenth Amendments, the passage of federal antilynching legislation, and democracy for the "colored
millions" worldwide who were the world's majority. Their final act was
the submission of their petition to the House of Representatives to
make known these Black political demands.[8]

Such an internationalist race-conscious stance of anti-imperialism
had been the key tenet of Harrison's political thought. Throughout the
first half of the 1910s, he had been the opinion setter in the world of
Harlem radicalism in his capacity as a tireless organizer and consum-
mate theoretician operating first within the orbit of socialists and later
as a leading independent Black intellectual-activist. It is not at all an
overstatement to say that the future leaders of New Negro radicalism,
such as A. Philip Randolph, Chandler Owen, Marcus Garvey, Richard
B. Moore, and Cyril Briggs, could not have acquired the necessary political vision and idioms to achieve political and intellectual maturity and
in turn shape their own radical politics without first being transformed
by Harrison's captivating oratory, courage to speak truth to power, and
breadth of knowledge. He was an intellectual mainspring or, as Randolph put it, "the father of Harlem radicalism." During the years surrounding the First World War, he not only gave a form to an emergent
race consciousness within the Black public sphere but also increased
the tempo of the radicalization of the masses and leaders by pushing
them to move in a racial groove to help transform existing Black political culture and leadership.[9]

Particularly important to the development of racial militancy was
the launching of Harrison's organization called the Liberty League and
its newspaper, the *Voice*, in the summer of 1917. It marked the ascent
of "the first organization and the first newspaper of the New Negro
Movement," as Perry emphasizes. Carving out a space of resistance to
make known the new political voice, Harrison gave categorical unity
to the political consciousness and identity of a determined, assertive,
and militant Black American called the "New Negro." At the time, as
Harrison worked his way into Harlem to stake out the field of political action independent of the dominant currents of American radicalism, the emergent Black metropolis was rapidly being transformed by
the influx of migrants from the Jim Crow South and the Caribbean and

the exodus of the white middle class. Coinciding with this changing demographic urban landscape was the beginning of President Wood-row Wilson's second term and America's entry into the First World War. While Wilson's vision of a new world order, couched in the language of international cooperation and democracy, appealed to a wide audience, Harrison's Liberty League and the *Voice* categorically repudiated the Wilsonian liberal internationalist project. Intervening in this political culture with a strong clear vision, Harrison guided his peers on how to navigate the grounds of struggles that shifted with world-historic developments occurring at local, transnational, and global levels: rampant racial violence and state repression, labor radicalism, Caribbean and southern Black migration, the First World War, the Russian Revolution, the Irish rebellion and its revolutionary nationalism, and prospects for African liberation. All of this deepened New Negroes' resolve to fashion the collective right to self-determination and to quicken the pace of racial militancy.[10]

Although both Trotter and Harrison issued a counterpolitical statement against Wilsonian internationalism in the form of a "Fifteenth Point," ultimately they were not the catalysts that set the racial struggle in motion on the international stage in Paris. Acknowledging that diplomacy at the 1919 Paris Peace Conference, especially its deliberations, negotiations, and decisions, would be dictated by Anglo-American powers, Japan sought to attain equality with the imperial powers of the West and did so by invoking the language of racial equality. The Japanese delegation was certainly cognizant of this imperialist power politics. But Japan's diplomatic strategy at the Paris Peace Conference was shaped as much by external factors as by domestic pressure groups that saw the international politics of racial discrimination as leverage to expand Japan's political and economic spheres of influence in East Asia. Although major newspapers in Japan often pronounced that "the object of the League's formation will not be fully realized, it would seem, so long as Japanese and other colored races are differentially treated in white communities," the Japanese government was only remotely interested in attacking the stronghold of white supremacy.[11] In Paris, Japan pursued its own imperial ambitions and colonial interests by demanding the control of the islands in the South Pacific, especially the Marshall, Mariana, and Caroline Islands, as well as of the German concessions in Shantung, China. Nonetheless, Japan's race-conscious diplomatic maneuver did shake up the nature of the debate. The racial-equality clause proved effective in strengthening imperialist Japan's position within the global racial polity. Such was the irony of race.[12]

Arriving in Paris, the leaders of the Japanese delegation, Baron Makino Nobuaki and Viscount Chinda Sutemi, took this issue to Colonel Edward M. House, President Wilson's most trusted adviser, to figure out a way to accommodate Japan's concern. In talks with Makino and Chinda in early February 1919, House remained attentive to Japan's demand and expressed that the problem of the color line was "one of the serious causes of international trouble, and should in some way be met."[13] In the end, both parties decided to introduce the racial-equality clause by way of seeking an amendment to the religious-freedom article (Article 21) in the covenant of the League of Nations. On February 13, 1919, Japan presented the following draft: "The equality of nations being a basic principle of the League of Nations, the High Contracting Parties agree to accord as soon as possible to all alien nationals of states, members of the League, equal and just treatment in every respect making no distinction, either in law or in fact, on account of their race or nationality."[14] The delegates representing the British empire and the United States opposed the amendment. They interpreted Japan's demand for racial equality as directed at achieving unrestricted Japanese immigration to countries such as England, Australia, Canada, and the United States. Thus, Lord Robert Cecil of the British empire and Australian Prime Minister William Morris Hughes organized strong opposition. Cecil declared on the floor that the proposal was divisive and would lead to "interference in the domestic affairs of State members of the League." For the same reason, he added that the International Council of Women's demand for gender equality would not be considered in drafting the Covenant of the League of Nations.[15]

After repeated negotiations and revisions, the Japanese delegation dropped all the referential connections between "race" and "equality" and presented a revised version that endorsed "the principle of equality of nations and just treatment of their nationals." Italy and France as well as other countries, such as China, Greece, Serbia, Brazil, and Czechoslovakia, all voted for this revised amendment on April 11, 1919. By 11–6, it was passed. However, Wilson, presiding as the chair of this session, did not honor the result. He justified that "in the present instance there was, certainly, a majority, but strong opposition had manifested itself against the amendment and under these circumstances the resolution could not be considered as adopted." Japan did not pursue the fight for racial equality at the last session of the League of Nations Commissions.[16]

When the racial-equality clause was introduced in Paris, it took on a life of its own within the context of imperialist diplomacy. It generated Anglo-Americans' apprehension and their determination to protect the system of white supremacy. While Cecil cast Japan as a troublemaker of the international community for introducing the contentious race question, Wilson insisted that issues of race and racism "play[ed] no part in the discussions connected with the establishment of the League."[17] As historian Gerald Horne discusses in *Race War!*, the U.S. embassy in Tokyo was assigned to do damage control after the racial-equality proposal was unilaterally tossed. It sent an official statement to the Japanese press to explain that the proposal was rejected "due to the fears of the British and American delegates that it had a bearing, not only on the immigration question, but on the treatment of subject races such as Indians and Negroes in their dominions." With irony, Horne comments, "The Japanese could either be comforted by the fact that they were allegedly not the primary target of white supremacy, or wonder why the United States was incapable of making meaningful distinctions between 'races.' Others, perhaps, may have begun to think they had more in common with the despised U.S. Negroes than they had imagined."[18]

White nations' response to Japan was aimed to dissemble. Their determination to reject the racial-equality clause was intertwined with their unwillingness to give up property and colonial interests in white supremacy. During the Paris Peace Conference, A. Philip Randolph and Owen Chandler explained the logic of colonial and racial domination in this way: "Those who hold vested property interests and privileges under a given social system will resist with desperate determination any assault upon that system by the advocates of a new, a different social doctrine."[19] Although Western leaders sought to suppress the debate surrounding the problem of the color line at the Paris Peace Conference, the globality of race was a social and political fact that could not be denied. Amid contradictions, the great powers had vested interests in shaping the discourse of race, especially since they all vied to rationalize their claims to control Germany's former colonies in Africa and Asia and to further consolidate their empires. Even when they eschewed a direct reference to the language of racial equality, their endorsement of the virtues of democracy and internationalism was *racial* at every turn because of colonialism and imperialism. Hubert Harrison offered the most succinct summary of the construction and function of white justice and property rights, the key political tenets buttressing imperialism and colonialism:

> The white race assumes an affirmative answer in every case in which the national property of darker and weaker races are concerned and deny it in cases in which their national property rights are involved. It seems strange that whereas the disturbances occurring in our own southern states are never considered sufficient to justify the destruction of their national sovereignty, on the one hand, such disturbances occurring in Hayti [*sic*] or Mexico are considered a sufficient reason for invasion and conquest by white Americans. The same is true of England, France, and Italy. . . . The truth is that "might makes right" in all these cases. White statesmen, however, often deny this at the very moment when they are using "force without stint, force to the utmost" to establish "rights" which they claim over territories, peoples, commerce and the high seas.[20]

Ironically, the same criticism also applied to Japan. While the Japanese delegation raised the banner of racial equality to set up a new international standard for diplomacy and cooperation in Paris, the Japanese colonial government suppressed Koreans' struggle for self-determination and tightened the grip of colonial rule. It had no interest in trumpeting the right of colonized and racially oppressed people for self-determination. When the Chinese learned that the German concessions in Shantung had come under Japanese control, intellectuals and students gathered at the Gate of Heavenly Peace in Peking on May 4, 1919, and challenged the legitimacy of Japanese and Western imperialism. Commonly known as the May Fourth Movement, an outburst of political and intellectual activities awakened the people struggling to seek radical solutions to create a new nation. Nationalist China debated the crisis of modernity and struggled to define its own path toward peoplehood and nationhood. The anti-imperialist Chinese nationalists opposed the decisions made at the Paris Peace Conference and mobilized protests locally and globally. On the day of the signing of the Versailles Treaty, Chinese students in Paris took direct action. They blocked the Chinese delegates from entering the signing ceremony. Consequently, the treaty was signed without their presence on June 28, 1919.[21]

## To Manifest Race Consciousness at the Peace Conference

Like the Japanese, the leading voices of the New Negro movement looked to the Paris Peace Conference, and like the colonized subjects under Japanese rule, they knew that imperialists lied and evaded the realities of violence and oppression by capitalizing on the euphoria of democratic aspirations. New Negro intellectual-activists in America were not interested in presenting their political demands without consideration of the rights of Africans and people of African descent to complete their struggle for self-determination (as W. E. B. Du Bois and Blaise Diagne, a Senegalese leader and a high commissioner of French West Africa, essentially did at the Pan-African Congress convened in Paris in February 1919). These intellectual-activists presented a bold critique.[22] Shortly after the armistice in November 1918, Hubert Harrison set the currents of anti-imperialism and anticolonialism in motion within the New Negro movement culture in this way:

> When Nations go to war, they never openly declare what they WANT. They must camouflage their sordid greed behind . . . [a] phrase like "freedom of the seas," "self-determination," "liberty," or "democracy." But only the ignorant millions ever think that those are the real objects of their bloody rivalries. When the war is over, the mask is dropped, and then they seek "how best to scramble at the shearers' feast." It is then that they disclose their real war aims. . . . Africa's hands are tied, and so tied, she will be thrown upon the peace table.[23]

Harrison aptly pointed out the operating principles at the core of the Peace Conference and the League of Nations. Determined to discuss the future of colonialism in Africa, the imperialist scramble for colonial possessions all over the world, and the racist hypocrisy of Wilsonian liberal internationalism, he placed these issues in the front and center of his political activity during the First World War era.

For Harrison, such a sharp critique of imperialism and colonialism came out of his serious engagements with the category of race in political struggles. As Harrison once explained, "The feeling of racial superiority which the white races so generally exhibit is produced by the external fact of their domination in most parts of the world. That same fact, by the way, produces in the minds of the masses of black, brown and yellow peoples in Africa, Asia and elsewhere what is called in psychology a protective reaction; and that is their race-consciousness." It was this firm grasp of the dialectics of race that guided the essential intellectual and political work that he performed as the leading voice of New Negro radicalism. He was at work in organizing a forum from which "race consciousness" would emerge, both in political activity and thought, "to furnish a background for our aspirations, readers for our writers, a clientele for our artists and professional people, and ideals for our future." What he found in race consciousness was the incubator of new knowledge that could become, as Perry puts it, "a necessary corrective to white supremacy" and "a strategic component in the struggle for a racially just and socialist society."[24] Later writing for Marcus Garvey's weekly newspaper, the *Negro World*, Harrison clearly explained his method of how to evoke and utilize race consciousness to articulate the discourse of Black radicalism and internationalism informed by anti-imperialism and anticolonialism. Published in 1920, this article was titled "The Line-Up on the Color Line":

> In the face of these facts the first great international duty of the black man in America is to get in international touch with his fellows of the downtrodden section of the human population of the globe. . . . We need to join hands across the sea. We need to know what they are doing in India; we need to know what they are doing in China; we need to know what they are doing in Africa, and we need to let them know what we are doing over here. We must link up with the other colored races of the world, beginning with our own, and after we have linked up the various sections of the black race the black race will see that it is in its interest and advantage to link up with the yellow and brown races.[25]

Throughout late 1919 and early 1920, numerous New Negro intellectuals took up the task of Harrison's call to "link up" among Africans
and peoples of African descent, as well as with the "yellow and brown
races." Given this heightened race consciousness in the New Negro
movement, when the Japanese delegation introduced the question of
"Color" on the international stage, this action took on powerful meanings among New Negro intellectual-activists. In fact, Japan's place in the
world of race and empire served these New Negro intellectual-activists'
aim well. It helped them affirm their collective ethos, best captured in
the words of Marcus Garvey, expressed in late 1918: Africans and people of African descent looked to Japan with a promise and a hope that
it would "succeed in impressing upon her white brothers at the Peace
Conference the essentiality of abolishing racial discrimination."[26] Cyril
V. Briggs, writing in December 1918 for the periodical *Crusader*, for
which he served as an editor, urged readers to move through the experience of race and in doing so to "link up" to achieve clarity of purpose
in the struggle for a new society in Africa and the African diaspora.
He emphasized that the New Negro demands comprised the following
core principles: "that the full rights of citizenship be granted to all people of Color, that all discrimination because of Color be made illegal,
that self-determination be extended to all nations and tribes within the
African continent and throughout the World, and that the exploitation
of Africa and other countries belonging to people of Color herewith
cease."[27] For these intellectual-activists, the process of constructing the
iconography of Japan became the touchstone to mount a critique of the
imperialist power and politics of "Color," or the theory and practice of
white supremacy that Harrison called the "international Color Line."
Their pro-Japan provocation made the culture of liberation productive for their internationalism and allowed race-based acts of political
insurrection to emerge at the local level.

A surge of the New Negro grassroots campaign to "link up" in late
1918 came to the notice of government authorities. On January 5, 1919,
retired Major Walter Howard Loving, a Black American informer who
worked for the U.S. Military Intelligence Branch of the Army, recognized the political radicalization in Harlem and reported that "New
York 'soap box orators' are beginning to invade this city, and their presence must carry some significance."[28] Loving's observation was not

an overstatement. Despite ideological and political differences, Black American and Caribbean activists busily organized meetings and converged at various points; their political activism presented itself as an "invading new society" of sorts.[29] They participated in each other's local projects and frequently shared the same stage to articulate their perspectives on peace making in the immediate aftermath of the First World War. Many of them entered the debates over war, peace, disarmament, and global racial justice and communicated their commitment to help establish what Marcus Garvey once called the "Racial League" to counter Wilson's plan for the League of Nations.[30]

At the National Race Congress for World Democracy meeting in Boston, for instance, William Monroe Trotter, Ida B. Wells-Barnett, Madam C. J. Walker, Reverend Matthew A. N. Shaw, and seven other leaders were elected to represent the Black American peace delegation, although participants of this meeting, in the end, excluded women from taking part in the delegation.[31] Garveyites, too, organized a delegation of their own, which included A. Philip Randolph, Wells-Barnett, and Eliezer Caddet.[32] Moreover, on January 2, 1919, with Marcus Garvey in attendance and financial assistance from Walker, Harlem's prominent Black leaders formed a short-lived organization called the International League of Darker Peoples.[33] The following leaders became the officers of the organization: Rev. Adam Clayton Powell, president; Isaac B. Allen, first vice president; Lewis G. Jordan, second vice president; Madam C. J. Walker, treasurer; A. Philip Randolph, secretary; and Gladys Flynn, assistant secretary. They agreed to submit a Black American peace proposal, and Randolph drafted it.[34] In the March 1919 issue of the *Messenger*, Randolph described the overall thrust of their peace-making strategy under the striking editorial title "Internationalism":

Carry the Negro problem out of the United States, at the same time that you present it in the United States. The mere fact that the country does not want the Negro problem carried out to Europe is strong evidence that it ought to be carried there. William Monroe Trotter has caught the point and gone to Europe to embarrass the President of the United States, who has been making hypocritical professions about democracy in the United States which has not existed and does not exist. . . . The international method of dealing with problems is the method of the future.[35]

The U.S. government closely monitored New Negro leaders' political activities in Harlem and noted, in particular, the solidarity between Black America and Japan in localized projects. According to the Bureau of Investigation report coming out of New York City, Garvey allegedly "preached that the next war will be between the negroes and the whites unless their demands for justice are recognized and that with the aid of Japan on the side of the negroes they will be able to win such a war."[36] Garveyites, indeed, paid close attention to the mainstream media's view of Japan's role in the upcoming Peace Conference, citing a *New York Times* article which reported that "Japanese newspapers are suggesting that Japan and China raise the race question . . . with the object of seeking an agreement to the effect that in the future there shall be no further racial discrimination throughout the world." Garvey's *Negro World* also cited the report that Japan was "coaching China how to enter the Peace Conference."[37]

Marcus Garvey and members of the Universal Negro Improvement Association (UNIA) welcomed Japan's assertiveness and interpreted it as a hopeful sign: "This report is very suggestive. In it can be seen immediate preparation by the yellow man of Asia for the new war that is to be wagered [*sic*]—the war of the races. This is not time for the Negro to be found wanting anything. He must prepare himself, he must be well equipped in every department, so that when the great clash comes in the future he can be ready wherever he is to be found."[38] The Garveyites rallied behind the coming "war of the races" and at times invited Japanese speakers to their meetings to reinforce the idea of a race war. As Gerald Horne and Reginald Kearney have argued, such a vision of "a coming of racial Armageddon" enabled them to express their desire for liberation from white supremacy. For instance, John Edward Bruce, a journalist, a pan-Africanist, a UNIA officer, and a longtime supporter of Hubert Harrison's militant political activism since Harrison's early days at St. Benedict's Lyceum in the early 1900s, where he began community-based activism, wrote a short story in which Japan and the United States were at war with each other and Japan triumphed. Bruce wrote, "The Philippines and Hawaii . . . were lost to America and the flag of Japan waved proudly from the fortifications lately occupied by American troops."[39]

The concerns of U.S. authorities never ceased. The report prepared by the joint legislative committee investigating seditious activities in the state of New York commented that some members of the International League of Darker Peoples were actively propagating ways "to unite with the darker races, such as the Japanese, Hindus, etc., with the whites" and imagining the "broader movement," in which "Japan may come to their aid in their struggle for amancipation [*sic*]." Walker, too, had come under the surveillance of the Military Intelligence Branch of the Army, for she played an important role in the International League of Darker Peoples. She was especially instrumental in arranging a meeting with S. Kurowia, a publisher of the Tokyo newspaper *Yorudo Choho* and one of the Japanese representatives selected to participate in the Paris Peace Conference.[40] The report indicated that the International League of Darker Peoples held a conference on January 7, 1919, "in honor of S. Kurowia, of the Japanese Peace Conference," during which the participants resolved to demand "the abolition of colored discrimination, freedom of immigration, revision of treaties unfavorable for Africa, abolition of economic barriers, self-determination for Africa."[41] In 1918–1919, keeping Japan in sight, the supporters of the Black American campaign to organize the world for peace and global racial justice converged politically, although they did not necessarily share the same politics.

Notable during these several months preceding the Paris Conference was Black women's participation, especially how they made their presence known even as they faced marginalization within the male-dominated Black public sphere. Wells-Barnett, a towering crusader for racial justice and a veteran antiracist and feminist activist, and Walker traversed the nerve centers of New Negro radicalism by assuming key leadership roles in the Black internationalist efforts. Although the expression of racial militancy emanating from the New Negro movement was anchored by the tropes of war and militarism and suffused with gendered assumptions, with the idea that international and domestic politics were male-oriented spheres, Wells-Barnett and Walker commanded influence as "helpmates and leaders," to borrow historian Ula Y. Taylor formulation, within this emergent Black counterpublic sphere. The nature of their engagement with New Negro radicalism reveals how they not only made the currents of anti-imperialism, anti-colonialism, and Black nationalism active during this period but also helped cultivate the culture of liberation, from which a distinct Black feminist tradition that Taylor calls "community feminism" could emerge. According to Taylor, most instrumental in the shaping of this Black feminist tradition during this era of the First World War were the first and second wives of Marcus Garvey, Amy Ashwood-Garvey and Amy Jacques-Garvey. In particular, Jacques-Garvey, in her capacity as the associate editor of the *Negro World*, published writings that cast women as both helpmates and leaders capable of playing a leading role in community and nation building; she made the practice of "community feminism" central to the Garvey movement.[42]

So, too, did the core member of Cyril Briggs's African Blood Brotherhood, Grace Campbell. As a steadfast organizer, Campbell translated "community feminism" in the service of revolutionary socialism and pan-Africanism and entered the orbit of Harrison's, Randolph's, and Chandler Owen's community-based activism in Harlem in the late 1910s and early 1920s. The leading Caribbean radical intellectuals and key forces in the Socialist and Communist Parties, Claude McKay and Richard B. Moore, who often collaborated with Campbell through local projects, regarded her as a central figure in New Negro radicalism. Particularly noteworthy is Moore's remembrance. Several decades later, in the 1960s, he characterized her as one of the deeply enmeshed community activists and militant socialists who "emphasized the liberation of the oppressed African and other colonial peoples as a vital aim." Moreover, highlighting the essential quality of Campbell's "community feminism," Moore mentioned that Campbell was a "humanitarian social worker who maintained, largely from her own earnings, a needed home for deserted young mothers." Moore knew she was a rarity within the orbit of these socialists, for as a militant woman, she was virtually alone; but she held a key position, for instance, in the "Harlem variety of socialism," the Twenty-First Assembly District Socialist Club, a product of Harrison's community-based activism during the years in which he worked as an organizer for the Socialist Party in the early 1910s.[43]

Indeed, in these self-conscious, deliberate, and politically committed ways, Campbell sustained the work of the African Blood Brotherhood throughout the years surrounding the First World War, making her home a meeting place and an office for the Brotherhood and helping to organize the People's Educational Forum, a counterpublic sphere established by Black socialists and communists of the New Negro movement that incited debates over the direction of the movement. As historian Minkah Makalani emphasizes, thanks to Campbell's organizing work, the African Blood Brotherhood did bring women into the organization, although issues of women's rights did not appear in the pages of the *Crusader*. Recognizing that Campbell was "one of the most important and least known members of the black left from the First World War to her death in 1943," historian Winston James set the historical record straight in his book *Holding Aloft the Banner of Ethiopia*.[44] Like Moore's acknowledgment of the outstanding features of Campbell's political thought and activity, James, too, captures the place and function of "community feminism" within New Negro radicalism:

> [Campbell] was able to lead primarily because her comrades recognized her commitment, selflessness, and even goodness. Campbell, who remained single all her life and had no children, unlike many of the members of the black middle class around her, did not simply sit down on her relatively fat civil service salary. She tried, in the spirit of the National Association of Colored Women's Club, to lift as she climbed, extending her own resources to help those in need. She evidently came to the conclusion that the problems of black people in America required something more radical than relief—important though relief was. Like the rest of the [African Blood] Brotherhood, Bolshevism appeared to her to have been the solution.[45]

Although the vision of Wells-Barnett and Walker did not center on revolutionary Marxism as in Campbell's politics, all of these women were part of the currents of New Negro radicalism that recognized the efficacy of pro-Japan provocation in making their race-conscious political engagements productive for the articulation of counterpolitical statements that categorically repudiated the dominant political idioms of peace and democracy couched in the discourse of Wilsonian liberal internationalism. Likewise, although the key leaders of the clubwomen movement, such as Mary Church Terrell, Mary Talbert, Addie Hunton, and Margaret Murray Washington, did not follow the lead of Campbell, who ultimately used the racial-uplift motto of the Black American Clubwomen movement, "lifting as we climb," in the service of Bolshevism,

they nonetheless entered the international terrain of struggle to syn-
thesize the local and global causes of peace and racial justice during
this period. For some members of such groups as the Women's International League for Peace and Freedom and the International Council of
Women of the Darker Races, as Michelle Rief has shown, the so-called
Japanese question did enter into their political imagination, for it was
taken up as the topic of discussion among the members.[46]

Jessie Fauset, then the literary editor of the *Crisis* magazine and
also in this distinct Black feminist tradition, evoked the mood of New
Negro radicalism in the wake of the 1917 East St. Louis race riots. In a
letter to the editor of the periodical *Survey*, she presented an instance
of white mob violence against a Black woman and her baby to make
known the stupendous barbarism and savagery that was so pervasive
and widespread not just in the United States but across the world, laying the groundwork for pro-Japan provocation. The symbolic significance of her narrative strategy was that it not only "carried specific historical resonance in light of the history of sexual terrorism visited upon
Black women in slavery and freedom," writes Robin D. G. Kelley, but
also linked up with the cases of state violence in places such Turkey,
Russia, and Belgian King Leopold's Congo.[47] Fauset wrote,

> A people whose members would snatch a baby because it was Black
> from its mother's arms, as was done in East St. Louis, and fling it into a
> blazing house while white furies held the mother until the men shot her
> to death—such a people is definitely approaching moral disintegration.
> Turkey has slaughtered its Armenians, Russia has held its pogroms, Bel-
> gium has tortured and maimed in the Congo, and Turkey, Russia, Bel-
> gium are synonyms for anathema, demoralization and pauperdom. We,
> the American Negroes, are the acid test for occidental civilization. If we
> perish, we perish. But when we fall, we shall fall, like Samson, dragging
> inevitably with us the pillars of a nation's democracy.[48]

At once indignant and convinced, like many of the leading male New
Negro internationalists, Fauset was acutely aware of the "white problem" and interpreted it as a sign of the moral and political bankruptcy
of so-called modern civilization.[49]

The repeated patterns of pogroms against what Harrison called the "colored majority" were clear evidence of the white world's "descent to Hell," as Du Bois described in an essay published in 1920, titled "The Souls of White Folk."[50] During this period of the First World War, Fauset was indisputably one of the sharpest critics of the white-supremacist underpinnings of imperialism and colonialism, and her expression of "community feminism" in *Survey* powerfully conveyed her conviction that the insurgent democratic tradition of the Black freedom struggle represented the only hope for the survival of humanity. On this ground of a critique of white supremacy via pro-Japan provocation, despite differences in political orientations, these leading Black women leaders and activists found the political language to articulate their enmeshment in both a Black internationalist and a feminist ethos.

Alongside "community feminism," which facilitated convergence within the thought and activity of New Negro radicalism, stood New Negro intellectual-activists who debated the dynamics of race and class to cultivate a culture of liberation via pro-Japan provocation. By the late 1910s and early 1920s, for instance, Randolph and Owen of the *Messenger* were already known as the leading critics of the race-conscious worldview of Garveyites, emphasizing the struggle for a socialist society rather than Black empire building as Marcus Garvey and his followers did. Yet they, too, interpreted the problem of the existing world system in racial terms and globalized the race question to challenge the international politics of racial discrimination. They were especially incensed with the imperialists' systematic suppression of the race question in order to consolidate their empires at the Peace Conference, which enabled them to solidify the "international Color Line."[51] In one editorial published in March 1919, they expressed their indignation in this way: "There must be no more Belgiums. There may be Congo massacres of innocent Africans by Belgians, though. There may be Memphis and Waco (Texas) burnings of Negroes. Hush! Don't raise the race issue!"[52] By way of linking the case of genocide in the Belgian Congo with the campaigns of white terror in the United States, Randolph and Owen presented the Black American map of anticolonialism.[53] When lines drawn from one locale to another were connected, their cognitive map revealed the nexus of race and empire.

Thus, when Japan introduced the racial-equality clause during the League of Nations Commissions meeting in early 1919, Randolph and

Owen responded with great enthusiasm and entered the currents of anti-imperialism and anticolonialism. They quickened the flows by issuing the following indictment against the arrogance of the white race in March 1919:[54]

> Japan raised the race issue and threw a monkey wrench into the league of white nations which well nigh knocked the peace conference to pieces. It was successfully side-tracked, however. This question would not bear the slightest examination by the American peace commission which has its vexatious Negro problem and which excludes Japanese immigrants by a gentleman's agreement. Nor could Great Britain face the issue with her West Indian colonies and her India. Australia, a British dominion, excludes both Negroes and Asiatics.[55]

Randolph and Owen integrated the symbolic significance of Japan's struggle for the racial-equality proposal to develop a countermap of Wilsonian liberal internationalism, rendering visible the white-supremacist underpinnings of debates and discussions that ensued at the Paris Peace Conference. In their political imagination, Japan functioned as a device to communicate and represent the interconnectedness of the problems of racism, imperialism, and colonialism and the racial politics of immigration.

Although Randolph and Owen identified with Japan in the wake of the appearance of the racial-equality clause at the Paris Peace Conference, that did not mean that they looked to Japan as the leader of the colored world in the future race war, as some of the Garveyites did. Inspired by a Marxist interpretation of the world capitalist system, both of them were grounded in class analysis and well armed with theoretical insights to scrutinize the Japanese imperialist state and colonial projects in Asia. Even as they expressed enthusiasm for Japan's diplomatic strategy that exposed the real face of colonial powers and the white supremacy of Wilsonian internationalism, they remained critical, arguing that Japan was not interested in challenging the "international Color Line," let alone putting pressure on the United States to end the practice of Jim Crow. In the May–June 1919 issue of the *Messenger*, Randolph and Owen included a lengthy cautionary note to explain the significance of Japan's race-conscious intervention in world politics:

A word of warning, however, to the unsuspecting and to those not thoroughly versed in social science. The Japanese statesmen are not in the least concerned about race or color prejudice. The smug and oily Japanese diplomats are no different from Woodrow Wilson, Lloyd George or Orlando. They do not suffer from race prejudice. They teach in the Rockefeller Institute, wine and dine at the Waldorf Astoria, Manhattan or Poinciana, divide financial melons in Wall Street, ride on railways and cars free from discrimination. They care nothing for even the Japanese people and at this very same moment are suppressing and oppressing mercilessly the people of Korea and forcing hard bargains upon unfortunate China.[56]

Similarly, in an editorial titled "Japan on American Lynching," published in August 1921, Randolph criticized elements of the Japanese ruling class for capitalizing on the savagery of racial pogroms in America to prepare the Japanese masses for war. with a kind of fatalistic zeal "never to come under the yoke of American imperialism." They also expressed discontent toward Japanese imperialist propaganda on the grounds that it could animate, in Black America, a social and cultural movement guided by wishful thinking that could actually impede their fight for Black equality and a socialist society, as, in their minds, Garvey allegedly did. They were concerned that if such a race war were to begin, "the Negroes will be the front line trench men against Japan. . . . (The lowest group of any population always serves as cannon fodder during a war.)" The antiwar and anti-imperialist editorial closed with the following remarks that were sharply critical of Japanese imperialism and colonialism: "We hardly need to say that we are in favor of exposing American hypocrisy. Nor is it out of place here to expose the utter hypocrisy of Japan which brutalizes Chinese, oppresses most shamefully the Koreans, crushes and abuses the Japanese working-classes, and disenfranchises more Japanese—*in Japan*—than the United States disenfranchises Negroes in the South."[57]

Engaging with the dialectic of race and class in the context of world politics, Harrison also knew that Japan was no different from other white imperial powers of the West. He wrote, "The secret of England's greatness (as well as of any other great nation's) is not bibles but bayonets—bayonets, business and brains. As long as the white nations have a

preponderance of these, so long will they rule. Ask Japan: she knows."[58]
Throughout this period, Harrison discussed the political imperative to
help achieve unity among the "colored millions" in order to resist imperialism and colonialism and to overthrow white supremacy. However,
never included in this internationalist solidarity scheme was imperialist
Japan. For him, Japan was merely an "index," as he once put it, for his
main political concern was always with the lives of the restless Black
masses in the United States and darker peoples under colonial domination, especially those in Africa and its diaspora. Although Randolph
and Owen would be in disagreement, "If Japan should take up arms
against any white nation at this time," Harrison wrote, "it would be 'all
Hell let loose'—and they know it."[59] Characteristic of Harrison's effort
to carry out an anti-imperialist critique of world affairs to manifest race
consciousness via pro-Japan provocation, he argued in the midst of
the Washington Conference of 1921–1922 that "England's Asiatic alliance with Asia" was to stifle the coming unity between India and Japan.
He explained,

> The mere existence of a colored great power in Asia is a tremendous
> stimulant to Asiatic self-assertion. Add to this fact that this colored
> power has defeated successively two white powers [Russia in 1905 and
> Germany in 1915] and driven them from Asia's eastern front, and it will
> be seen what trouble it could stir up in India with its 150,000,000 peo-
> ple if it should, in a spirit of unfriendliness assume the role of liberator
> or leader.[60]

After the Paris Peace Conference ended, Cyril Briggs of the *Crusader* and Andrea Razafinkeriefo continued to critically assess the
significance of Japan's invocation of the race question, in a manner
similar to Harrison's framing of Japan as merely an "index" in the
worldwide struggle for Black liberation. In other words, Briggs's and
Razafinkeriefo's symbolic solidarity with Japan was not wedded to the
"class-first" principle like Randolph and Owen, nor was it built on
the "race-first" principle like Garvey. These two intellectual-activists
navigated the dialectic of race and class flexibly to bring coherence
to Black radicalism and internationalism in the mass movement and
social and political thought. Critical of the hero-worship dynamic of

the Garvey movement, which crippled the capacity of Black masses to hone the necessary skills to become critical thinkers capable of engaging with the conflicting and contingent nature of the politics of race, they demanded from intellectual-activists rigor and creativity. Both Briggs and Razafinkeriefo proved themselves as leading Black internationalists with skills to capture the infinite variety and complexity of the politics of race to enable acute analytical advances. Their pro-Japan provocation aided this process of bringing radical Black internationalism into sharper focus.[61]

## Disarmament Dissenters

New Negro intellectuals' internationalist outlook and race consciousness remained salient in the aftermath of the 1919 Paris Peace Conference, and their commentary on Japan continued to appear in the margins of their political discussions. When the great powers of the West and Japan congregated to set the general framework for a new diplomacy in East Asia during the Washington Conference of 1921–1922, Hubert Harrison, Chandler Owen, A. Philip Randolph, Cyril V. Briggs, and Andrea Razafinkeriefo developed sharp criticisms of the underlying imperialism and white supremacy of this new international system.

At this conference, the United States, Great Britain, Japan, and France, along with other nation-states such as Italy, the Netherlands, Belgium, and China, held a series of talks to establish the terms of disarmament and the basis of a new order. As in the 1919 Paris Peace Conference, the United States assumed world leadership and challenged the old structure of power diplomacy. Its primary objective was to abrogate the foundation of the imperialist scramble for territories, resources, and colonies and to replace it with a U.S.-led Open Door policy, which would guarantee the great powers' access to the market in China. The U.S. government called on world leaders to organize a consortium, which would foster "international cooperation" and enable Western powers to derive power and wealth from trade with China. Meanwhile, the great powers of the West excluded the Soviet Union from participating in this consortium and forced Italy, Japan, Germany, and China to fall in line and accept subordinate roles within this newly reorganized international system.[62]

The Washington Conference reminded Japan of its tenuous status as a great power. The combination of diplomatic pressure, the necessity of securing foreign markets for domestic economic growth, and the retention of great-power status influenced Japan's decision to concede to the U.S.-led reorganization of East Asian affairs. By the end of the conference, Japan had come to accept the new era of imperial diplomacy and gave up much of its wartime gains, including its control of the Shantung peninsula in China. The United States and Great Britain also pressured Japan to accept an unequal ratio of capital ship tonnage in the name of disarmament and subsequently weakened Japan's naval power in Asia. In the end, Japan agreed to the liquidation of "all existing treaties between the powers and China [and] replaced them with the Open Door principles so long espoused by the United States."[63] Contrary to the great powers' rhetoric of liberal internationalism, the main purpose of the conference was not to guarantee peace in postwar East Asia but to figure out ways to exploit China and other colonies under European rule in the region. This new diplomacy intensified the contest for supremacy in Asia, and Japan struggled to maintain its status within this globalized racial polity.

Throughout this period of the Washington Conference, New Negro intellectuals and writers were vocal opponents of the terms of disarmament and international agreements to institute a new order in the Pacific. They argued that imperialists' pursuit of power and property interests encouraged the drive toward the reconstitution of white supremacy in East Asia. Harrison's precise analysis struck at the operating logic of the "international Color Line": "So long as the will-to-be-free of these darker millions is limited by the will-to-power of the white people of Europe and America, just so long must these white people stay armed."[64] Likewise, in the following poem published in the January–February 1922 issue of the *Crusader*, Razafinkeriefo condemned the white-supremacist objective of the conference on disarmament through the creative use of rhyme:

> *The Reason*
> The conference is quite ill at ease
> In regards to their friends, the Chinese.
> There's no country finer

To exploit than China—
The Japs must not get all the cheese.[65]

Razafinkeriefo, a Madagascar-born and leading poet of New Negro radicalism, showed a keen understanding of the ways in which the Anglo-American alliance vied for white supremacy in East Asia. His poem simultaneously mocked and exposed the arrogance and anxiety of the white world. For New Negro intellectuals who were cognizant of the dialectic of race and class, Western countries' resistance to Japan's struggle for racial equality, especially their militantly defensive posture toward Japan's assertiveness in the international system, served them well. It enabled them to manifest race as the terrain of political struggles that were shaped by the conflicts for "the titles to possession of the lands and destinies of this colored majority in Asia, Africa, and the islands of the sea," as Harrison once described it.[66] Harrison and Razafinkeriefo were collaborators, and they always found ways to combine their intellectual and artistic talents. For one, along with Briggs's *Crusader*, at which Razafinkeriefo served as a staff member, Razafinkeriefo's poems were always included in the newspaper Harrison edited, be it Harrison's own *Voice* or Garvey's *New Negro*. Indeed, if Harrison was the "voice of Harlem radicalism" during the First World War period, then Razafinkeriefo was undeniably, as Jeffrey Perry reminds us, its leading poet. Projecting the ethos of the racial militancy of the New Negro movement, he sought to increase the pace of this political struggle.[67]

Razafinkeriefo's poem titled "Disarmament," published in the January–February 1922 issue of the *Crusader*, represented a critique in the best tradition of Harrison's Black radicalism and internationalism. Most illuminating was how Razafinkeriefo's poetry intersected with Harrison's serious engagement with the Black theater, especially the most dominant and popular forms of entertainment at the time, vaudeville and comedy. Both men found these forms of human drama, especially creative exchanges, encounters, and expressions, instructional, for they struck at the essence of human existence in a society built on the racial subordination of Black Americans and other people of color.[68] Using rhyme to produce particular sound and literary effects, Razafinkeriefo presented a commentary on the absence of real disarmament in the existing world:

*Disarmament*
O, Gentlemen! why not disarm
The hordes who daily do us harm,
Who ply their trade relentlessly
On suffering Humanity?

Disarm the bed-bug,
Disarm the flea,
Disarm the mosquito,
The cootie and bee.
Disarm the barbers of their tongues
And back-yard songsters of their lungs.

But while there's money to be got
By sending folks off to be shot;
Just keep your side-arms at your hips
And hold on to those battleships.
For, my last pair of socks, I'll bet
That we are booked for more wars yet.[69]

Razafinkeriefo adopted myriad forms and styles and used humor to communicate the dangers of continued armament and how it threatened world peace. He was a master at capturing the ethos of ordinary Black working people. Instead of naming weapons of mass destruction and explicitly criticizing Western powers for making the world unsafe for people of color, he named insects, especially those that bite, sting, suck, and cause ill feelings, harm, and pain, to convey the grievances of Black people. The language showed evidence of the musical style of slave songs, especially work songs that were composed as Black workers performed daily activities and interacted with fellow workers.[70]

The poem, moreover, avoided denouncing the imperialist and white-supremacist underpinnings of the Washington Conference in a politicized language informed by Marxism, as Randolph and Owen often did. Instead, it relied on what historian Lawrence W. Levine calls "Black laughter," which "provided a sense of the total Black condition not only by putting whites and their racial system in perspective but also by supplying an important degree of self and group knowledge."[71]

Humor embedded in this poem possessed an explanatory power. Syncopating the rhythms especially through rhyme, Razafinkeriefo projected what Robin D. G. Kelley calls the "freedom dreams" of ordinary folk, particularly their desire to disassociate from aggressive militarism and their readiness to inhabit a new life after the overthrow of white supremacy.[72]

The differences in politics and political language between Randolph and Owen of the *Messenger* and Razafinkeriefo's artistic expression appear most explicitly when their rhetorical strategies are analyzed in juxtaposition. Unlike Razafinkeriefo's poem, which relies on the creative and lyrical use of language to manifest the revolutionary potential of race consciousness at the grassroots, the *Messenger*'s December 1921 editorial went straight to the Marxist critique of imperialism and colonialism. Randolph and Owen explained that an emphasis on "scrapping of some battleships" among the Five Powers, the United States, Great Britain, Japan, France, and Italy, at the Washington Conference concealed the real aims of international capitalist states: the exploitation of the resources and people of China in the name of the Open Door policy. They explained,

> Our readers should understand that this conference is not called to disarm. It was called to parcel out, divide up and emasculate China with a sort of gentlemen's agreement as to the spheres of influence. That is all which is meant by the "open door" and the Far East or Pacific question. Open the door to America, Great Britain, France and Japan to go into China and rob the helpless people of their iron, coal and oil.[73]

Yet Randolph and Owen, like Razafinkeriefo but presenting their position in a qualitatively different tone, sharply pointed to the problem of the proliferation of weapons of mass destruction: "What about poison gas, airplanes, submarines and torpedo boats? These are the modern, more deadly instruments of war. A ton of Lewisite gas is more deadly than the entire American navy."[74] The editorial explicitly stated that conditions for disarmament could never be found in the world capitalist system as long as a "bone of contention in trade routes, commerce, concessions, spheres of influence, underdeveloped territories, weaker peoples, cheap land and cheap labor will ever exist."[75] The Washington

Conference was nothing but a conference to bring together race, class, and militarization.

In a characteristically perceptive manner, New Negro intellectual-activists' protest against the disarmament conference also emphasized the impact of militarization on the home front. They emphasized that the imperialist club's obsession with world domination severely damaged the civic sector of the U.S. economy and contributed to an increase in living costs and taxes, which burdened ordinary working people, especially racially aggrieved populations. Chandler Owen, for instance, explained, "This apparent desire for peace . . . is not found to be the motivating cause of the conference by students of world politics. We find, on the contrary, that the burdens of taxation for maintaining armies and navies have soared so high that it is no longer possible to shift all of those loads on the working people, but any further assessment must, as they will, fall upon wealth. This, to say the least, is not a rosy anticipation." Harrison concurred, arguing that "a state of unstable subordination in domestic affairs" in the lives of the poor was a direct outcome of "the permanent need of the police machinery of the State." Owen concluded that "if each of them [imperialist powers] continues to pile up this huge burden upon the tired and bending backs of the working people, it must plan to face civil war at home—the revolt of the people—a revolt which may metamorphose into a revolution and sweep away the very foundations of the old order of society—the tottering system of capitalism, and its foster child, a dogged but doddering imperialism." Owen's call for mass political action was fused with Razafinkeriefo's poetic chant to "disarm," and together their utterances carried the tune of radical Black internationalism.[76]

Like Owen, Briggs of the *Crusader* dreamed of "the revolt of the people." However, Briggs's position was different from that of Randolph and Owen and ideologically close to Harrison's race-conscious activism. The central concern of his Black liberation movement was the radicalization of the home front. Arguing that the "final success will depend upon the degree to which the opinion of the Negro masses have been mobilized and their minds prepared for the necessary sacrifice,"[77] Briggs took a position characterized by unwavering commitment to anti-imperialism, anticolonialism, and African liberation. As an advocate of a Black-led movement guided by revolutionary Marxism, he, like Harrison and

Razafinkeriefo, turned to pro-Japan provocation to index the broader aim and ambition of the struggle against white supremacy. Writing in the wake of the Red Scare and Red Summer of 1919, yet "still marked by tremendous optimism on the part of large sections of the revolutionary forces around the world," as historian Winston James writes, Briggs made known "gathering war clouds" between the United States and Japan, as well as between the United States and Mexico. The purpose of his message was not to apprehend "a war to force acceptance of the doctrine of white superiority upon Japan" or to wait for "the American Negro [to be] . . . called upon to shoulder *his* share of the white man's burden" in the war of aggression against both Mexico and Japan. Defiantly, Briggs put forth the mission and strategy of Black radicalism and internationalism. Writing in capital letters, he issued a call for his readers "NOT TO FIGHT AGAINST JAPAN OR MEXICO, BUT RATHER TO FILL THE PRISONS AND DUNGEONS OF THE WHITE MAN (OR TO FACE HIS FIRING SQUADS) THAN TO SHOULDER ARMS AGAINST OTHER MEMBERS OF DARKER RACES."[78]

As a leader of the African Blood Brotherhood, Briggs worked out an uncompromising race-conscious program for his organization that was anti-imperialist and rooted in the local struggle against the system of racial exploitation.[79] Presenting the position of New Negro radicalism in the form of pro-Japan provocation, he urged his Black American readers and supporters not to be an accomplice in the white-supremacist project.

> The Negro who fights against either Japan or Mexico is fighting for the *white man* against himself, for the *white race* against the darker races and for the perpetuation of *white domination of the colored races*, with its vicious practices of *lynching, jim-crowism, segregation and other forms of oppression* in opposition to the principle advocated by Japan of Race Equality, and there are things that, we are convinced, *no loyal Negro* will do.[80]

Essentially, Briggs proclaimed that those who would fight on behalf of the U.S. imperialist power against Japan or Mexico were a part of the socially and historically constructed category called the "white race" and compromised the principled political aim of the struggle for racial equality and justice, the very issue that Japan helped to internationalize during the 1919 Peace Conference. Yet far from being blind to Japan's imperialist ambitions and colonial projects, he was merely trying to establish race as grounds for resistance. His pro-Japan provocation was designed to manifest race consciousness, or to incite a movement in a racial groove, but was not the kind of narrowly conceived racial politics intended to incite a race war, as the rhetoric of Marcus Garvey was. Rather, he aimed to mobilize the fight for Black liberation on the home front and elsewhere in Africa and communities of the African diaspora, while linking up in "common cause," as Briggs wrote, "with the Indians and the Irish Republicans, with Soviet Russia and the Turkish National-ists and with all other forces now, or in the future, menacing the British empire in particular and the capitalist-imperialist world in general."[81] In other words, like Harrison, Briggs was interested in coalition work, not with imperialist Japan but among oppressed peoples worldwide to forge a new identity by taking the internationalist position guided by the revolutionary struggle for socialism.

As the Washington Conference neared, Briggs instructed his read-ers and supporters to be cognizant. Calling the Washington "Disarma-ment" Conference "the conference for white supremacy in the Pacific," he instructed his readers and supporters who were in the orbit of New Negro radicalism to adopt an internationalist position and to "work out a program for co-operation and co-ordination of effort that would give the last smashing punch to the dying system and usher in a new era of genuine freedom for the workers of all races." He wrote, "Negroes, Hindus, and other members of the Darker Races do not have to bear a brief for imperial Japan in order to be interested in the maneuvers of the white race against the only colored nation that has so far success-fully challenged the vicious principle of white supremacy."[82]

Such a tactical and flexible engagement with the politics of race, via pro-Japan provocation, was his main concern; ultimately it would strengthen the resolve among darker peoples to take a strong stance against white supremacy in solidarity with each other. Throughout, guiding Briggs to shape this discourse of Black radicalism and inter-nationalism was a clear vision that at the center of "the invention of the white race" was the making of the system of social control, as both Har-rison and Theodore Allen argued in different times, to keep the "colored majority in Asia, Africa, and the islands of the sea" in the condition of bondage.[83] Thus, he recognized that the utility of pro-Japan provocation was to be found in carving out the culture of liberation capable of attacking all things white in religion, science, law, and world affairs, so as to make known the lies of modern civilization and the root causes and consequences of social misery. Razafinkeriefo understood this general orientation quite well, and he captured it in the following poem published in the *Crusader* in October 1921:

> *Civilization*
> With all your Christian churches
>   And all your lofty creeds,
> With all your modern progress
>   The heart of man bleeds.
>
> With all your law and order
>   Which you proclaim a cure
> You've doubled greed and hatred,
>   The world is more impure.
>
> With all your talk of Justice
>   And grand Democracy,
> The weak are still exploited
>   And robbed of liberty
>
> If hypocrites amongst you
>   These statements would deny
> Let them come forth and answer,
>   And I will ask them why
>
> Are Africa and Ireland
>   Beneath the tyrant's feet,
> Deprived of rights and freedom,
>   That, which all men hold sweet?
>
> Why are unhappy Egypt
>   And India kept down;

Enslaved, forced to contribute
Toward an alien crown?

And what of valiant Haiti,
Whose liberty has fled;
Because of Southern Crackers—
What of her murdered dead?

What of your leading nations,
Their mob-rule and unrest;
Their crimes, which are increasing,
Which has the Bible blessed?

Tear down your Jim-crow churches,
Burn up your lying creeds;
And find a true religion
Which you'll express in—deeds![84]

In the immediate aftermath of the First World War, the iconography of Japan as a race rebel and a racial victim helped to open another space within the culture of the New Negro movement to critique white supremacy. By the mid-1920s, however, gone was the application of New Negro intellectual activists' pro-Japan provocation, which at critical conjunctures in the context of war and revolution and unending state-sanctioned white terrorism had brought together multifaceted, race-conscious political and intellectual activities to shape Harlem radicalism. Increasingly, the New Negro movement began exhibiting ideological orientations that laid the groundwork for the flowering of the cultural movement called the Harlem Renaissance, which veered away from the currents of anti-imperialism, pan-Africanism, and revolutionary Black nationalism that characterized the radical tendency. In the pages of the leading presses of New Negro radicalism, such as the *New Negro* and the *Messenger*, for instance, prominently featured were narratives and representations of race progress and race pride that emphasized Victorian gender conventions, to set "a new standard of feminine beauty as part of the New Negro cultural aesthetic," as Kevin K. Gaines describes.[85]

Moreover, becoming pronounced were New Negro intellectual-activists' criticisms of Japan's imperialist pursuits in Asia. Writing in 1920, the leading Black socialist, A. Philip Randolph, said, "So much, yet so little, of value has been said about the Japanese problem that we need to examine its real content. Analyzing it carefully, we find the whole thing growing out of the capitalist system." Randolph elaborated his analysis in this way: "Now just as America was not 'fighting to make the world safe for democracy,' nor England for the rights and protection of smaller nationalities, so the United States will not be fighting Japan because she is yellow in color and different in race." The focal point of his criticism was the relentless expansion of capitalism and colonialism worldwide, and his point was that Japan was no different from white imperialists. Taking the same position, the key members of the African Blood Brotherhood—Briggs, Grace Campbell, Claude McKay, and Dutch West Indies–born Otto Huiswoud (the first Black American to link up with the Communist Party), all joining the Workers Party and becoming pioneer Black Communists by 1921–1922—never again made statements of pro-Japan provocation.[86]

Eventually, Randolph's ongoing engagement with "the Japanese problem," as a socialist leader increasingly concerned with the plight of the Black working class, led to his entry into the politics of immigration, where he took the side of restrictionists. Among the Black intelligentsia, he was, as historian Daryl Scott has commented, "virtually alone."[87] While he considered the passage of the 1924 Immigration Act, which barred the entry of Asian immigrants completely and limited the entry of immigrants from Europe through the system of national origins, a step "in the right direction," he was not content. Stating that the law did not go "far enough," his quibble centered on variations in the method of exclusion, or how immigrants were racialized differently. Although Randolph's opinion deviated from the dominant anti-Asian position of the American Federation of Labor and mainstream America slightly, his explanation for his support of this new legislation nonetheless reinforced that position:

No race line should be drawn, none against nationality or religion. We favor shutting out Germans from Germany, the Italians from Italy, the Russians from Russia, the Irish from Ireland, the Japanese from Japan,

the Hindus from India, the Chinese from China, and even the Negroes
from the West Indies. The country is suffering from immigration indigestion. It is time to call a halt on this grand rush for American gold,
which over-floods the labor market, resulting in lowering the standard
of living, race-riots, and general social degradation. The excessive immigration is against the interests of the masses of all races and nationalities
in the country—both foreign and native.[88]

Meanwhile, on the other side of the Pacific, the defeat of the racial-
equality proposal at the Peace Conference, combined with a major
setback at the Washington Conference in 1920–1921 and the growing
anti-Japanese movement in the United States that pushed the passage of
the Immigration Act of 1924 through Congress, strengthened the pan-
Asianist orientation in Japanese foreign policy throughout the 1920s
and 1930s. Eyeing an aggressive imperialist pursuit of territorial expansion through wars to consolidate Japan's colonial power and to establish
a new order in Asia, the Japanese civilian and military leaders began
fashioning a race-conscious discourse against an Anglo-American
world order based on white supremacy. These leaders made this ideological language, which cemented the spectacle of Japan's struggle with
white supremacy in the international system, central to the imperialist
state's propaganda.[89]

Responding to this politics of race that was beginning to emerge in
U.S.-Japan relations was W. E. B. Du Bois. Although he was roundly
criticized by the leading intellectual-activists of New Negro radicalism
for rallying behind Wilsonian liberal internationalism during the First
World War era, by the early 1930s, on matters of race-conscious political activism, he began donning the ideological mantle of Hubert Harrison, ironically, the very person who earlier mounted the most rigorous criticism of Du Bois's place in Black political leadership. Following
Harrison's revolutionary orientation, some twenty years later, Du Bois
began working at the intersection of "the race radicalism of Garvey
and the class radicalism of Randolph and Owen" to make this dialectic
fundamental to the Black liberation struggle. As the next chapter will
elaborate at length, the making of Du Bois as a radical Black internationalist in the 1930s and 1940s was punctuated by his repeated pro-
Japan provocation. In his capacity as the leading Black intellectual, he

sought to quicken the anti-imperialist, anticolonial, and Black national-ist currents by projecting the dream of a coming unity between pan-Africa and pan-Asia. Just before resigning from the editorship of the *Crisis* and departing from the National Association for the Advance-ment of Colored People in 1934 to take an independent course of politi-cal action, he issued the following political challenge in the form of a call for transpacific strivings to manifest race consciousness:

> Listen to a word from twelve little black millions who live in the midst of western culture and know it. . . . Unmask them, Asia; Remember Japan that white American despises and fears you. Remember China that Eng-land covets your land and labor. Unite! Beckon the three hundred mil-lion Indians; drive Europe out of Asia. . . . Let the yellow and brown race, nine hundred million strong take their rightful leadership of mankind. . . . Get together China and Japan, cease quarreling and fighting! Arise and lead! The world needs Asia.[90]

2

W. E. B. Du Bois's Afro-Asian Philosophy of World History

In April 1937, shortly after returning from the world tour, W. E. B. Du Bois's outlook on prospects for Black liberation appeared in his weekly column for the *Pittsburgh Courier*. Both international travel and distance allowed him to take stock of the fate of white supremacy amid turmoil in the world. For seven months, he traversed turbulent European nation-states, including Nazi Germany and Stalin's Soviet Union, the Russian frontier via the Trans-Siberian express train, Manchukuo (a Japanese puppet state since 1931), fractious China, and imperialist Japan. The trip allowed him to calibrate the optics of race. He explained, "I have had pause in space and time and spirit; a chance to look at this American scene from afar and of studying it and rethinking our problem with something of calmness and detachment." He continued,

It is so easy to miss the forests for the trees, particularly in a problem like ours which is so beset with little annoyances, personal matters, small occurrences which in and of themselves are as nothing compared with the thunder of the world's highways. But all these things continually reduce the Negro Problem to a matter of the party last night, next door, in this impossible flat; the occurrences in school; the question of wages and savings; and the immense uncertainty of the future. But after all, and despite this, the broad highway is there, the great path along which we walk toward the future of the Negro in America and in the world, and the future of the world itself.[1]

Expressing how he achieved this analytical clarity and philosophical integrity with regard to his lifelong commitment to the study of what he often called a "race concept," he reminded his readers that the so-called Negro Problem, viewed in the broader context of the movement of world history, was "the thunder of the world's highways." The problem of the color line was not a mere domestic concern and a local issue of inequality at work and in school. Nor was it a problem related to individual psychology or cross-cultural communication. It was a powerful force that uprooted, transformed, and united people of color and various minorities and nationalities around the world, consequently shifting the terrain of the struggle for Black liberation in an animating way. Indeed, in the October 1936 issue of the *Aryan Path*, a periodical published and circulated in India, Du Bois explained that "no matter what [Black America's] destiny in America, its problems will never be settled until the problem of the relation of the white and coloured races is settled throughout the world."[2] He was certain that the struggle for Black freedom in America was linked to myriad racial struggles on the world stage.

Du Bois's bold declaration that contained in the "Negro Problem" was the theory of world revolution signaled the maturation of his Black radicalism and internationalism. The big picture that he cognitively mapped—the forests he identified—grew out of his negotiation with modernity in crisis, where competing languages of governmentality, liberalism, fascism, and communism vied for ideological and political supremacy. Du Bois put himself in the middle of this space ever more self-consciously after the 1936 world tour to search for alternative routes to reach the world's highway to resolve the fundamental problem of the modern world, or white Europe, a term he often used to connote the

foundations of modernity—namely, racism, colonialism, and imperialism—which endowed whiteness tremendous categorical weight as
well as explanatory and shaping power to control and divide the world's
majority—people of color—in Africa, Asia, Europe, and the Americas.
Building on his masterpiece *Black Reconstruction in America: An Essay
toward a History of the Part Which Black Folk Played in the Attempt to
Reconstruct Democracy, 1860–1880*, which was published in 1935, Du
Bois articulated this Black internationalist ethos, laying both the theoretical and epistemological foundations to help guide the shifting configurations of political struggles and emancipatory possibilities locally,
transnationally, and globally.[3]

But Du Bois's rumination on whiteness and resistance to it was
increasingly being punctuated by not only the ascendancy and militancy of Japan as a nonwhite world power during the period of looming
clouds of a race war spreading across the Pacific but also his own persistent pro-Japan defense, even as the facts of Japanese atrocities across
Asia and the false promise of Japan's leadership in pan-Asianism became
glaringly evident. At best, his pro-Japan articulation was utopian in its
orientation and intent. In developing the theory of transpacific striving to overcome whiteness, Du Bois affixed the symbolic and political
significance of race-conscious Japan's defiance against white Europe to
a certain condition, characteristic, and possibility and linked it to the
local significance of the struggle for Black freedom to intervene in prevailing discourses about race and revolution. His theoretical orientation
was undeniably informed by Marxian dialectical historical materialism, but his philosophical intervention was simultaneously a critique
of the underlying Eurocentrism of the whole edifice of Enlightenment
thought, including that of Western Marxism. The presence and growing strength of Japan, a nonwhite nation within the global white polity,
helped him communicate the promise of transpacific strivings within
the context of the Black public sphere.[4]

The purpose of this chapter, thus, is to examine Du Bois's intellectual
project of developing a new racial philosophy of human emancipation,
or what I call the Afro-Asian philosophy of world history, which, he
contended, could unleash new kinds of knowledge and critical resistance to white supremacy within Black political life. Situated within the
specific historical conjuncture of the 1930s and 1940s, Du Bois's reflec-

tion on a nexus between the Black world and Japan, albeit laden with contradictions and serious shortcomings in his critique of Japanese imperialist politics and complicity with uninterrogated gendered and sexual politics, influenced his transformation as a theorist of Black radicalism and internationalism. The analysis of this particular intellectual formation requires the contextualization of Du Bois's positionality. That is to say, it requires an investigation into how Du Bois organized the racial past so as to incite collective action out of the wreckage of the racist present and ultimately to carry out the work of human liberation into the future of race, while occupying a specific moment in time, during which Japan's ascendancy in the existing world of race and empires in the 1930s and 1940s challenged the terms of white supremacy. Grappling with "the question of the contingent relation the present has to both the past and future," he sought to generate, to borrow the words of critic and postcolonial theorist David Scott, "the historical idioms and historical rhythms in which our own present might yield to us a desirable future" via pro-Japan provocation.[5]

In the final analysis, however, Du Bois's historical discourse—anchored by praise of Japan's racial struggle on the world stage, or the conceptualization of Japan as "the stand-in for the lost historical agency capable of resisting being swept into the ceaseless flow of history,"[6] to use the framing of historian and critic Harry Harootunian—could not guarantee the promise of human emancipation. What Du Bois failed to overcome was "the demand of criticism," as David Scott puts it, at a particular historical conjunction in the 1930s and 1940s. His historical discourse, which was worked out searchingly during the period of Japan's Fifteen Years War (1931–1945) in Asia, a time marked by a renewed interest in and the vigorous return of a pan-Asianist orientation in Japanese foreign policy and widespread atrocities, bore a resemblance to the project of interwar Japanese thinkers' and philosophers' desperate and tortuous valorization of the racial construction of pan-Asianism to justify colonial expansion, subjugation, aggressive militarism, and violence throughout Asia.[7] Ironically, this very problem of theoretical abstraction in dominant discourses of the past and the present was what Du Bois struggled to overcome as a historian writing *Black Reconstruction in America* and a critic occupying "an historically constituted field of ongoing moral argument." Up against the epistemic and moral weight of white Europe, Du Bois had to both sharply and flexibly delineate "the lines and play of forces (what might count and what might not as a possible intervention)" to overcome what Scott calls "the problem of strategy for criticism."[8]

## Not a Black Groove but a Racial Groove

Soon after Du Bois returned from the tour of the Japanese empire in late 1936, he sent the rough sketch of a book-in-progress to his publisher, Alfred Harcourt. The book was tentatively called "A Search for Democracy," he noted. In the proposal, he stressed the need to develop a new philosophical foundation to pursue an alternative to the existing world order:

> I want in this book to try to compare, in different countries that I have seen, the effort to carry on government in accordance with the popular will and especially to discuss the means and methods by which governments today are trying to face new problems of work and wage, income and wealth. I want to see how far I can induce Democracy, Fascism, and Communism to speak the same language and to draw into the picture of colored peoples of the world; the people of China, Japan, and India, and the peoples of Africa.[9]

Although the proposal was a rudiment of a much bigger project, Du Bois had nonetheless unveiled the critical analysis of the shifting configurations of world powers and the increasing significance of race in the project of making the world anew. When the wider world experienced the total collapse of capitalism as a dominant system, on the one hand, and the intensification of the struggle over power, land, and wealth among competing fascist, liberal democratic, and communist states, on the other hand, Du Bois set out to explain the nature of this crisis. "A Search for Democracy," much like the recently published *Black Reconstruction*, aimed at presenting a new kind of political theory that could animate the reconstruction of modernity and democracy. As a theorist of Black radicalism and internationalism, he was in a state of transition, as he sharpened the analysis of the connection between the Black freedom struggle in the United States and the self-determination of darker nations and people around the world. Japan was a part of his overall design.

While the wider world slipped into turmoil and despair and America experienced impasse, Du Bois found himself in a moment of creative outburst despite a bitter experience of resignation from all posts he held in the National Association for the Advancement of Colored People (NAACP) and the *Crisis* magazine in 1934. His departure from the movement was interpreted as a break from his past, the tradition of Black struggles he helped to develop since the launching of the Niagara Movement in 1905. To be sure, one of the central reasons behind his resignation was a growing disparity between him and board members of the NAACP over the association's future course of political action in light of the impact of the Depression on the lives of the Black working class.[10] However, his determination to struggle for Black equality did not change; only the scope and method changed.

Unlike other members of the NAACP, who remained committed to "attack lynching, to bring more cases before the courts and to insist upon full citizenship rights," Du Bois proposed a new orientation. It was called voluntary self-segregation, which was designed to create cooperative Black societies. Calling for racial solidarity across class lines, he declared, "The only thing that we not only can, but must do is voluntarily and insistently to organize our economic and social power, no matter how much segregation it involves."[11] Instead of trying to integrate into the mainstream with American working people during the New Deal era, he pursued an alternative path and stressed the need for independent thinking and collective action. The conceptualization of this new political action was decidedly informed by the dynamics of race and class, as well as by his determination to infuse global perspectives to create a new outlook on the future of race.

Du Bois was convinced that New Deal liberalism did little to safeguard the lives of the Black working class even though Franklin D. Roosevelt (FDR) set out to improve the living standard and social welfare for all Americans. Black working people in agriculture, manufacturing, and services increasingly faced the "strongholds of color caste, . . . [which] was as strong in 1930 as in 1910 . . . and in certain points of view, even stronger."[12] Each piece of Roosevelt's New Deal legislation— the Agricultural Adjustment Administration, the Civilian Conservation

Corps, the National Recovery Administration, and the Federal Housing Administration, to name only a few—was inadequate in enforcing the equal distribution of public-works jobs and relief funds. Moreover, the Second Hundred Days' two landmark laws—the Wagner Act, which guaranteed the rights of workers to form and join labor unions and to bargain collectively to improve their wages, benefits, and working conditions, and the Social Security Act, which provided old-age pensions and unemployment insurance—failed to challenge the institution of white supremacy head-on. The failure to place an antidiscrimination clause in the provisions of the Wagner Act not only narrowed the scope of workers' democracy but in fact allowed racist labor unions to act as "exclusive bargaining agents" to protect the property interests in whiteness. The Social Security Act, too, did not address the needs of the poorest of the poor; it denied pensions and benefits to agricultural and domestic workers, most of whom were workers of color, both men and women.[13]

Writing in 1934 and anticipating intense white resistance as the FDR administration declared the New Deal for America and affirmed the government's responsibility and commitment for the social welfare of all Americans, Du Bois lamented, "We could wish, would pray, that this entrance [into the New Deal] could absolutely ignore lines of race and color, but we know perfectly well it does not and will not, and with the present American opinion, it cannot." He believed that the institution of white supremacy in America was as strong in the time of the New Deal as it was in the period of slavery and its aftermath because the structure of racial domination was "built and increasingly built on the basis of the income [whites] enjoyed and their anti-Negro bias consciously or unconsciously formulated in order to protect their wealth and power."[14]

Even labor unions affiliated with the Congress of Industrial Organizations (CIO), which raised the banner of racial egalitarianism, did not stir a sense of hope for Du Bois. Unlike many Black intellectuals who were radicalized by progressive labor politics on the home front and advocated for Black workers' participation and inclusion in labor struggles, he showed very little faith in organized labor. In his quest for democracy, he instead looked beyond the U.S. nation-state, especially at the intersection of Black nationalism and Marxism, to challenge the "American exceptionalist belief that the United States was the world's exemplary nation-state and the bearer of universality in the world system."[15] For him, America was not the incubator of new universals, even when American labor radicalism in the 1930s showed signs of a new beginning.

Du Bois instead entered the global currents of racial struggles and argued that the movement toward voluntary self-segregation in Black politics and life was not only in accordance with the trend in world affairs but more important inevitable, despite the fact that increasing separation among nation-states might "lead to jealousy, greed, nationalism, and war." He explained that separation was

> inevitable to Jews because of Hitler; inevitable to Japanese because of white Europe; inevitable to Russia because of organized greed over all the white world; inevitable to Ethiopia because of white armies and navies; inevitable, because without it, the American Negroes will suffer evils greater than any possible evil of separation: we would suffer the loss of self-respect, the lack of faith in ourselves, the lack of knowledge about ourselves, the lack of ability to make a decent living by our own efforts and not by philanthropy.[16]

Thinking through the problem of political representation for myriad despised subjects, ranging from Jewish people and Russian communists to Japanese and Ethiopians, in the world dominated by the property interests in whiteness, Du Bois asserted that voluntary segregation was "not aimless, but to one great End," for there existed "power to entrench ourselves for a long siege against the strongholds of color caste."[17] In fact, he claimed that voluntary self-segregation presented "schemes for internationalism in race relations." He explained that the "underlying thought has been continually that [new racial philosophy] can and must be seen not against any narrow, provincial or even national ground, but in relation to the great problem of the colored races of the world and particularly those of African descent."[18]

Far from being divisive, voluntary self-segregation was conceived of by Du Bois as the basis for building the international working-class movement. His rationale was that "labor" was the objective reality for darker people, and that was not always the case for the majority of white workers worldwide, for as Du Bois observed, they "were compensated in part by a sort of public and psychological wage . . . [or] given public deference and titles of courtesy because they were white." Writing in *Black Reconstruction*, he explained the futility of looking for seeds of labor insurgency solely in the United States: "The South is not interested in freedom for dark India. It has no sympathy with the oppressed of Africa or of Asia. It is for the most part against unions and the labor movement, because there can be no real labor movement in the South; their laboring class is cut in two and the white laborers must be ranged upon the side of their own exploiters by persistent propaganda and police force. Labor can gain in the South no class-consciousness." Missing in Black intellectual-activists' thinking, Du Bois knew, was such an internationalist foresight combined with a critical inquiry into the "race concept" as they joined CIO-led labor insurgency across the United States. Their frame of reference remained nation-bound and color-blind, seeing the unity of the integrated American working class rather than the struggle for Black autonomy linked to other racial struggles worldwide as a vehicle for historical and revolutionary change.[19]

Ultimately, Du Bois insisted on the globality of race, which, he argued, facilitated the formation of a new black radical politics that moved on both national and global scales. But Ralph Bunche, an emerging young scholar at Howard University, took issue with Du Bois's race-based political analysis and collective action. In "The Programs of Organizations Devoted to the Improvement of the Status of the American Negro" (1939), published in the *Journal of Negro Education*, Bunche flatly rejected Du Bois's program of voluntary self-segregation, or a call to forge racial solidarity among businesses, workers, educators, and religious leaders to improve the welfare of the race. It "would offer no hope for the betterment of the Negro masses," Bunche wrote, since the primary cause of unemployment, disenfranchisement, and poverty would remain intact. The arrangement of cooperative relations between Black labor and Black capital to overcome the system of racial exploitation was futile "within the walls of white capitalism" unless the problem of the whole system of capitalism was called into question.[20]

Moreover, Bunche wrote that Du Bois's race-conscious political program would produce reactionary and conservative movements. For instance, the "Don't Buy Where You Can't Work" campaign—boycotts and picketing directed at white and Jewish employers who refused to hire Black workers—led to "sort of blind, suicidal emotionalism" when it attracted popular support in cities, such as Chicago and New York, in the 1930s. Bunche argued that such "racial generalizations and prejudices are luxuries which the Negro can ill afford" and denounced Black leadership's failure to be "rational and bold enough to wage a vigorous campaign against Negro anti-Semitism."[21]

Bunche's criticisms against race-based activism did not stop there. What he observed in the politics of race among Black leaders was a narrow outlook that was woefully ill prepared to infuse global perspectives to link up the global struggles against the horrors of fascism and wars abroad and Jim Crow at home: "The white American may recoil with horror at the German barbarisms against the Jew. But the American Negro cries, 'Hitler be damned, and the Jew too; what about the Jim Crow here?'"[22] Bunche continued,

> In a world in which the major issues affecting the future of humanity are increasingly defined in terms of fascism, with its fundamental racial and totalitarian dogmas, versus democracy, imperfect as it has been for minority groups, no Negro organization makes any serious attempt to define these issues in terms of Negro interest, or to align the full power of Negroes with those forces which are struggling heroically to preserve the last vestiges of human liberty in a world gravely threatened with enslavement. Negro organizations herald the Gaines case and the anti-lynching bill while the eyes of the rest of the world are turned on Munich, Prague, and Memel, Albania, Spain and China.[23]

Putting an emphasis on the declining significance of race, he called for a turn to focus on economics and broad political and philosophical concerns, such as fascism and the fate of humanity. Taking a "cue from the share-croppers' and tenant-farmers' unions formed in the South," Bunche argued that the struggle to overcome a society built on racial subordination was possible. He wrote, "Under oppressive conditions identity of economic interests can overcome racial prejudices, and . . . black and white unity is possible."[24] He saw no salvation in race-based activism, let alone the struggle for equality in courts or through ballot boxes. He saw interracial unionism as an agent of social change.

Du Bois did not agree with Bunche's primacy of class over race, although he was impressed with his global perspectives on fundamental human problems. The point of contention between Du Bois and Bunche came down to a difference in the way they approached the race question in America and the world at large. While Bunche saw race as a particular problem in the broader context of the movement of world history, Du Bois insisted it to be at the front and center of human and economic transformations in the modern world.

In the final analysis, Bunche explained that Black leaders and organizations defined the parameters of their thinking and action "entirely in a black groove." "In a world in which events move rapidly and in which the very future of themselves and their group is at stake," he continued, "they are unable to see the social forests for the racial saplings. They, like Hitler, although obviously for different reasons, think that 'all that is not race in this world is trash.'"[25] Du Bois responded to Bunche's repulsion toward all forms of race thinking by arguing that the struggle for Black freedom would "necessarily be racial in effect" because it would have to face the realities of Black Americans' experience, especially their degraded and alienated human qualities as the *racially* oppressed, which were results of their historical experiences with slavery and racial capitalism. Moreover, the struggle for Black freedom would evolve in racial terms because its aim is to revolutionize these very realities of life, including the socially and historically constructed ontological category called race, as well as the very corruption of this concept that denied them human dignity and advancement.[26]

By way of expanding the metaphors of forests and saplings that Bunche used, Du Bois explained the contradictory nature and power of the ontological category called race: "the way to the social forest is through the racial saplings; or better, as it must appear to most of us today, the way to the saplings which are growing into the future social forest, is through the present stark and thick trunks of ancient trees with almost impassable undergrowth; through which the American Negro and other colored groups must force and cut a way."[27] While Bunche discouraged the struggle for Black freedom from moving in a "black groove," Du Bois insisted on the imperative to move in a "racial groove." He saw something usable in racial strivings. He believed that darker nations and people in the modern world, by moving in a racial groove, would find the "stark and thick trunks of ancient trees with almost impassable undergrowth" and, in so doing, transform the old ties of kinship and communal practices to forge new forms of solidarity across multiple color lines not just in America but globally. To move in a racial groove, thus, was a step toward that direction; it was central to his theory of transpacific striving.[28]

## Theorizing and Historicizing a Third Path

Around this time, Du Bois had the same conversation about the impera- tive of a movement in a racial groove with an Indian intellectual named N. S. Subba Rao. Like Bunche, Rao objected to Du Bois's insistence on the race-based struggle for liberation from the interlocking system of white supremacy and industrial exploitation. His contention was that the Du Boisian race-based project of human emancipation would only reinforce existing tensions across the color line and, worse, further cre- ate conditions for "war and . . . the prolonging of that awful path of blood through which humanity has staggered thus far." Yet, for Du Bois, the denial of race consciousness would lead to "the path of humilia- tion and degradation, of insult and suppression, which . . . will be much more disastrous to the world's future than anything else could possibly be." While Du Bois acknowledged limited strategic options available for darker nations and people around the world in their racial struggles for humanity, with one path leading to war and another to humiliation, he was convinced that there existed "a third path—a path that will not range the forces of the world into" these two paths. For him, the basis of this third path was the Afro-Asian philosophy of world history, and the way in which he related to Japan and its political ambition was also shaped by this same conviction.[29]

Central to Du Bois's framing of a third path was his reading of Marxian historical materialism, particularly his grasp of labor as truly human property, sensuous human activity, and ontological category. Just as the philosopher Herbert Marcuse concluded by closely study- ing Karl Marx's *Economic and Philosophic Manuscripts of 1844* when it first became available in 1932 that labor was "the real expression of human freedom," Du Bois, independently of Marcuse, also considered this concept's philosophical foundation as a centerpiece in understand- ing the Marxian theory of revolution called historical materialism. In other words, Du Bois reached the same conclusion as Marcuse did, that embodied in the concept of labor were, borrowing from Marcuse, "original forms of communication, essential relationship[s] of men to one another" that would enable people of color—the world's laboring majority—to become aware of key ontological elements of historical materialism, specifically people of color's existence, alienation, and aspiration and the world's future. And as Marcuse believed, Du Bois, too, was convinced that this insight into human objectification was "not mere theoretical cognition or arbitrary, passive intuition, but *praxis.*" Elaborating with a great insight Du Bois's relationship with Marxism during the period in which he completed *Black Reconstruction*, the great historian of race Sterling Stuckey has argued in *Slave Culture* that Du Bois regarded this growing self-awareness of the Black working class as the nucleus of a workers' democracy, a center lane on a highway moving in the direction toward the emancipation of labor.[30]

Writing *Black Reconstruction* in the 1930s, Du Bois continued to assign, as in his early years, utmost confidence in the potential of human consciousness emerging out of the movement in a racial groove to become a revolutionary force to be reckoned with. In the 1930s, Du Bois was reworking the key idiom of Marxism, labor, to develop a new blueprint of striving in the context of the material and social reality of the Black working class and darker nations and peoples that had to contend with the objective reality of race and its corruption. Thus, emphasized in his project of reclaiming the ontological category of labor for people of color and restoring the field of sensuous human activity for them, first and foremost, was the imperative of fighting the curse of white Europe, which included but was not limited to objectification and reification that stifled human dignity, creativity, and advancement. From this vantage point, he instructed that people of color had to think primarily about how to relate with one another through race: "They must always stand as representatives of the coloured races—of the yellow and black peoples as well as the brown—of the majority of mankind, and together with the Negroes they must face the insistent problem of the assumption of the white people of Europe that they have a right to dominate the world and especially so to organize it politically and industrially as to make most men their slaves and servants."[31]

Simultaneously, however, Du Bois was fully aware of the danger of inserting the concept of race as a stand-in for the concept of labor to invoke Marxian historical materialism as "the lever of the revolution," to borrow Marcuse's words.[32] Ever more sensitive and attuned to the contradictory concept of race and how it related to class, nation, and capitalism, he wrote to Rao,

> If now the coloured peoples—Negroes, Indians, Chinese and Japanese— are going successfully to oppose these assumptions of white Europe, they have got to be sure of their own attitude toward their labouring masses. Otherwise they will substitute for the exploitation of coloured by white races, an exploitation of coloured races by coloured men. If, however, they can follow the newer ideals which look upon human labour as the only real and final repository of political power, and conceive that the freeing of the human spirit and real liberty of life will only come when industrial exploitation has ceased and the struggle to live is not confined to a mad fight for food, clothes and shelter; then and only then, can the union of darker races bring a new and beautiful world, not simply for themselves, but all men.[33]

If what informed Du Bois's preoccupation with race and world revolution during the 1930s was such a philosophical inquiry into "the one real and final repository of political power" called labor, then *Black Reconstruction*, the foundational text for understanding the Du Boisian Afro-Asian philosophy of world history, published during the same period, was his intervention into the discourses of the past and the present to interpret strivings of people of color, specifically Blacks, Indians, Chinese, and Japanese, as agents of historical and social change capable of ushering in a better future.

In *Black Reconstruction*, Du Bois resorted to the production of a counterdiscourse because he was convinced that the existing field of historical studies reduced the agency of the colored world to the level of abstractions. He found this systematic impoverishment of the theory of agency in the discipline of history detrimental to the enterprise of history making in the present. History was "for our pleasure and amusement, for our inflating national ego, and giving us a false but pleasurable sense of accomplishment." The structure of modern historiography, Du Bois believed, resembled the structure of the commodity.

It had repeatedly demonstrated its refusal to represent the humanity of the colored world in its fullness.[34] The problem of ahistoricism was something more than "mere omission and difference of emphasis," Du Bois wrote. It was integral to the production of myths, fictions, and racist ideologies, all of which functioned as systems of rationalization to make the American nation-state virtuous and whiteness normative.[35] He wrote *Black Reconstruction* to eliminate "the Blindspot in the eyes of America, and its historians," that consistently suppressed, as he wrote, "so clear and encouraging a chapter of human struggle and human uplift," made palpable by the self-emancipation of the Black workers, ex-slaves, and their pursuit of "abolition-democracy" during the Reconstruction period. "Black" in the title *Black Reconstruction* was hermeneutics to revolutionize the existing systems of knowledge production and cultural criticism; it was conceived as a political category of struggle.

In *Black Reconstruction*, Du Bois emphasized that historians failed to grasp what it meant for four million enslaved Blacks to struggle against racial exploitation and to emancipate themselves from it during the American Civil War and throughout the Reconstruction era, especially "in the midst of nine billion bitter enemies, and indifferent public opinion of the whole nation." He wrote, "The unending tragedy of Reconstruction is the utter inability of the American mind to grasp its real significance, its national and world implications. . . . We are still blind and infatuated to conceive of the emancipation of the laboring class in half the nation as a revolution comparable to the upheavals in France in the past, and in Russia, Spain, India and China today."[36] This insurgent movement led by Blacks and other proponents of "abolition-democracy" was, as he conceptualized it in terms of the language of labor radicalism, a "general strike," in which the "withdrawal and bestowal of labor decided the war." To put it another way, the emancipation of slaves, as David Roediger has also reinforced, represented "the greatest uncompensated revolutionary seizure of property (that is, slaves) in history prior to the Soviet revolution" and was so contagious that it also radicalized white workers and disenfranchised women to seek their own jubilee in the aftermath of this war.[37]

Du Bois was aware of the significance of this connection between Black freedom and labor. Within the historical development of the colored world, Du Bois argued that "labor" appeared as objective reality, revealing sensuous human activity directed toward revolutionizing all objects of life to make the existing world anew, including the American nation.[38] With this in mind, he strongly believed that "there will be no world labor movement which does not begin with black Africa, brown India, yellow Asia, [because] all other so-called movements end in nationalism, colonial imperialism and war."[39] His argument was that the historical development of the colored world produced a distinct culture of liberation from which labor's own realization of its object could potentially be achieved.

While the emancipation of labor would not be easy, Du Bois explained that "the quickest way to bring the reason of the world face to face with this major problem of human progress is to listen to the complaint of those human beings today who are suffering from white attitudes, from white habits, from the conscious and unconscious wrongs which white folk are today inflicting on their victims. The colored world therefore must be seen as existing not simply for itself but as a group whose insistent cry may yet become the warning which awakens the world to its truer self and its wider destiny."[40] In other words, the Du Boisian formulation of working-class internationalism was a revision of Western Marxism, designed to assign categorical unity to the insurgency of the colored world, which crystallized at the very moment when the oppressed found themselves standing at critical historical conjunctures, becoming aware of their capacities to break all categories of domination, including race and other alienated qualities found in their own labor.

Du Bois's strong sense of conviction about the presence of a third path in the 1930s was derived from this grasp of the revolutionary tendency within the readiness of the Black masses to revolt against existing society and its structure of thought and how such an act opened up new political, theoretical, and epistemic possibilities during the period of the American Civil War and Reconstruction. While historians characterized ex-slaves' cries for freedom as "gangs of dirty Negroes howling and dancing; poverty-stricken ignorant laborers mistaking war, destruction, and revolution for the mystery of the free human soul," or dismissed such dreams of emancipation altogether as "foolish, bizarre, and tawdry," Du Bois identified something at once ecumenical and revolutionary. Du Bois lyrically captured the essence of jubilee that revealed itself most explicitly through the expression of Black masses' surrealism:[41]

> Suppose on some gray day, as you plod down Wall Street, you should see God sitting on the Treasury steps, in His Glory, with the thunders curved about him? Suppose on Michigan Avenue, between the lakes and hills of stone, and in the midst of hastening automobiles and jostling crowds, suddenly you see living and walking toward you, the Christ, with sorrow and sunshine in his face?
>
> Foolish talk, all of this, you say, of course; and that is because no American now believes in his religion. Its facts are mere symbolism; its revelation vague generalities; its ethics a matter of carefully balanced gain. But to most of the four million black folk emancipated by civil war, God was real. They knew Him. They had met Him personally in many a wild orgy of religious frenzy, or in the black stillness of night. His plan for them was clear; they were to suffer and be degraded, and then afterwards by Divine edict, raised to manhood and power; and so on January 1, 1863, He made them free.[42]

Du Bois was a brilliant student of Black religion and understood the social and historical dynamics of human passion. Indeed, as Stuckey has emphasized in *Slave Culture*, "the whole range of the religious experience in the countryside [while Du Bois was a student at Fisk University] was a primary source for his exploration of slave religious consciousness and behavior that he would write about in *The Souls of Black Folk* and in *Black Reconstruction*." What he saw in Black religion and more broadly in slave culture was not heathenism or primitivism. Where there was enormous joy of freedom, Du Bois found the brutal reality of slavery and a path toward humanity: "What connects that sadness and joy is the courage to life, the capacity to confront tragedy without wincing and thereby allow the human spirit to assert itself undiminished," writes Stuckey. In "the tragic soul-life of the slave," Du Bois located the nature of spiritual strivings, the transformative power of the expression of Black self-affirmation, which served as an essential guide to replot the narrative of racial struggles in world history.[43]

Du Bois might have understood what Karl Marx meant by an objective sensuous being, which was interpreted as the essence of the ontology of labor. According to Marx, "To be sensuous is to *suffer.*" He explained in *Economic and Philosophic Manuscripts of 1844*, "Man as an objective sensuous being is therefore a *suffering* being—and because he feels what he suffers, a *passionate* being. Passion is the essential force of man energetically bent on its object."[44] While the dominant scholarship distorted "unshakable historical facts" about the Black freedom struggle with adjectives such as "shrewd," "notorious," and "cunning," Du Bois found the "Truth" in what Nikhil Pal Singh calls "Black worldliness." Du Bois insisted that the task of a historian is to deliver this Truth, a sensuous world that Black workers inhabited and nurtured called "labor," for there one would find the real meaning and practice of freedom and humanism.[45] Struggling against the one-sidedness of Reason, called Eurocentrism, in the discourses of the past and the present, Du Bois deconstructed white Europe and its claims to rationality, civilization, and democracy and sought to validate and valorize, by way of presenting *Black Reconstruction* as a counterdiscourse, the philosophical and historical basis of the third path. The struggle for Black humanity during Reconstruction was a proof of Black labor's capacity to revolutionize all objects of life to actualize freedom, for, as he insisted, it "did not fail where it was expected to fail."[46] The task of a scholar engaged in the history of the present, according to Du Bois, was to make this pursuit of a third path a political reality on a global scale.

Aiming to recall and renew this tradition of historical Black struggles in the 1930s and 1940s and to carry this project forward worldwide, Du Bois became increasingly preoccupied with how Japan might relate to Black worldliness and with finding ways to reach a third path to overcome the effects of white Europe, just as Black masses did in their efforts to reconstruct American democracy during the Civil War and Reconstruction. Assessing the success of Japan's modernization since its historic encounters with white Europe in the mid-nineteenth century, Du Bois wrote in his *Pittsburgh Courier* weekly column that in Japan's "very pride and accomplishment lies danger." He explained, "The Europe which she copied was not perfect land. The technique of industry which she mastered, the capitalistic regime which she adopted so successfully has, as all thinking men see today, threatening, if not fatal tendencies." In an affirming tone, he made his point clear:

> Her attitude toward China is the main case in point. . . . Japan forgets the danger of capitalism. Unbridled production cannot continue indefinitely. Cheap labor is not in the end cheap for the nation that seeks to build prosperity on it. If Japan today, avoiding temptation, raised the standard of living among her laborers [in China and other parts of Asia], she could still compete with the world and at the same time develop a mass of workers who would be the most intelligent and gifted the world has ever seen.

He expressed hope that Japan would grasp the significance of the politics of race and power "not in terms of capitalistic advance . . . [but] primarily in terms of human culture" to actualize history, which meant the unification of East Asia to resist and overcome white Europe structured by capitalist imperatives. He declared, "In the nineteenth century Japan saved the world from slavery to Europe. In the twentieth century she is called to save the world from the slavery to capital."[47]

Surveying the global topography of race from East Asia while traveling through the region in the winter of 1936, Du Bois articulated a new historical discourse via pro-Japan provocation, validating and valorizing Japan as an incubator of new universals. He essentially argued that the crisis in East Asia resulting from the expanding Sino-Japanese War and Japan's resistance to white Europe presented Japan with an opportunity to take a giant step in the movement of world history to complete its destiny: pan-Asian liberation from white Europe under Japanese leadership. Du Bois's conception of the Afro-Asian philosophy of world history gained legitimacy in his thought and emerged as a rigidly conceived intellectual property during this period. Irony was not of his concern, for he did not discern how the ahistoricity of his own discourse reinforced the very problem and structure of Eurocentrism, which was deeply embedded in modern thought and life and which he relentlessly criticized and sought to overcome.

As much as Du Bois desired, Japan, unlike Black America and other communities of the African diaspora, was not concerned with vindicating its humanity in the white-supremacist world, nor was it struggling for political autonomy and legitimacy, let alone legal affirmation on the world stage. As a sovereign territorial state, it had all of that. By the 1930s, starting with Japan's invasion, conquest, and colonization of Manchuria, followed by its departure from the League of Nations and its declaration of full-scale war with China and throughout Asia in the name of pan-Asianism by the end of the decade, Japan had established a space of its own in the global white polity, securely tied up with its own and competing empires, colonies, and diplomacy. Black America had not.

This difference in the conception of "nation" between Black America and Japan was obviously crucial in fashioning a new historical discourse capable of mounting a critique of Eurocentrism and articulating how to overcome it. The Japanese imperialist state did not possess a concept of human culture that could be mobilized in the service of world-historic transformation to bring an end to the domination of white nations, although it certainly proclaimed that it did to justify the policy of pan-Asianism throughout Japan's Fifteen Years War (1931–1945). Moreover, Japan was not a proletarian nonwhite nation, although it did create a façade as an anti-imperialist nation in opposition to white Europe. The ontological concept of labor could never be derived from the state even when this state was not white; it had to come from the "basic experience of the [masses] to constitute a practical, sensuous activity and the original philosophy of labor," as the preeminent scholar of Japanese history Harry Harootunian puts it, keenly aware of the immanent difficulties of organizing an intellectual movement to overcome the problems of modernity when thinking on a world-historic scale.[48] Ultimately, the fundamental problem of Du Bois's pro-Japan provocation was his failure to critique the Japanese imperialist state's racial propaganda. Instead, he fueled the power of the state through the legitimation of the Afro-Asian philosophy of world history.

## The Failure of Du Boisian World History

Upon Du Bois's arrival in Nagasaki, Japan, on December 3, 1936, a journalist from *Osaka Mainichi Shimbun* (Osaka Daily Newspaper) sat with him and asked him how he interpreted the turmoil in world politics. Although the accuracy of this reporting is in question, given that by

then an elaborate system of state propaganda existed in Japan, the journalist reported that Du Bois prophesized that "the next World War will
undoubtedly be a race war," as long as the global problem of the color
line remained unresolved, and argued that the unity of the colored
world held a key to reconstructing democracy and modernity in the
present.[49] During the course of Du Bois's tour through East Asia in the
winter of 1936, he reiterated this line of argument to elevate the political stakes and to communicate the importance of cultivating kinship
and fraternity based on race among darker people and nations around
the world.

However, his formulation of coming unities between pan-Africa and
pan-Asia depended on a romantic view of historical destiny and intellectual leadership that was persistently articulated through a gendered
structure of thought and sexual politics. In Du Bois's assessment of the
rise of "colored" Japan as one of the important episodes in the movement of world history, in other words, one finds his preoccupation with
assigning radical political agency at the nexus of race and heterosexual
masculinity. What came out of this politics, or "processes of governmentality," as Roderick Ferguson writes, were "the gender and sexual
economies of African American intellectual formations" that held the
constitution and reproduction of gender and sexual normativity as
the essential requirement in the struggle against the global racial polity. In Du Bois's efforts to develop a mode of political belonging that
moved on local and global scales to assist Black subjects to articulate
goals and dreams of human emancipation, he enunciated the pro-Japan
position, valorizing the new form of radical agency that was not only
decidedly heteropatriarchal but also predicated on the regulation and
management of Black female subjects. Du Bois's pro-Japan provocation could not dislodge itself from this power, the gendered and heterosexist logic of domination underpinning white Europe. This section
indexes this failure in Du Bois's Afro-Asian philosophy of world history
by closely tracking his "itineraries of power" as he occupied one of the
nerve centers of the Japanese empire, Manchukuo, especially how, from
there, he ruminated on the state of Sino-Japanese relations, the future
of pan-Asia.[50]

While Du Bois acknowledged to the *Osaka Mainichi Shimbun* journalist that he was an autodidact with regard to his knowledge of Japan,

he did convey his intellectual interest. He told the reporter that he was eager to learn more about the Ainu, the indigenous people of Hokkaido, the northernmost region in Japan, and briefly touched on the status of American Indians as a point of comparison. Since he made a reference to indigenous people on both sides of the Pacific, one of Japan's leading daily newspapers mistakenly identified him as the father of American Indians' struggle for sovereignty.[51] This mistake revealed much about how he studied and surveyed this new terrain in East Asia. His method of evaluation and interpretation in East Asia was at every turn informed by an American perspective on race, as well as his determination to grant human agency to the colored world in the discourses of the past and the present. As he toured Manchukuo, China, and Japan in November–December 1936, he began shaping the global topography of race cognitively to replot the narrative of a racial history of the modern world and to establish the Afro-Asian philosophical basis of historical materialism.

For Du Bois, this work of replotting the globality of race entailed undoing the history of whiteness from American and global perspectives. His intellectual project was clear: to articulate the new political imagination to explore possibilities for pan-nonwhite mobilizations against the political alliance of what Du Bois called the "Nordic race." The choice of the topic for his formal address in Manchukuo in mid-November 1936, the first stop in his itinerary across the Japanese empire, was characteristic of Du Bois, who had been exploring how to combat this "Nordic" system of exploitation and domination from multiple fronts.[52] When Du Bois arrived in Hsinking (now Changchun), this new capital in Japanese-occupied northeast China, Manchuria, was in the midst of major construction to become the center of a "new" Asian nation called Manchukuo. Since the Manchurian Incident of 1931, the Japanese had begun building this puppet-colonial state through aggressive militarism, imperialist racism, Japanese migration and settlement policies, the coercive and repressive mobilization of populations, which entailed violence and labor exploitation, and the state control and management of the economy by the Southern Manchuria Railroad Company (SMRC). Although the Japanese had placed the last emperor of the Manchu dynasty, the young Puyi, as head of this new state in 1933, the Japanese political and economic elites associated with the SMRC, the officers of the Imperial Japanese Army in Manchuria called the Guandong Army, and the leaders of the fascistic Concordia Association were actually in charge of political, military, social, and economic affairs.[53]

Particularly important to Manchukuo state builders during this nascent period of colonial state formation was the concept of the East Asian Cooperative Body (*toa kyodotai*). Guided by "the idea that a collectivized Asian economy provided a step towards a more 'just' social order," Manchukuo state builders imposed, through war, militarism, and fascistic cultural politics, their racial construction of pan-Asian unity from above and carried out brutal colonial projects and large-scale structural transformations, all the while framing Japan's action as a work of an anti-imperialist nation resisting white Europe and its racialized imperialist system of exploitation. Du Bois witnessed this "birth of a new nation" in Hsinking. Most likely, he was swept up by utopian discourses that were central to imperialist state propaganda when he met and dined with statesmen, officials, and business leaders who were centrally involved with the Japanese imperialist project of building a colonial state.[54]

The members of the SMRC's Employees Club (*Mantetsu Shainkai*), to whom Du Bois delivered his formal talk in Hsinking, were individuals not only familiar with Marxian political and intellectual orientations but also influenced by the transnational vision of egalitarianism and cooperation to pursue "a viable alternative to Marxist-Leninist development of a just society."[55] According to historian Prasenjit Duara, these members "advocated racial harmony" in Manchukuo and across Asia and held the utopian notion of Manchukuo as a place where "they could realize a vision that many considered impossible to achieve in the established society of Japan." It was "arguably the only place that held a romance for Japanese." Much like the Manchurian Youth League, the members of the SMRC's Employees Club insisted on cooperation among the "five races" in Manchukuo—Han, Manchu, Mongol, Korean, and Japanese—as a basis for building a new "multiracial" state under the leadership of Japan to achieve the unification of East Asia. In fact, some of the members were most likely "painfully aware that Japanese interests in Manchuria were doomed without some kind of compact with the Chinese communities or . . . cooperation between races or nationalities and the rejection of colonialist attitudes."[56] Given the salience of race consciousness manifested through their expression of the dream of pan-Asia, when Du Bois declared in his talk that "the current striving for political equality by various colored races the world over is a movement for the better of human intercourse, building a firm basis for lasting world peace," such a pronouncement struck a chord in them.[57] Both Du Bois and the Japanese settler-colonialists entered the process of identification and began moving in a racial groove.

Strikingly, Du Bois's talk centered on the historical critique of whiteness, especially its "origins, social reproduction, and vulnerabilities," all of which were presented from the vantage point of the historical Black struggles to bring an end to white supremacy in America.[58] Du Bois's main argument resonated with the writer for *Manchuria Daily News* so much that this writer was able to identify the essence of Du Bois's main argument. The writer used the following quote derived from Du Bois's talk to make the point: "There was no color prejudice in ancient or medieval eras: it is a product of a comparatively recent epoch, when the advance of technical advances enabled the Nordic race to master the material resources of the world."[59] The importance of this statement, from the point of view of dialectical historical materialism, was that, on one hand, the institutionalization of white supremacy had been the driving force of Western imperialism and colonialism. Indeed, Du Bois, at the outset of this talk, took the task of a materialist critique, by way of resetting the historical context of British colonial America with a race-making project at its center, to explain how America swiftly organized itself into a society built on the racial subordination of Blacks and Indians:

From the beginning America never has been really a white man's country. The aborigines . . . were Indians, a copper-colored race. And soon as the white colonists from Europe started settling there early in the 17th century Negroes from Africa came in increasing numbers to do the hard basic work c.f. the plantations in Americas. Not all the Negroes migrating to America were slaves at first. Some came as contract laborers but gradually they were all reduced to the status of slaves. The tide of Negro immigrants to America rose in the 18th century and reached its climax in the first half of the 19th century. The prosperity and expansion of the cotton and tobacco plantations in the southern states required an increasing amount of slave labor.[60]

The significance of Du Bois's remark about the origins of whiteness was that the formation of whiteness as a category was tied to such "grand historical processes" as slavery, European imperial expansion into the New World and Africa, and colonization worldwide. Rather than "casting it overwhelmingly as an identity, disembodied from social relations," as David Roediger writes, Du Bois took seriously this crucial moment in the racial history of America, during which "the idea that owning a white skin had tremendous value," or had the power of money, acquired categorical unity. Du Bois set out to communicate this history of the construction of what Cheryl Harris calls "whiteness as property" in the United States to the audience of the members of the SMRC's Employees Club.[61]

On the other hand, in terms of a Marxian dialectical materialist critique, the significance of Du Bois's invocation of white supremacy as "a product of a comparatively recent epoch," as he put it in this talk, was that it articulated the horizon of possibilities. Presenting the imperative of a race-making project dialectically, Du Bois pointedly highlighted that the constitution of the so-called Nordic race was inseparable from the dominant systems of rationalization that were made and remade in recent times through "the advance of technological sciences" in law, philosophy, natural sciences, sociology, economics, history, and education, to name just a few. Far from being a permanent fixture, although reified as such, he argued, this configuration of racial power would not stay white forever. It was a matter of time before "the worship of the Nordic totem" would come to an end because race, or as he referred to it in this talk, "the color question," had become a crucial site of contradiction both locally and globally.[62] His contention was that the system of racial exploitation and the grounds for resistance to this system were being pulled into the vortex of struggles. The European scramble for Africa from the late nineteenth century to the early twentieth century globalized this terrain of racial struggles in important ways and engendered new formations and possibilities. He explained to the audience of the SMRC's Employees Club,

If the United States was an isolated country its color problem may have been settled as a local issue. But after the European colonists plunged into Africa in the last century the color question came to the fore as a world issue. The Americans later started color agitation against the Mexicans, Chinese, Japanese in the States, and even against the darker whites from Italy and the Balkan lands. The color question is now acute all over the world.[63]

Clearly, for Du Bois, race was a political category, not a biological category. In his mind, those who were subjected to the wrath of white supremacy in the United States included not only Asians, Mexicans, and Africans and people of African descent but also "darker whites," southern and eastern Europeans.[64] The so-called race question crossed multiple color lines. If racialized subjects were to reflect on how to locate potential for convergences in the shared racial past, as Du Bois sought to do in this talk in Hsinking, then possibilities for the local and global projects of pan-nonwhite mobilizations against the "Nordic race" could become something other than a mere rhetorical stance. Du Bois assigned utmost confidence in this politics of race and its power to render the "acuteness" of the so-called color question that was capable of exceeding the boundaries governing and dividing darker nations and people and engendering the communities of solidarities against the "Nordic race." The whole point of presenting this, to borrow Roediger's exacting phrase, "short, inglorious, and hopefully finite" history of whiteness in America from the colonial period to the rise of the Jim Crow South in the early twentieth century and the relationship of this history to European expansion in Africa from the late nineteenth century, thus, was to suggest that change was necessary and possible.[65]

However much Du Bois's Hsinking talk represented a strategic practice of criticism to help forge a broad front against white supremacy, his articulation of the unity of darker nations and people, repeated throughout his sojourn across the Japanese empire, could not dislodge itself from imperialist Japan's racial propaganda. Ultimately, Du Bois was unable to emphasize the impossibility of guaranteeing a just social order through such a theoretical abstraction. One of the ways to explain this problematic in Du Bois's thought and methodology is to consider

Du Bois's deployment of the literary convention and narrative form of "Romance" as a propagandistic strategy to engender "a black internationalist response to both U.S. racism and Euro-American imperialism." What one finds in Du Bois's engagement with the pedagogy of propaganda is, as Alys Eve Weinbaum argues, "a highly troubling heterosexual logic of narrative resolution particular to the genre of [Romance]." For him, this genre suffused with gender and sexual politics functioned as the platform to rework the idioms of Black radicalism and internationalism to articulate imperatives of not just unity between pan-Asia and pan-Africa but also trained leadership to complete the historical destiny of this solidarity project. His eagerness to reproduce the meanings and idioms of the significance of such racial struggles worldwide as the incubators of the ontology and epistemology of radical political agency for darker nations and peoples, Weinbaum explains, "all too often created unanalyzed, racially essentialist representations of reproductive heterosexuality."[66] The unpacking of Du Bois's reflection on Manchukuo, how he constructed the narrative form and convention of Romance as an instrument of political protest, in many ways helps explain why Du Bois recalled his meeting with Matsuoka Yosuke (1880–1946), the vice president of the SMRC who later became a foreign minister during Prince Konoe Fumitaro's second term as the prime minister of Japan, in glowing terms.

Indeed, while in Manchukuo, Du Bois exhibited nothing but admiration and respect for Matsuoka and continued to speak of him in high regard thereafter, although he was then a colonial bureaucrat who helped to set Manchukuo on the path to state-led industrialization and modernization with brutal consequences and later led the "Greater East Asian Co-Prosperity Sphere" movement with Tojo Hideki, which resulted in destructive and horrifying wars on an unspeakable scale. As a principal architect of imperialist Japan's policies in Asia, he intensified the repression and brutality of the imperialist state, while creating a façade that Japan was the "liberator" of Asians, fighting in a race war against the white world to achieve a sphere of prosperity throughout Asia.[67] Du Bois wrote in his column for the *Amsterdam News* in March 1940, describing the nature of his meeting with Matsuoka in the following way:

We sat and talked together about the world and color prejudice. I already knew of him as the man who had demanded that the League of Nations openly declare the equality of all races. When the League refused; when England and France declined because of their fear of the United States to consider the subject, Matsuoka arose and led Japan out of the League. That fall day in Singking [*sic*], we talked about democracy—that broader democracy that sees no color line. Such a democracy, said Matsuoka, only Japan could lead.[68]

Both Du Bois and Matsuoka were in agreement concerning Japan's place in the world of race and empire and its capacity to resolve the unfinished struggle for democracy. Both men concurred that powerful "colored" Japan was on its way to entering the new stage of human development by disavowing the curse of white Europe. Du Bois saw in Matsuoka a man of conviction who could be presented as an embodiment of, to borrow Wahneema Lubiano's words, "a strategic will to constitute a new institutional and ontological object of knowledge" for the oppressed nationalities and races under the spell of white Europe so that they could pursue the alternative model of modernization, much like how the Russian Revolution and the Marxist-Leninist program of development showed the alternative path to human emancipation during the First World War era. Indeed, building on Matsuoka's remark that "Japan was the most communistic of modern states, . . . [for] there had never been that strong sense of individual ownership of property that characterized so many people," Du Bois concluded that Matsuoka was trying to live up to "the responsibility of proving to the world that colonial enterprise by a colored nation need not imply the caste, exploitation and subjection which it has always implied in the case of white Europe."[69]

Du Bois turned to history as a tool to defend Japan's claims to China's northeast and to constitute Japanese imperial legitimacy as an ontological and institutional fact, just as Matsuoka did when he mounted a revolt against white Europe when the League of Nations' Lynton Commission report upheld Chinese sovereignty over Manchuria in 1932. Du Bois's historical account of "colored" Japan's emergence onto the world stage, which was dominated by white interests and polities, further reinforced his depiction of Matsuoka as an admired revolutionary leader who took an independent political and diplomatic action to reject the terms of white Europe. Du Bois's mythos of Romance was built around the figure of Matsuoka as a man of action and determination "whose life could be thought as an exemplary and which in consequence could be deployed for didactic and inspirational purposes." An outcome of this "figuration of the heroic" was the articulation of critical agency, the projection of radical heterosexual masculinity as a crucial work of racial vindication and solidarity among darker nations and people.[70]

Before leaving Manchukuo for Tientsin (now Tianjin), China's second-largest port city after Shanghai, Du Bois contemplated the recent history of East Asia to search for the meaning of Manchukuo. The region surrounding Dairen was, as Du Bois wrote, a "historic ground," where Japan and "white Europe" contested for power and wealth through territorial expansion, investment, militarization, and colonization, while China defended its sovereignty in this region. He wrote, "Today I stood where, in 1905, Japan blockaded the Russian fleet in yonder shining harbor of the Yellow Sea and, creeping the great harsh peaks of these wild mountains, made Europe surrender to Asia."[71]

In narrating the unfolding events of the recent past with epic momentum and framing this movement of history in the context of European and U.S. imperialism and colonialism in the nineteenth and twentieth centuries, Du Bois constructed the image of a confident Japan and sketched the process by which it emerged as a race rebel of sorts, which culminated in Matsuoka's decision to leave the League of Nations in 1933 to take an independent path to pursue the development of a new society and a new East Asian order. For Du Bois, Japan's colonization of Manchuria was conceived as a decisive moment in world history, a historic leap. It marked Japan's departure from its dependency to white Europe. He wrote,

Manchuria is the natural mainland of the isles of Japan. She wrested it from China in the war of 1895, but Europe made her surrender it. Then the Russians calmly walked in and took it. They extended the Siberian railroad through it and, seizing the harbor of Port Arthur, fortified it and built the city of Dalny. Along came Germany and seized the Peninsula of Shantung, just south, and fortified that. Already England had seized

Hong Kong, while France was in Indo-China. Japan was surrounded with guns pointed at her heart. Then came the Russian-Japanese war, and Japan secured the extreme point of the cape as a lease, but Russia was still behind her and Germany at her side. After the World War, the situation changed. Japan said to England, who held India, Hong Kong, half of Africa and all the continent of Australia; to France, who had North Africa and Syria; to America, who held half of Mexico, Puerto Rico, the Philippines and the Canal Zone: I need Manchuria more than you need any of these territories. Manchuria today has no government, but is in the hands of roving bandits. Its land and materials are absolutely necessary to my development and expansion as a nation. Moreover, there was one thing more which Japan did not say aloud, but which was even more true: Unless I take Manchuria now, when you can't stop me, you will seize it at the very first moment you can. England, France and America, gorged with the loot of the world, suddenly became highly moral on the subject of annexing other people's land. No! they said, and Japan walked out of the League of Nations and took Manchuria.[72]

Suffused with racial romanticism, Du Bois constructed this saga of Japan's sovereignty claims to characterize Manchuria as a "natural mainland of the isles of Japan." Although his use of the word "natural" to define the relationship between Japan and China could potentially be interpreted as his failure to escape the nineteenth-century theory of scientific racism, he described this relationship in this way to posit race as a political category of kinship and fraternity.

In fact, the concept of race was not simply the political idiom anchoring Du Bois's prose of protest and narrative of Japan's heroic conquest of China's northeast. It functioned as an incitement to Matsuoka, to borrow from Roderick Ferguson's theorization, which animated an incitement to revolutionary heterosexual masculinity. Race, in this instance, helped articulate the gendered and sexual *discourse of Matsuoka*. In other words, this discourse made "an art of the self," as Ferguson explains, "intended to connect the fashioning of the self to the management of family, economy, and state." Indeed, Du Bois's historical interpretation revealed the extent to which he was fixated on seeing Japan's struggle for Manchukuo, via the figuration of Matsuoka, as a struggle to conserve the culturally, socially, and historically conceived grouping called race. Du Bois was at work in this transpacific project of the "conservation of races" to articulate a heteropatriarchal authority that was capable of guiding striving "by race organization, by race solidarity, by race unity to the realization of that broader humanity which freely recognizes differences in men, but sternly deprecates inequality in their opportunities of development." Such was the function of the discourse of Matsuoka: an enabler of heteronormative transpacific racial formation. It indexed, as the following passage shows, a disastrous turn in Black radicalism and internationalism and hence the failure of the Du Boisian intellectual project.[73] Du Bois declared,

> I have been in Manchuria for only a week. But in that time I have seen its borders north, west and south; its capital and their chief cities and many towns; I have walked the streets night and day; I have talked with officials, visited industries and read reports. I came prepared to compare this colonial situation with colonies in Africa and the West Indies, under white European control. I have come to the firm conclusion that in no colony that I have seen or read of is there such clear evidence of
>
> (1) Absence of racial or color caste;
>
> (2) Imperial law and order;
>
> (3) Public control of private capital for the general welfare;
>
> (4) Services for health, education, city-planning, housing, consumers' cooperation and other social ends;
>
> (5) The incorporation of the natives into the administration of government and social readjustment.[74]

Du Bois's denial of truths was absolute. He would not acknowledge that Black America and Japan did not occupy the same space of a racial promise. Nor did Black America and Japan share the same political stakes and problems from which the criticism of Eurocentrism would be mounted or the work of vindicating the colored world would be carried out. However, in order to present a deeper analysis of this problem of racial romanticism that was linked to gender and sexual normativity, one would have to further interrogate the interplay of race, sexual politics, and empire that appeared in his opinions about the imperative of pan-Asian unity in Sino-Japanese relations.

When Du Bois ruminated on how to develop the argument against the theory and practice of white supremacy in solidarity with Japan and China, he often inverted the dominant eugenicist rhetoric of reproduction that called on white women to keep the nation racially pure and homogeneous. Specifically, relying on the "spectral presence" of a Black woman and her "reproductive capacities," he argued that nations and people of color had to ensure the integrity of the unity of the colored world, no matter how much self-segregation it involved.[75] Speaking as the representative of the pan-African movement, Du Bois hoped that Japan and China would come around the circle to mend their differences, avoid race suicide, and struggle for the unity and liberation of the colored world. He wanted these "two cousins" in Asia (as he called these nations to highlight kinship) to face Africa and understand the true meaning of spiritual and cultural striving rather than turning to white Europe for sources of renewal, uplift, and salvation.

In Du Bois's grappling with how to overcome white Europe, Africa was always a vortex, for, as he explained to the SMRC's Employees Club in Hsinking, "after the European colonists plunged into Africa in the last century [that is, the nineteenth century], the color question came to the fore as a world issue." In the Black world, Du Bois thought Japan and China would find, as Weinbaum explains, "the life-giving goddess of the entire world," who would sing sorrow songs and help project an alternative political imagination. According to Weinbaum, "the universal message of [sorrow] songs . . . has been *reproduced* by black mothers not as a biological destiny, but as a cultural inheritance of universal significance."[76] Yet neither the presence of Black women nor their agency was acknowledged in his discourse of Black radicalism and internationalism. It was buried. Moreover, even if their agency was not entirely absent, it figured only marginally, as evident in the prospectus for his unpublished manuscript "A Search for Democracy," which he presented to his publisher, Alfred Harcourt, soon after he returned from the 1936 world tour.

Interestingly, Du Bois told the publisher that he would distill in the form of a novel the dynamics of the rapidly changing international system, a wide variety of racial struggles on the world stage, and how they were all tied to local politics of race and power in the United States. In terms of the novel's global focus, transpacific consideration, technique of narration, and structure of narrative, the book was similar to *Dark Princess* (1928), in which he explored the dynamic connection between Black America and India to fashion a more expansive conception of Black internationalism. While at the center of *Dark Princess* was the romance between Matthew Townes, a young African American man, and Royal Highness Kautilya of Bwodpur, an Indian princess, his new work centered on the platonic relationship between a Black male professor and his "woman friend." He wrote to the publisher soon after he returned from the 1936 world tour:

> I want to put this book into popular form by beginning with the difficulty of discussing problems and politics and economics in a small, southern, Negro college. Then I am sending my colored professor on leave of absence without pay and having him correspond with the woman friend whom he had left behind. She writes from time to time about democracy in America and particularly the practical application of democracy in committees, boards of trustees, group organization, and local government. He, on the other hand, writes of democracy in England and France, of Hitler and the Nazis, and of Russia. Then he plunges into the contradictions and implications of the new political and economic revolution in China and Japan and its inevitable extension in other parts of the East. He then comes back to the newer aspects of the African question, disenfranchisement and land monopoly in South and East Africa, the conquest of Ethiopia, and industry and raw materials in West Africa, and the influence of all this on incipient war in Europe.[77]

As the male protagonist of this story drifts from the American South to England, France, Nazi Germany, Russia, China, and Japan and returns to Africa, all the while thinking of his points of departure, the American South and a "woman friend," he seeks to underscore the problem of white Europe and its global and local significance. The protagonist's world tour makes the transnational space of inquiry become productive for a new theoretical analysis and formation.

The main character, a professor of color at a small Black college in the South, is a man in motion in this plot. Like Du Bois, this male character travels around the world, including East Asia, witnesses the world on the verge of being turned upside down, and records his assessment and analysis. The main concern of this male protagonist, as well as of Du Bois, is to bring together coeval modernities—fascism, liberalism, and communism—and to explain a way out of the crisis of the existing world. A woman he leaves behind, on the contrary, discusses workings and limits of democracy in committees, boards of trustees, group organization, and local government. The story was designed to connect the local and the global through these two characters' exchange of insights into the politics of race and power.[78]

But the female character enters into this discussion without political authority, a quality only assigned to the male character. This man is purported to be the only person fit to venture into the realm of the unknown—Manchukuo, China, and Japan—to bring home the new institutional and ontological insights to bear on the local practice of American democracy. Du Bois explained that the male character, not the female friend in America, "plunges into the contradictions and implications of the new political and economic revolution in China and Japan and its inevitable extension in other parts of the East," and this male protagonist emerges out of negotiation with the consequences of modernity with clarity in thought and aim. The female character, meanwhile, is subordinated, despite her key role in supplying information, or facts, empirical or otherwise, to help articulate a call to racial globality. Denied her is access to the dialectical inquiry, and buried in the name of racial solidarity across the global color lines are her gender consciousness and its place in the shaping of the discourse of Black radicalism and internationalism.[79]

In Du Bois's journalistic writings, in which he discussed and analyzed the significance of Sino-Japanese relations for the unity of the colored world, however, the "spectral presence" of a Black woman appeared as a guide to help him achieve cognitive clarity as he worked through what he called "the contradictions and implications of the new political and economic revolution in China and Japan." She was present all along, although her critical agency was never named, and precisely because of this "lack of embodiment," Du Bois made theoretical and analytical advances.[80] The proof appeared most tellingly as he persistently characterized animosity between Japan and China as a case of race suicide that needed to be avoided if the colored world were to be constituted as

a radical form of governmentality whose power was derived from revolutionary heterosexual masculinity. Figured in his transpacific call to
racial globality was the inverted eugenicist discourse of reproduction,
which activated the logic of white heteropatriarchy.[81]

While Du Bois was in Shanghai, for instance, the Chinese elites were
awestruck by his woefully inadequate grasp of Sino-Japanese relations
when he asked the following questions intended to collectively explore
the potential of racial solidarity within the colored world:

> How far do you think of Europe as continuing to dominate the world,
> or how far do you envisage a world whose spiritual center is Asia or the
> colored races? You have escaped from the domination of Europe politi-
> cally since the World War—as least in part; but how do you propose to
> escape from the domination of European capital? How are your work-
> ing classes progressing? Why is it that you hate Japan more than Europe
> when you have suffered more from England, France, and Germany, than
> from Japan?[82]

Understandably, there was, as Du Bois put it, "a considerable silence"
after he posed these questions. In response, Chinese men defended
that China was working to realize a unified nation, amid the civil war
between the Kuomintang nationalists led by Chiang Kai-shek and communists led by Mao Tse-tung. They expressed that the Kuomintang was
working to overcome "the danger of European capital . . . by the method
of establishing [its] own capitalistic control and the political power of
taxation and regulation." Although the domestic economy remained
unstable and workers suffered low wages, these men insisted that China
was trying to liberate itself from the spell of Europe and to establish
an independent republic. However, they emphasized that at every turn
their efforts were hindered and hampered by the Japanese.[83]

Although Du Bois learned the extent of the antagonism between
China and Japan as he moved southward from Manchukuo and admitted that he had failed to probe the deeper problem of this conflict, he
remained sympathetic to Japan. Instead of denouncing the Japanese
imperialist state and its colonial rule and violence across Asia, he saw
the Sino-Japanese conflict as "a vivid, real thing and a major threat to

the peace of the world" since it involved a tragedy of race suicide among Asians and hence the greater possibility of the continued dominance of white Europe: "With China and Japan in understanding and in co-operation the domination of Europe—the enslavement, insult and exploitation of the darker majority of mankind is at an everlasting end. But with China and Japan in rivalry, war and hatred, Europe still con-tinues to rule the world for her own ends."[84]

Even in the midst of Japanese military aggression southward in China, which led to the destruction and occupation of Beijing and Shanghai in July–August 1937 and the Nanking massacre in December–January 1938, Du Bois emphasized the importance of achieving unity between "two cousins," the Japanese and the Chinese, to reproduce racial globality. He argued that "the cause and blame of this war [the Sino-Japanese War] lies on England, and France, and America; on Ger-many and Italy; on all those white nations, which for a hundred years and more, have by blood and rapine forced their rule upon colored nations." In a logic that echoed Japan's rationalization for expansion and colonization in Asia, he explained that Japan went "into a horrible and bloody carnage with her own cousin" to prevent Asia from falling under the domination of white Europe. He wrote, "Japan believes that colored nations are going to escape this fate in the future if they orga-nize themselves in self-defense."[85]

This discourse of Du Bois, couched in the language of race suicide, increasingly turned into harsh indictment against China. Criticizing China's unwillingness to cooperate with Japan in the revolt against white Europe, he presented China as an Asian version of Uncle Tom. He wrote,

> Even while China was licking the European boots that kicked her and fawning on the West; and when Japan was showing her the way to free-dom; China preferred to be a coolie for England rather than acknowl-edge the only world leadership that did not mean color caste, and that was the leadership of Japan. It was Japan's clear cue to persuade, cajole, and convince China, but China sneered and taught her folk that Japa-nese were devils. Thus the straight road to world dominance of the yel-low race was ruined in Asia by the same spirit that animates the "white

folks' nigger" in the United States. Whereupon Japan fought China to save China from Europe, and fought Europe through China and tried to wade in blood toward Asiatic freedom.[86]

This perspective was not at all at odds with the popular sentiment within the Black community. "When all was said and done," writes Gerald Horne, "many Negroes simply had a high opinion of Japan and the Japanese and a correspondingly low evaluation of China and the Chinese."[87] Thinking again of Manchukuo as a model, Du Bois wrote, "The control of Asia by Asiatics could not possibly have such frightful results as the exploitation of Asia by Europe has already had. Let England and America get out of Asia, and clean up their own mess in the Western World."[88]

As the United States expressed its determination to save China from Japanese aggression, Du Bois's transpacific call for racial globality became more pronounced, as he refused to play politics by the terms of white supremacy. In a letter addressed to Du Bois on January 24, 1940, Secretary of War Henry L. Stimson tried to enlist him in the campaign to oppose Japan's imperial advances, but Du Bois did not accept Stimson's invitation to join the fraternity of white men.[89] In fact, he publicly expressed a resounding indictment against white supremacy in his *Amsterdam News* column:

> I know perfectly well what America and Mr. Stimson want in Asia. They want low wages, cheap raw materials and increased private profit. They do not care a rap for the Chinese. They have excluded them from America by law and they propose to keep up that exclusion. They raise against them and the Japanese, the color bar and regard them as "lesser breeds without the law." They want China and if possible Japan as the backyard for their industrial and commercial activities, and they have been fighting toward this end ever since Commodore Perry bullied helpless Japan into admitting "American civilization." I hold no brief for war whether carried on by Japanese or English or Germans or Americans; but if ever a continent had reason to fight and fear the Americans bringing gifts, it is the continent of Asia. P.S. Moreover, I don't remember Mr. Stimson's protest on Ethiopia.[90]

Insisting that the same dynamics of race and imperialism that demonized Japan, exploited China, and spread "race war" clouds across the Pacific also excluded and disenfranchised Asian immigrants in the United States, he called on Black Americans to "think straight in this crisis." He wrote, "Not love for China, but hate for Japan motivates Stimson and the United States; Chamberlain and England. The way out is for young China and young Japan to get into an indissoluble alliance and save the world for the darker races. For if the yellow people commit suicide they will serve the noblest purposes of white folk."[91] To highlight his transpacific call for racial globality to the Black readers of *Amsterdam News*, he laid bare Stimson's white blind spot (as his *Black Reconstruction* did in the realm of American historiography), reminding the Black readers that Stimson never reached out to support the Black nationalists' and internationalists' campaign to defend and save Ethiopia in the aftermath of Italian invasion in 1935.

In Du Bois's encounters with Japan and China in the 1930s and 1940s, he exercised conceptual power to steer the intellectual and political currents of the Black public sphere in a new direction. He wanted to animate the different ways of imagining kinship and alliance based on race and to incite the formation of the transpacific culture of liberation against European imperialism and colonialism. Du Bois's transpacific strivings produced a set of ideas and meanings about race and culture and transformed them into symbolic capital for darker nations and people so that they could constitute themselves as new racial subjects. However, such a nexus of race and culture produced the traps of racial essentialism rather than a culture of liberation capable of articulating the qualitatively different discourses of the past and the present. Even when Du Bois forged solidarity with Japan in the context of anti-imperialist nationalist struggles to resist the terms of white supremacy and invested in this politics to present the future of race for darker nations and people, he could not eradicate the weight of the racial past, nor was he able to avoid "racist detritus" in the present.[92] To be sure, his Afro-Asian philosophy of world history was a counterdiscourse that guided his analysis of the meaning of Japan and its pan-Asian project in the context of European expansion worldwide. But because of his preoccupation with giving moral, epistemic, and political authority to the concept of race at a scale exceeding the nation-state and because this concept of race was wedded to "heterosexual gender and sexual norma- tivity," he could not extricate himself from the strong shaping force of colonial and capitalist modernity.[93]

Yet in the aftermath of the destruction of a race war, as the next two chapters will detail, the culture of liberation made palpable by the anti- imperialist, anticolonial, and nationalist currents within Black Ameri- can political and intellectual life opened a new horizon of possibilities toward Black and Third World liberation, peace, and social justice on the other side of the Pacific. It offered diverse constituents of radical social and intellectual movements in postwar Japan and occupied Oki- nawa essential resources and creative energies to help organize critical agency toward ends that Du Bois desired and desperately and tortu- ously justified in the 1930s and 1940s. Japanese scholars in the 1950s and 1960s and Okinawan activist-intellectuals, dissenting American GIs, both Blacks and whites, and peace activists from mainland Japan and the United States during the late 1960s and early 1970s stepped into the transpacific culture of liberation, forming collectives at the grassroots to call into question the supposed universality, exceptionalism, and virtue of American democracy. In the process, they helped carve out a discursive space for the rearticulation of Black radicalism and inter- nationalism to incite new desires for human liberation. Characteristi- cally perceptive in reflecting on "the experience of Japan" after atomic bombs were dropped on Hiroshima and Nagasaki in August 1945, which brought an end to the horror of "a war between nations of dif- ferent colors," Du Bois showed that he was already thinking ahead. In anticipation of the renewal of the race-making project at the beginning of what Henry Luce referred to as the "American Century," he sought to highlight to the readers of his August 25, 1945, column in the *Chicago Defender* the coming of new political dynamics and challenges:

> So far as Japan was fighting against color caste, and striving against the domination of Asia by Europeans, she was absolutely right. But so far as she tried to substitute for European, an Asiatic caste system under a "superior" Japanese race; and for the domination and exploitation of peasants of Asia by Japanese trusts and industrialists, she was offering Asia no acceptable exchange for Western exploitation.

Uneasy, therefore, as we have been about war between the United States and Japan, and about our having as colored people to fight colored people possibly only for the benefit of white people, we have this to remember and sustain us: we are facing the beginning of the end of European domination in Asia. The ideas which Japan started and did not carry through, are not dead but growing.[94]

PART II

## Collectives

In the poetics of struggle and lived experience, in the utterances of ordinary folk, in the cultural products of social
movements, in the reflections of activists, we discover the
many different cognitive maps of the future, of the world not
yet born.
—Robin D. G. Kelley, *Freedom Dreams:*
*The Black Radical Imagination* (2002)

3

The Making of "Colored-Internationalism" in Postwar Japan

After taking detours through the ideologically heterogeneous terrain of a movement culture in postsurrender Japan in the late 1940s,
Nukina Yoshitaka (1911–1985) finally helped launch *Kokujin Kenkyu no
Kai* (Association of Negro Studies) in Kobe in June 1954, a collective
devoted to the international and diasporan study of Black life, culture,
and history. It was around this time, just before the inaugural meeting of *Kokujin Kenkyu no Kai*, that Nukina experienced an encounter
that was paradigmatic. He picked up a rare find at a used bookstore
in Osaka, one of the three hundred copies of the Japanese translation
of W. E. B. Du Bois's *The Negro* (1915), which first appeared during the
resource-scarce wartime period in 1944. It was translated by the Waseda
University professor of literature Inoue Eizo with a Japanese title, *Koku-
jinron* (Negritude Theory).[1] Reading *The Negro*, Nukina stepped into
a domain of world history that he had never known; it was a revelation. The historical accounts of Africa and its ancient civilizations and

achievements, as well as Africa's central role in the movement of world history, which *The Negro* chronicled, presented Nukina with what Du Bois called a "third path" to move through the epistemology of the tradition of historical Black struggles.

This chance encounter with Du Bois's movement of world history not only turned Nukina's world upside down, shattering the myths of the backwardness of Africans and people of African descent. It also awakened him never to "locate Black 'history' within the context of modern 'history' as merely one of the episodes," as Nukina once wrote but to establish the study of Black life, culture, and history as an independent field of inquiry into the "nature of the world's 'enlightenment' and 'progress,'" so as to find ways to resolve the causes and consequences of unresolved world-historic concerns. Just as the proponents and theorists of Negritude, such as Aimé Césaire and Leopold Senghor, plotted a revolt in modern thought by locating the beauty and grandeur of Black life and culture in the domain of history, the very place where the Western world found qualities antithetical to human progress, the effect of Du Bois's *The Negro*, a precursor of Negritude, on Nukina was characterized by an epistemic breakthrough. It enabled him to emphatically repudiate the legitimacy of Western humanism. Entering Black worldliness, he found a political possibility to engender new categories and creative energies to render visible an alternative path to human liberation.[2]

This chapter chronicles how *Kokujin Kenkyu no Kai* entered the currents of the Black liberation movement during the Civil Rights era of the 1950s and 1960s from Japan and in the process helped to give a form to the transpacific culture of liberation. Guiding the dynamics of transpacific strivings in *Kokujin Kenkyu no Kai* during the formative years of its formation was the practice of translation. In the same way in which the Japanese translation of Du Bois's *The Negro* helped Nukina achieve cognitive clarity and cement political commitment, the very task of translating the diverse texts and idioms of Black radicalism in collaboration became, for the core members *Kokujin Kenkyu no Kai*, the mainspring of "a shared ethos of communion," or a collective aspiration to experience a revelation and to help articulate the essence that would help sustain group life and identity, kinship and fellowship among each other, as well as with Afrodiasporic people in the struggle. As Nukina once described in a letter to Robert F. Williams, the African American

Nukina Yoshitaka (© 2011 *Kokujin Kenkyu no Kai*)

revolutionary then exiled in Fidel Castro's Cuba, *Kokujin Kenkyu no Kai* "is not only an academic research group but [also] moves against [all forms of] racial discrimination and participates in democratization movements in Japan."[3]

Indeed, for Nukina, there was a reason for naming the collective *Kokujin Kenkyu no Kai* rather than *Kokujin Kenkyu Kai*. He thought that the intervening *no*, the Japanese form of apposition, in between two noun phrases, *Kokujin Kenkyu* (Negro Studies) and *Kai* (Association) would project the image of a collective tied to the local community, where citizens not part of the academic world and left-leaning political groups would feel unencumbered to devote themselves to communal learning and to participate in the work of communion via the study of Black life, culture, and history. He longed for a space where masses not only produced knowledge that could transform themselves and society but also collectively owned this intellectual property. With-out *no*, he feared, a collective would be seen as strictly an academic endeavor without the presence of local people and their participation. His premonition proved correct, for the intervening *no* became the subject of mockery within the official circles of intellectuals. The work of *Kokujin Kenkyu no Kai* was often not taken seriously.[4]

Yet the collective engaged with collaborative research of the first order. While gathering, cataloguing, selecting, interpreting, and editing diverse texts with contradictory and conflicting political orientations, the members searchingly fashioned the pedagogy of human liberation called Black radicalism to produce new kinds of knowledge capable of bursting the boundaries of nations and modern political thought. A cat-alyst animating the collective's intellectual pursuit in the nascent years in postsurrender Japan was its eclectic orientation, especially its inter-est in the Marxist position on the "Negro Question," postwar Japanese Popular Front activism, the Esperanto movement, and antebellum uto-pianism and abolitionism. Traversing such diverse terrains of thought and activity, this group of progressive Japanese intellectuals and activ-ists found ways to organize a discursive space, or a culture of liberation, from which members could articulate deep desires on their part to pur-sue Black liberation. For them, this culture emerged as an entry point to participate in transpacific strivings. This chapter shows how this collec-tive's transpacific practice of translation enabled its members not only to link up with the political world of Robert F. Williams but also to con-struct their own distinct discourse of Black radicalism called "colored-internationalism." The story of this collective's coming into being as a collaborator in the Black liberation movement during the Civil Rights era demonstrates just how, for the participants of Afro-Asian solidar-ity, the category of race had less to do with personal identity than the politics of identification. This distinction made the work of antiracism productive in Japan.

## Curious Marxian Groundings

On June 22, 1954, *Kokujin Kenkyu no Kai* held its inaugural meeting on the campus of the Kobe City University of Foreign Studies. Convened by Nukina Yoshitaka, a professor of American literature and culture, a small group of eight, consisting of three professors, four local school-teachers, and one graduate student—all male in their twenties and thirties and acquaintances and former students of Nukina—set out to define the name, mission, and structure of this study group and to discuss the methodology of their inquiry into the Black world. They all agreed that they would set out to research the issues surrounding Black life, culture, and history broadly and to present their findings, both independently and collaboratively, at a monthly meeting and in a periodical of their own. Conscious of the global scope and reach of the study of the Black world, they resisted defining their intellectual and organizational endeavor in geographical terms. From the outset, *Koku-jin Kenkyu no Kai*'s framing of the experience of race exceeded not only national boundaries but also the existing conceptual language of race that was U.S.-centric.[5]

Varied research interests represented at this meeting revealed how the members stretched the boundaries of "race studies" in an animating way. The group's leader, Nukina, at the time had just completed a two-part article titled "On Abolitionists," which appeared in *Kobe Gaidai Ronso* (Journal of Kobe City University of Foreign Studies). Juxtaposing William Lloyd Garrison, Henry David Thoreau, and John Brown in relation to each other, he sought to identify a homegrown intellectual tradition in the history of abolitionism that could serve as a frame of reference to complete the unfinished struggle for democracy in the present. Nukina's colleague linguist Konishi Tomoshichi was then reading and interpreting African American folktales collected from former slaves during the period of Reconstruction to "decode" Black dialect and achieve basic comprehension, a project that consumed him ever since Nukina had handed him a copy of Joel Chandler Harris's *Uncle Remus: His Songs and Sayings* (1881).[6] Tamura Tetsuya, a junior high school teacher, sought to establish the connection between the Black world and Japan and to make "race studies" relevant in the context of Japan. He was particularly interested in exploring the status of the biracial children of Black servicemen within the Japanese educational system, as well as Japan's own "race question" involving *Zainichi* (Resident) Koreans who experienced, as colonialized subjects living in Japan, persistent discrimination, political disenfranchisement, and residential and school segregation.

While investigating the "race question" in Japan, Tamura was also hard at work on the translation of leading Black Marxist theoretician Harry Haywood's *Negro Liberation*. Published in 1948, Haywood's book reaffirmed the Communist International's 1928 position that Black-majority counties spread across the Jim Crow South, or the Black belt, constituted the oppressed nation and that Black people in this region possessed the right to struggle for self-determination as a part of the worldwide revolutionary struggle against imperialism. Categorized as the "Negro Question" within the international Communist movement, this theory saw a brief comeback in 1946 after the general secretary of the Communist Party of the United States of America (CPUSA), Earl Browder, was expelled and William Z. Foster assumed that capacity.[7] Thinking of how to define the significance of the experience of Japan's minority groups, especially *Zainichi* Koreans and "mixed-race" Japanese children, Tamura turned to the vision of the struggle for Black self-determination as a guide. The impact of Haywood's text on *Kokujin Kenkyu no Kai*'s collective consciousness appeared most explicitly in the first issue of *Kokujin Kenkyu no Kai*'s journal, *Kokujin Kenkyu* (Negro Studies), published in October 1956. On the mimeographed cover was a map representing the Black belt in the Jim Crow South, although the irony was that by the time this first issue was published, this Marxist position on national self-determination for African Americans was abandoned in favor of the CPUSA's support for the struggle for Blacks' equality as citizens of the United States.

Not bound to the rigid party line of the CPUSA, what mattered to this collective was the usefulness of this map of the Black belt in communicating how to narrate its own Black radical politics in relationship to civil rights struggles that were unfolding in the aftermath of the 1954 *Brown v. Board of Education* U.S. Supreme Court decision that declared school segregation based on race unconstitutional. Founded merely one month after this landmark decision was handed down, the collective was cognizant of the timing of its own emergence as a transpacific solidarity project in the context of this racial struggle. Until 1962, *Kokujin Kenkyu no Kai* used this cartographic motif as the journal's cover, changing the legend on each issue to carve out the discursive space for the articulation of Black radicalism.

The map on the cover of the August 1958 issue was a case in point.

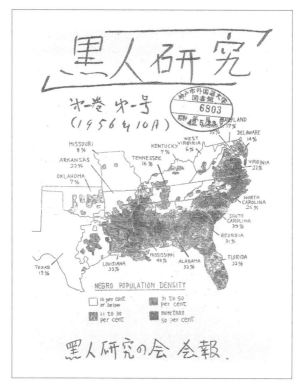

The cover of the inaugural issue of *Kokujin Kenkyu* (Journal of Negro Studies), published in October 1956 (© 2011 *Kokujin Kenkyu no Kai*)

It sharply presented the slow pace of school desegregation in the South since the 1954 *Brown* decision, revealing the pitifully low number of Black students attending integrated schools. However, the point of presenting this fact of white resistance was not to express *Kokujin Kenkyu no Kai*'s solidarity with the National Association for the Advancement of Colored People (NAACP), which was leading the desegregation campaign. Far from it—it represented the repudiation of the idea of integration into America as the hallmark of the American liberal democratic experience. In other words, it did not participate in mythmaking to present the United States as the exceptional state that stood for universal principles of justice, inclusion, and equality. As it turned out, the legends for this map were derived from the work of William L. Patterson, an African American attorney, a member of the CPUSA since 1926, and a leading figure of the Civil Rights Congress that fought hard against racism and political repression in the midst of the Red Scare. Patterson paid a high price for his radical politics, just as did Paul Robeson, W. E. B. Du Bois, and Alphaeus Hunton, all associated with the Council on African Affairs, in the form of legal charges, intense surveillance, and isolation.[8]

While the NAACP disassociated itself from left-leaning politics and took the position of anticommunism explicitly to try to achieve some civil rights progress from the federal government at the height of McCarthyism in the late 1940s and early 1950s, Black radical intellectual-activists such as Patterson, Hunton, Robeson, and Du Bois categorically rejected U.S. Cold War propaganda. They mounted a critique of the fascism of the American liberal democratic state and fought hard to prevent it from narrowing the scope and methods of the Black freedom struggle, which were at once antiracist, anticolonial, and anti-imperialist. The petition that Patterson's Civil Rights Congress drafted and submitted to the United Nations in 1951, called *We Charge Genocide: The Historic Petition to the United Nations for Relief from a Crime of the United States Government against the Negro People*, stood as the sharpest expression of the most radical tendency within the Black freedom movement. These Black radical leaders were a part of the political project that had been fashioning the discourse of Black internationalism throughout the Second World War and its immediate aftermath to link the momentum of the Black struggles at home with the waves of decolonization in Africa and the Caribbean to develop strategies for retribution for Africans and people of African descent in the African diaspora.[9]

And the Japanese intellectual-activists associated with *Kokujin Kenkyu no Kai* on the other side of the Pacific were also part of this project. During the collective's formative years, aiding it to move in the same groove as the intellectual-activists of the Black Left were the currents of Black radicalism that Robin D. G. Kelley has called the "Red dreams of Black liberation."[10] While English-language literature of the Black liberation movement and specifically that of a Marxist orientation was not readily available in Japan in the late 1940s and early 1950s because of the censorship policy of the U.S. occupation authority, it was not entirely impossible to obtain either. When *Kokujin Kenkyu no Kai* started in 1954, it already had its own library of Black studies humanities and social sciences literature that consisted of progressive periodicals such as *Political Affairs, Masses & Mainstream, Monthly Review*, and the *Nation* and books published by the CPUSA's International Publishers. As Nukina later admitted, he himself was one of the first to own a sizable collection of sources and documents that pertained to Black radicalism in the immediate postwar years, and if it were not for his deliberate efforts to explore the ideologically heterogeneous terrain of prewar and postwar Japanese Marxism, a collective aiming to carry out collaborative research in the field of Black studies would have materialized much later in postwar Japan. To put it another way, *Kokujin Kenkyu no Kai* found ways to embrace diverse ideological and cultural orientations and ultimately cultivated an ecumenical vision that could help make this discourse of Black radicalism relevant in postsurrender Japan precisely because creative energies decisive to the formation of this collective came out of a context that appeared seemingly far removed from the currents of Black radicalism, namely, the postwar Japanese Communist Party's Popular Front activism, the progressive wing of the prewar and postwar Esperanto movement, and the antebellum resurgence of interest in the transcendentalism of Henry David Thoreau.[11] Nukina was moving through unlikely routes toward Black radicalism, and it all began in the spring of 1946 upon his return to Japan from Java, where he had served in the Japanese Army for nearly four and a half years.

Nukina was one of the five million Japanese who were repatriated from various parts of Asia between October 1, 1945, and December 31, 1946.[12] While his precise role in Japanese-occupied Java is never documented in any of his published work, most likely he was a witness to atrocities or heard about the stories of massacres, brutal campaigns, and sexual exploitation that the Japanese military carried out throughout Asia. As a repatriated soldier, he bore the full responsibility of this war's consequences. Yet by anyone's account, Nukina was fortunate in the midst of what historian John Dower calls "shattered lives." He not only survived the war and repatriation. He also found a way to make ends meet within a mere one month of his return. Because of his prewar graduate training in American literature at Kyoto Imperial University and ties to the Kansai intelligentsia, he secured a teaching position first at Kansai University in Osaka as adjunct faculty and then at the

Kobe Municipal College of Foreign Languages several months later as a full-time professor.[13]

In the Kansai cities ravaged by repeated B-29 air raids, Nukina lived and worked through hunger, suffering, and destitution, rubbing shoulders with the unemployed, the homeless, ex-soldiers, disabled veterans, and orphans on the streets of Osaka and Kobe. Facing these reminders of war daily and the preeminence of the U.S. occupation authority, which controlled every aspect of the reform process, he contemplated the meaning of the war.[14] For Nukina, active participation in the causes of peace, antimilitarism, democracy, and social justice offered essential outlets for self-reflection and consolation. The dramatic mobilization and growing militancy of postwar social movements created a space through which he could come to grips with the recent past and its relationship to the present and future. He entered what Nukina's contemporary and a leading public intellectual Maruyama Masao called a "community of remorse" and sought "to make a new start and turn the 'rationed-out freedom' of the occupation into a spontaneous embrace of demilitarization and democratization."[15]

Nukina could hardly contain his excitement for the potential of a genuine democratic revolution, albeit one orchestrated from the top down by General Douglas MacArthur, the Supreme Commander of the Allied Powers (SCAP). Repatriated nine months after Japan's unconditional surrender on August 15, 1945, Nukina saw Japan's political and cultural landscapes undergoing astonishing transformations. Already MacArthur had unleashed various reform policies to facilitate the process of democratization. He freed political prisoners, especially prewar left-leaning critics, legalized the Communist Party, gave workers the right to unionize, enfranchised women, separated the state and Shinto religion, and attacked the concentration of power in the hands of the police and giant industrial conglomerates. The officials of the U.S. occupation authority also had put together a working group to draft a new constitution for Japan, in secrecy, and unveiled the draft, which was hermaphroditic, a synthesis of monarchism and commitments to peace and democracy, to the Japanese Diet in March 1946.[16]

Nukina especially welcomed the enormous popularity of Marxism, giving intellectuals like himself and the working masses political opportunities and analytical tools not readily available in wartime

Japan to pursue emancipatory projects from below that were capable of transcending the constraints of SCAP directives, the conservatism of Japanese elites, and the orthodoxy of Marxism itself. The U.S. occupation authority did not expect to see such a surge of political, creative, and intellectual engagements.[17] Especially at a local level, working men and women, students, and young intellectuals moved to the beat of a democratic revolution through participation in *sakuru* (cultural circles or, simply, collectives) of all types—studying and discussing myriad literary and social texts, organizing choirs, composing music, writing poems and personal essays, self-publishing their own mimeographed journals and chapbooks, and starting alternative schools. All of these cultural activities flourished against the backdrop of rapid unionization and labor militancy, where the Japanese Communist Party (JCP) wielded the most authority. Moreover, in February 1946 at the Fifth National Congress, by way of reaffirming the 1935 Comintern's directive, the JCP asserted the position of the Popular Front, placing a strong emphasis on the primacy of industrial unionism and solidarity with liberal and progressive elements, especially the U.S. occupation authority, to complete the Communist revolution.[18] The SCAP was not a reactionary force, according to the JCP, but an essential ingredient toward the struggle for a new society.

The intellectual-activists tied to the JCP recognized that in order to reach, organize, and mobilize disparate local sites, institutions, networks, and associations to make the Popular Front productive for revolutionary change, the JCP needed to facilitate the formation of a new culture. To this end, the JCP issued a cultural policy agenda to expand the foundation of party support, turning to Kurahara Korehito, a literary critic and leader of a prewar proletarian avant-garde, to take the leadership role, as he had done in the late 1920s and early 1930s, to make literature and art an integral part of the postwar class struggle. Among the young intellectuals of Nukina's generation who dabbled in the prewar proletarian literature movement, Kurahara was a revered figure. He was a leader of *Zen Nihon Musansha Geijutsu Renmei* (All-Japan Federation of Proletarian Arts), commonly known as NAPF (pronounced *nappu*), and later *Nihon Puroretaria Bunka Renmei* (Japan Proletarian Cultural Federation), or KOPF (pronounced *koppu*), established in 1928 and 1931, respectively. Kurahara spent much of the interwar and war

periods in prison and under house arrest. While other radical intellectuals committed apostasy during this period, he defiantly resisted it and
reemerged in the immediate postsurrender years to shape public discourse about culture and revolution.[19]

The context for Nukina's connection with Kurahara was in the prewar
Esperanto movement. Nukina certainly knew that the acronyms of prewar proletarian avant-garde organizations—NAPF and KOPF—were
derived from Esperanto translations: *Nippon-Artista Proletaria Federacio* and *Federacio de Proletaj Kultur-organizoj*. Discovering Esperanto
at age twelve in 1923, he explored this planned international language
on his own until he joined the Osaka Esperanto Study Group in 1928.
Later in 1935, his first year as a graduate student in American literature
at Kyoto Imperial University's Faculty of Letters, he became a member of *Nihon Esperanto Gakkai* (Japan Esperanto Society), which was
a national organization that replaced *Nihon Esperanto Kyokai* (Japan
Esperanto Association), Japan's first Esperanto organization established
in 1906.[20]

Nukina was attracted to the primary mission of the Esperanto movement: the creation of a whole new universal language to promote peace.
L. L. Zamenhof, a Russian-Jewish medical doctor who lived through
wars and conflicts on the Russian-Polish border, started the movement
in 1887, having become convinced that the teaching and learning of a
new planned international language would help mitigate the capacities of ethno-nationalism to generate much harm, violence, and misery
and ultimately help constitute a community of tolerance. Progressive
thinkers and anarchists around the world, guided by the Marxian principle that workers of the world did not have country, were drawn to
this movement, for they too believed in the potential of a new international language to transcend national allegiance to achieve the unity of
the international working class. In the early 1900s, Japan's leading anarchists, socialists, and communists, such as Osugi Sakae, Sakai Toshi-
hiko, and Yamaga Taiji, also played a central role in shaping this movement.[21] Nukina was moved by the utopian appeal of this progressive
wing of the Esperanto movement.

The local Esperanto group that Nukina joined in Osaka in 1928 and
in which he remained active throughout the 1930s was a part of such

a left-leaning Esperanto movement, which was in the orbit of NAPF and KOPF. Osaka remained the center of radical Esperanto activism, despite the intensification of state suppression of people associated with the Japanese Socialist Party and the JCP. Through small study groups, these Osaka-based Esperantists connected with each other and contributed to the shaping of the proletarian avant-garde. As early as 1920, influenced by anarchist Osugi Sakae, Fukuda Kunitaro began a study group and an Esperanto school for socialists, anarchists, and workers and helped to edit the Esperanto journal titled *Verda Utopio* (Green Utopia), whose articles were all written in Esperanto.[22] Another Osaka-based Marxian Esperantist, Ito Saburo, also operated at the intersection of the nascent proletarian avant-garde and the Esperanto movement. As a student active in *Nomin Rodoto* (Farmer-Labor Party) at the Osaka Municipal College of Foreign Languages, he organized an Esperanto study group in the mid-1920s. This group took a position of antimilitarism and anti-imperialism explicitly and organized numerous rallies and conferences bringing together diverse constituents of Japanese radicalism. The members of this group tirelessly infused Esperanto into the proletarian cultural movement and Marxism into the Esperanto movement to articulate this nexus in the service of revolutionary struggles. Later in 1932, Ito Saburo's collection of poems, *Verda Parnaso*, written in Esperanto, was published and received a wide readership within the international Esperanto movement.[23]

Although Nukina's involvement in the Osaka Esperanto movement and his intellectual pursuits at Kyoto Imperial University were interrupted by conscription, upon his return from Java, he reentered the local Esperanto scene. Soon he renewed his ties with those who were involved in the prewar proletarian avant-garde that had come to align with *Nihon Minshushugi Bunka Renmei* (Japan Democratic Culture League), commonly known as *Bunren*. That organization had come into existence in April 1946 as an extension of JCP's Popular Front activism and cultural policy directive led by Kurahara to coordinate the networks of alliances among affiliates in myriad cultural fields ranging from literature and theater to Esperanto. At the time, however, the Esperanto movement at a national level was experiencing a split resulting from differences in political orientations. In the end, a group of progressive

Esperantists led the Japan Esperanto Association in opposition to the Japan Esperanto Society, which preferred taking a neutral position in times of Cold War hysteria rather than becoming an affiliate of *Bunren*. Nukina led a busy life throughout the late 1940s as a head of the Hyogo prefecture chapter of the Japan Esperanto Association, shuttling back and forth between Kobe and Tokyo. It was during this period in which *Bunren* set up a Hyogo prefecture chapter that he began contemplating the idea of creating *sakuru* that would engage in the collaborative research of the Black experience.[24]

Between 1946 and 1950, Nukina shared the idea of starting *Kokujin Kenkyu no Kai* with diverse activists of varying academic, cultural, and political interests, all associated with *Bunren* and most of them based in Tokyo. However, responses he received from comrades showed a deep-seated racism that ran within the Japanese progressive community. None of them cared, much less saw the "Negro experience" as worth researching. Some thought the idea was a joke and laughed at him. The Esperantist poet Ito Saburo, however, was different. Nukina vividly recalled how Ito took the matter with a seriousness he had never encountered: "With an intent gaze, he listened to my story. . . . 'This is an issue of utmost importance; I absolutely concur,' he said with a deep understanding and care." As much as Nukina saw *Kokujin Kenkyu no Kai* as a critical alternative paradigm for social change in postwar and occupied Japan, he was unable to gather a critical mass at the time and thus had to put his pursuit on hold.[25]

Meanwhile, Nukina kept himself abreast of developments in and around the local Esperanto movement and struggled to weather the wrath of anticommunism. It had been creeping into Japanese everyday life as early as 1946 when SCAP-led democratization and demilitarization began reversing course, rolling back the centerpiece of the U.S. occupation authority's labor policy, public employees' right to strike, in the summer of 1948 and ultimately going after militant unions, both in the public and private sectors, with the sole purpose of purging labor-union activists tied to the JCP in 1949–1950. According to historian John Dower, as many as eleven thousand workers in the public sector lost their jobs six months before the Korean War began, and another eleven thousand workers in the private sector were forced out by the end of 1950. The Esperanto movement was affected by the Red Purge as well, ultimately causing the Japan Esperanto Association, the progressive wing of the movement, to disband in December 1950.[26]

However, progressive Esperantists in the Kansai region kept this movement going and helped revive it in the anticommunist climate. In part, their resilience had to do with the presence of *Kyoto Jinbun Gakuen* (Kyoto Humanities Academy), a short-lived alternative school for college-age youths that started in June 1946. Its motto was to inculcate the values of rigorous inquiry and self-activity, so as to nurture proactive students and critical thinkers. Placing an emphasis on debates and dialogues, both instructors and students created a collaborative learning space that was almost utopian. Not surprisingly, Esperanto was one of the elective courses at this academy. The founder and headmaster, Shinmura Takeshi, a product of the prewar Popular Front antifascist movement, was a son of one of the pioneer Esperantists, Shinmura Izuru, who was said to be the last Japanese to encounter the creator of Esperanto, L. L. Zamenhof. Students who discovered Esperanto at this academy began a *sakuru* called *Osaka Rodosha Esperanto-kai* (Osaka Workers' Esperanto Association) in 1947. Soon after the academy's utopian educational and social experiment came to halt in April 1950 and the Japan Esperanto Association dissolved in December 1950, these students and other local Esperantists, including Nukina Yoshitaka, reached out toward each other and launched *Kansai Esperanto Renmei* (Kansai Esperanto League), or KLEG, in March 1951. Nukina became the inaugural chairman of KLEG, and the group published a journal called *La Movado* (The Movement).[27]

One of the distinguishing features of KLEG's activities was a collaborative practice of translation, which Nukina made one of the central functions of *Kokujin Kenkyu no Kai*. The first Esperanto translation of the 1950 bestseller *Kike—Wadasumi no Koe* (Listen! The Voices from the Sea) was completed and published in September 1951, followed by another bestseller, *Genbaku no Ko* (The Children of Hiroshima), a collection written by survivors of the atomic bomb that appeared in September 1952. Both of these texts documented the Japanese war experience, its cruelty, destructiveness, futility, and tragedy. Giving voice to the voiceless, these texts resonated with the old and young generations struggling with unresolved feelings about the war and its memories. For many, these texts allowed them to ground their collective pursuit of repentance and atonement in the cause of antimilitarism and the hope for a bottom-up democratic revolution.[28]

In particular, *Kike—Wadasumi no Koe*, a collection of journal entries, letters, and poems written by seventy-five Tokyo Imperial University student conscripts killed in the war and published posthumously by the members of *Wadasumi no Koe* associations made up of leftist intellectuals, allowed individuals grappling with guilt and remorse to articulate a path to redemption and renewal. As Dower explains, "Although they wrote under military censorship and accepted, sometimes even embraced, the mission of dying for their country, there was an underlying hunger for life, not death, in what they wrote."[29] Indeed, unlike the conservatives who used the war dead to revive the temper of prewar nationalism in the context of the collective acts of repentance and atonement, the younger intellectuals of KLEG used the translation of *Kike—Wadasumi no Koe* to enlist the memories of "departed souls" in such a way as to articulate a requiem capable of resisting an emergent U.S. (and Japanese) Cold War imperialism.[30]

During this period, such an anti-imperialist orientation and commitment to peace defined the direction of Japanese social movements. Organized in 1950 under the leadership of Takano Minoru, labor unions affiliated with *Nihon Rodo Kumiai Sohyogikai* (General Council of Trade Unions of Japan), commonly known as *Sohyo*, for instance, took the position of antimilitarism and peace and rallied around the theme of independence from U.S. neocolonial military domination, which was most explicitly manifested in the U.S.-Japan Cold War alliance. Takano called the antiwar and pacifist orientation of *Sohyo* "a third force, which was distinct from the Soviet camp and the capitalist West." Seeking to transcend the binary politics of the Cold War, *Sohyo* presented a political alternative by imagining a transnational alliance with the Third World coming out of anticolonial nationalist struggles, especially in India, Ceylon, and Burma, that rejected the Cold War conception of liberal nationalism and internationalism embraced by the United States, Japan, and other Western European nations. Such a position of nonalignment soon crystallized at the 1955 Bandung Conference.[31]

Nukina was following the intellectual trajectory of Thoreau and coming close to articulating the self-activity of Black masses (ex-slaves) as the intellectual foundation of a collective devoted to the study of Black life, culture, and history. He was beginning to move in a racial groove as Du Bois theorized in the 1930s and 1940s and made known in his book *Black Reconstruction*.

## The Echo of Black Radicalism in Japanese

Around fall 1950, Nukina found a kindred spirit in a local high school English teacher, Furukawa Hiromi (1927–2012), a former student who happened to be an Esperantist. Furukawa had known Nukina for a while, at least since 1946, first as an English-language teacher at the Kobe Municipal College of Foreign Languages (later Kobe City University of Foreign Studies) who taught Ralph Waldo Emerson's *Nature* and *The American Scholar* and required students to write essays in English. After being afflicted with severe illness, in part because of malnourishment experienced during the war and in the immediate aftermath, he was in and out of school and struggled to make timely academic progress. While recovering, he read American literature in English voraciously and in the process came across Erskine Caldwell's writings. There he discovered the "other America," the realities of impoverishment, disenfranchisement, and dispossession in the South; it engendered a point of identification. Cognizant of widespread sufferings in postsurrender Japan, he described his research interest at the inaugural meeting of *Kokujin Kenkyu no Kai* as a study in the representation of southern U.S. race relations in novels written by white authors, such as Caldwell and William Faulkner.[35]

Furukawa's revelation from reading Caldwell's work merely confirmed what he had been questioning for a while. "Not so far from our school [the Kobe Municipal College of Foreign Languages]," Furukawa recalled, "army barracks in dark green had been set up. These were for black troops and the location was called the West Camp." The military camp for white GIs, on the other hand, was "set up close to the downtown . . . and was called the East Camp." Although Furukawa was one of many students who "hungered for American ways of life and went to see Hollywood films in the makeshift movie houses," his doubts about

American democracy's universalistic claims grew strong steadily in the late 1940s. Just as the preeminent American studies scholar David W. Noble had come to accept the fact that "many of the truths about the nation that [he] was taught as a child had turned out to be untruth," Furukawa, too, declared that he "could not write elegies for Emerson and his generation of male Anglo-American artists and intellectuals." He was faced with a paradigmatic crisis, and like Noble, he began "searching for new hypotheses."[36]

When Furukawa was reunited with his mentor at one of the local Esperantists' gatherings in Kobe, a case of chance encounter, he began participating in the building of this local Esperanto movement. Soon they discovered that each had a strong desire to think through race to unmask the face of American liberal democracy and render visible a new intellectual tradition. As English-language teachers, both Furukawa and Nukina were particularly bothered by the Eurocentric contents of textbooks supplied by the American occupier, which systematically wrote out sufferings and injustices created and perpetuated by racism and capitalism. Refusing to embrace America as "a timeless space" endowed with boundless opportunities and promises where one could achieve emancipation from totalitarianism, fundamentalism, and militarism, they called into question the ideology of American exceptionalism. This moment of cognitive clarity was a repudiation of the bourgeois nationalist vision of American democracy that informed the politics of the U.S. occupation authority. Moved upon reading Nukina's recently published "On Abolitionists," which brought together the intellectual traditions of William Lloyd Garrison, Henry David Thoreau, and John Brown and delineated the path toward the Black radical tradition, Furukawa enlisted himself in Nukina's project to begin *Kokujin Kenkyu no Kai*. Together with other members, he explored a new paradigm for the pedagogy of human liberation and quickly emerged as one of the group's most skilled translators of the Black radical tradition.[37]

It is not an overstatement to assert that almost every project *Kokujin Kenkyu no Kai* pursued could not have been carried out without translating into Japanese the words, sentences, idioms, and meanings found in texts they studied. In fact, this practice of translation was central to the group's efforts to establish the connections between Japan and the Black liberation movement. Since *Kokujin Kenkyu no Kai* never recruited during its nascent formations intellectuals and activists of African descent to be core members and to participate in their collaborative research endeavor, the individual members had to amass knowledge about the Black world entirely from texts written in English or scholarly publications and news clippings written in Japanese. Moreover, this task of translating one linguistic and cultural convention to another was made all the more difficult in the case of translating African American prose and its aesthetic qualities. Despite these limitations and challenges, the members of *Kokujin Kenkyu no Kai* studied the texts with care and analytical sensitivity and always listened to what critic Brent Hayes Edwards calls "the sound of another tongue." Moving recursively through this experience of race, they looked for equivalent idioms in Japanese simultaneously to present the original anew and to stretch the boundaries of the African diaspora from Japan.[38]

The most notable example of the transpacific practice of translation appeared in Furukawa's three-part essay published in the journal *Kokujin Kenkyu* in 1959–1960, which explored the blues and jazz poems of Langston Hughes collected in *The Weary Blues* (1926), his first book of poetry.[39] Furukawa understood the task of a translator. Juxtaposing his Japanese translations with commentaries on Hughes's poems, Furukawa cultivated what the critic Walter Benjamin once called "the kinship of languages." Coming into contact with Hughes's poems for the first time in the early 1950s, he explored Hughes's rhythms, rhymes, and syntax and the myriad forms of his verses, while turning to James Weldon Johnson's *The Book of American Negro Poetry* to gather tools for interpreting the modes of Black cultural production. This engagement with Hughes's creative process helped him deepen his appreciation for African American expressive culture. But more important, Hughes's poetics enabled Furukawa to produce in the translated language an "echo of the original" and in doing so to "*describe* the workings of the music itself."[40] Explaining the task of translation in terms of creating the music, Benjamin wrote, "the language of translation can—in fact, must—let itself go, so that it gives voice to the *intentio* of the original not as reproduction but as harmony, as a supplement to the languages in which it expresses itself, as its own kind of *intentio*."[41] Occupying the space where Black literature and music met, harmony in translation was indeed what Furukawa achieved as a translator of Hughes's

blues poetry. Instead of reproducing the original to achieve authenticity, he diverged from the original while supplementing it. Such was the
dynamic culture of liberation from which the members of *Kokujin Kenkyu no Kai* linked up with the currents of Black radicalism to fashion
the pedagogy of human liberation.

Furukawa's translation of Hughes's "Caribbean Sunset" and "The
South," two poems that dramatize the horrors of the Middle Passage
and white terror in the Jim Crow South, best illustrates how the practice
of translation helped organize a discursive space for the rearticulation
of the dream of Black liberation in Japanese, making this deep desire
on the part of Black Americans to materialize freedom audible and palpable to the members of *Kokujin Kenkyu no Kai*. In the Japanese translation of the four-line short verse "Caribbean Sunset," the most obvious
alteration is the structure of the original version, which is constructed
of six syllables in the first three lines and ten syllables in the last line. In
the Japanese translation, the first line contains two five-syllable phrases,
followed by two phrases that are seven syllables and six syllables in the
second line. Then, in the third line, all three "sounds of phrases" appear
in the order of seven, five, and six syllables. When read and recited,
Furukawa's smartly plotted linguistic intervention helps establish a new
cadence in Japanese. The Japanese translation departs from the original, taking a detour of sorts, and reemerges with different sounds. Yet
the Japanese translation retains the essence of the Black ethos in the
original, which is presented with the economy of haiku in lyrical lines,
because Furukawa's translation preserves one of the defining features of
Hughes's blues poetry, "a syncopated insistence and urgency," as Yusef
Komunyakaa puts it.[42]

In the Japanese translation of "The South" as well, Furukawa has
adjusted the structure of the original. In this poem, Hughes deliberately
inverts the racialized and dehumanizing characterizations directed at
Blacks to present a sharp contrast between the Jim Crow South, hope-
lessly devoid of humanity, and southern Blacks' search for a new beginning in the North, albeit still uncertain. The most striking change in
Furukawa's Japanese translation, although small, appears at the outset.
Reversed is the order of the first two lines, which sets in motion a different rhythm, reinforced by an entirely new rhyming scheme in Japanese. Specifically, out of this alteration, the Japanese word for the South,

*nanbu*, acquires an aesthetic, lyrical, and sonic authority independently of the original. Progressively, the Japanese translation sets a different tempo, and ultimately it helps constitute the iconography of *nanbu* to capture the scene of white terror, the aftermath of lynching. Despite this change, Furukawa's translation retains the blues poetics of the original, designed to accentuate—all in the same breath—the inhumanity of the white South and the presence of Black suffering and yearning, because he grasps the allegory of the South that governs the entire thrust of this poem.

Even in the moment of mistranslation, the blues is heard in the language. Such is the case in Furukawa's efforts to translate the soundscape of "Lenox Avenue: Midnight." His translation maintains the tempo of this three-stanza poem fairly consistently until it hits a wrong note, to use a musical idiom, in the second stanza. Rendered visible in this instance of mistranslation is Furukawa's unfamiliarity with the Harlem cityscape. Not realizing that Hughes's poem refers to the sound of automobiles on Lenox Avenue, he has sought to make audible the sound of city trains (*shiden*). Of course, *shiden* run not above but down below Lenox Avenue. Yet this Japanese word performs a crucial function in Furukawa's imagination. Like a blot on his cognitive map, it takes him back to a specific moment in time, as he recalled in his memoir, when he was beginning to cultivate the kinship of language with Hughes's work on his train ride to and from the high school where he taught English. His mistranslation, thus, exhibits one of the essential musical qualities: the power of music to organize imagination and to make this imagination move recursively through time and space. It helped him transport to a place other than Harlem, possibly in the vicinity of Kobe, Japan, where he learned not only to "listen" to Hughes's blues and jazz poetry but also to respond to the call to translate a transpacific poetics of Black musical aesthetics. Indeed, it confirms Brent Hayes Edwards's assertion that "the possibility of black internationalism is heard to be a matter of music."[43]

If Furukawa's (mis)translation revealed the dynamic musical quality of Black radicalism, then the first decade of this collective's existence could be best interpreted as one that involved a series of attempts, through the practice of translation, to comprehend the epistemology and aesthetic governing the Black liberation movement. In other words,

Furukawa Hiromi, circa 1970 (© Furukawa Hiromi)

what the members of *Kokujin Kenkyu no Kai* were aiming to do was to "release in [their] own language," as Walter Benjamin once explained, "that pure language which is under the spell of another, to liberate the language imprisoned in a work in [their] re-creation of that work." Elaborating the essence of this creative process of making something anew immanent in the practice of translation in terms of the polynomial functions of "the tangent to a circle," Benjamin described how the working through seemingly incompatible principles in translation, freedom and fidelity, could potentially unlock the calculus of human liberation. He wrote, "Just as a tangent touches a circle lightly and at but one point, with this touch rather than with the point setting the law according to which it is to continue on its straight path to infinity, a translation touches the original lightly and only at the infinitely small point of the sense, thereupon pursuing its own course according to the laws of fidelity in the freedom of linguistic flux."[44] *Kokujin Kenkyu no Kai* negotiated fidelity and freedom in translation in that space where a tangent meets a circle when it began preparing, in 1964, the publication of its first anthology containing Japanese translations of the writings of leading African American intellectual-activists involved in the Black liberation movement.

Published in 1966, *Amerika Kokujin Kaiho Undo: Atarashi Niguro Gunzo* (The Black American Liberation Movement: The New Negro Crowd) marked *Kokujin Kenkyu no Kai*'s tenth anniversary. Two principal editors responsible for coordinating the acquisition of selected documents and copyright permission, as well as for the whole process of editing and proofreading Japanese translations, were Furukawa Hiromi and Akamatsu Mitsuo, who served as an editor of the journal *Kokujin Kenkyu* from 1958 to 1962.[45] What precipitated from this collective endeavor to translate the literature of the Black liberation movement was that it set in motion the group's efforts to inhabit the space and time of the shifting grounds of race and to organize a repository of shared hopes for a new society to produce the echo of Black radicalism in Japanese translations. In other words, the making of this anthology helped constitute the space of diaspora, through which Japanese intellectuals fashioned "the model for dialogue and exchange" to participate in the network of Afrodiasporic activists and writers that included John Henrik Clarke of *Freedomways*; Julian Mayfield, then the editor in chief of *African Review*, in Kwame Nkrumah's Ghana; and Robert F. Williams, an editor of *Crusader* and an exiled revolutionary in Fidel Castro's Cuba. This anthology-making project also brought an indispensable collaborator, Nakajima Yoriko, a steadfast Japanese supporter of Williams's revolutionary activity. While studying abroad in the United States in the late 1950s and early 1960s as a graduate student in political science, Nakajima was sucked into the vortex of the currents of Black radicalism. Shortly after returning to Japan in December 1961, she emerged as a key member of *Kokujin Kenkyu no Kai*, infusing a global vision of racial struggles and steering the members to recognize independent Black political action in solidarity with Third World liberation movements—not integration into American society—as the incubator of new universals in the United States and beyond.[46]

Consistent with *Kokujin Kenkyu no Kai*'s eclectic intellectual gen-
esis, the defining feature of this anthology was unevenness, although
the group tried to give it editorial coherence by stretching the arc of the
Black liberation movement as much as possible. Collected are the diversity and heterogeneity of political visions, experiences, and strategies.
It opened with the works of W. E. B. Du Bois: "Negro People and the
United States," an opening article of the inaugural Spring 1961 issue of
*Freedomways*, and "Behold the Land," a keynote address at the Southern
Youth Legislature in Columbia, South Carolina, delivered on October
20, 1946, which appeared in *Freedomways* in the Winter 1964 issue. Fol-
lowing these two selections were the works of "Black American Libera-
tion Movement" participants and icons (in order of appearance): pacifist
and Congress of Racial Equality (CORE) assistant community relations
director Robert B. Gore's "The Principle of Nonviolence" (1962); Martin
Luther King Jr.'s widely circulated "Letter from Birmingham Jail" (1963);
Julian Mayfield's "Challenge to Negro Leadership: The Case of Robert
Williams" (1961); Nakajima Yoriko's "The Cuban Revolution and the
American Negro of the South: An Eyewitness Account of the Robert
Williams Incident and Its Aftermath" (1965); Malcolm X's 1962 speech
at Yale University; and James Baldwin's "My Dungeon Shook: Letter
to My Nephew on the One Hundredth Anniversary of Emancipation"
(1963). The last section of the anthology was structured by the follow-
ing three selections from *The New Negro* (1961), an anthology edited by
Matthew H. Ahmann, then executive director of the National Catholic
Conference for Interracial Justice: Fisk University president Stephen J.
Wright's "The New Negro in the South" (1961); psychologist Kenneth B.
Clark's "The New Negro in the North" (1961); and a transcription of a
1961 radio broadcast symposium titled "The Negro in American Cul-
ture," featuring Nat Hentoff, James Baldwin, Alfred Kazin, Lorraine
Hansberry, Emile Capouya, and Langston Hughes.[47]

Nukina's introductory essay further complicated the presentation of
the thematic focus of this anthology.[48] Calling it "In Place of a 'Preface'" in his subtitle, he chose to do something unorthodox. Rather than
explaining the contents of this collection and how it was organized,
he presented a manifesto of sorts. It was a radical departure. Written
in September 1965 against the backdrop of the growing strength of
Black militancy in the wake of the 1965 Watts rebellion, the intractable

problem of structural racism in the areas of education, employment, and housing in the midst of postwar progress and prosperity and legislative civil rights victories, and the buildup of the U.S. war in Southeast Asia, he produced the discourses of international antiracism and antiimperialism in his essay. Presented in the best pan-African tradition of Black left thinkers such as W. E. B. Du Bois, George Padmore, Paul Robeson, and W. Alphaeus Hunton who shaped the culture of Black internationalism in the 1940s, his politics was informed as much by the Black revolutionary nationalism of Williams and post–Nation of Islam Malcolm X as by the Marxist critique of war, imperialism, and racism. In many ways, this substitute for a preface served a critical function as a "discursive frame" from which the mission and activity of *Kokujin Kenkyu no Kai* could be made anew amid a revolutionary ferment.[49]

Yet the most startling aspect of Nukina's manifesto was its seemingly anachronistic and incongruous title, "*Gendai no Niguro America-jin*" (Contemporary Negro Americans), which had the potential to skew his revolutionary political outlook. Since the founding of *Kokujin Kenkyu no Kai*, Nukina had expressed his preference for the use of *Niguro-jin*, as opposed to simply *Niguro* in Japanese. Echoing W. E. B. Du Bois's repudiation of "Negro" in lower case and sensitive to the politics of the naming controversy in Black life and culture, Nukina claimed that *Niguro* in Japanese would not highlight the significance of the capitalization of "Negro," especially the singular history of the struggle of Africans and people of African descent to be constituted as a people in America. Concerned with restoring that sense of the movement toward peoplehood, he translated Black Americans as *Niguro-jin* or *Niguro America-jin* by adding the Japanese word for "people" (*jin*). Yet, interestingly, the terrain of racial nomenclature shifted constantly in Nukina's essay and throughout the anthology, for various terms of designation other than *Niguro-jin*, such as *America Koku-jin* (Black Americans) and *Koku-jin* (Black people), coexisted. Such disjunctures in translation evinced a deep desire on the part of Japanese intellectuals to focus on the very process of traversing across and if possible connecting variations in the articulation of Black liberation. In essence, they engaged with the hallmark of the practice of diaspora: a call to translate race as a catalyst for resistance amid the constantly shifting grounds of race to help establish "the structure of a diasporic 'racial' formation."[50]

While choosing variation over defining Black liberation movement literature monolithically, *Kokujin Kenkyu no Kai*'s anthology nonetheless gave expression to a rather coherent conception of racial politics. Collected in the middle of this anthology were paired articles about Williams's life and political activism, written by Julian Mayfield and Nakajima Yoriko. At this conjuncture, when Mayfield and Nakajima fashioned themselves as collaborators in Williams's racial struggles, the diverse intellectual lineages seemed to converge to create a crease. From this enfolded section, "where the collection itself is collected," to borrow Edwards's useful formulation, *Kokujin Kenkyu no Kai* cultivated the Black radical tradition of localized political projects that were guided by the racial militancy of Williams and his supporters and the momentum of the Third World liberation movements. Nakamura's letter to Williams written on February 26, 1966, indeed highlighted this political position of editorial orientation: "Although it is not formally expressed in [an] editorial note in the book, considerable emphasis of this book was placed on your case and your idea which stands against iron adherence on non-violence and a great hope for future development of negro leadership is placed on *you* [throughout] this book."[51]

If this Black radical tradition anchoring *Kokujin Kenkyu no Kai*'s first anthology were to be manifested in the music of freedom and the sound of struggle, it would be heard in in the musical activism of *We Insist! Max Roach's Freedom Now Suite*. This comparison is not merely an academic exercise, as it is solidly grounded in concrete political reality. Released in 1960, Max Roach's *We Insist!*, featuring vocalist Abbey Lincoln and tenor saxophonist Coleman Hawkins, was originally a project-in-the-making in collaboration with Oscar Brown Jr., a Chicago-based singer, songwriter, and activist, that was intended to mark the centennial of the Emancipation Proclamation in 1963. Yet inspired by the militancy of youth in the Civil Rights Movement, marked by the direct action of the Student Non-Violent Coordinating Committee in 1960 and the promises of African liberation movements stretching beyond the pan-African guiding leadership of Nkrumah's Ghana, the album was quickly put together, albeit without Brown's consultation and input. Thus, explored in *We Insist!* were "three themes that were prominent in politically oriented jazz circa 1960: the African American experience with slavery, the contemporary freedom struggle, and an affinity with Africa." One of the notable compositions, "All Africa," featured a chant of Lincoln naming various African nations, backed up by the singing of Nigerian conga drummer Michael Olatunji in Yoruba in the background and "a steady polyrhythmic groove, facilitated by Olatunji's conga drums and Afro-Cuban percussionists Ray Mantilla and Tomas Duvail," all of which helped assemble Afrodiasporic sounds to make political statements and demands musically.[52]

This collaboration between Lincoln and Roach continued on such albums as Roach's *Percussion Bittersweet* (1961) and *It's Time* (1962) and Lincoln's *Straight Ahead* (1961) and extended well beyond the spaces of rehearsals and recording sessions. Frequently visiting Lincoln and Roach's penthouse apartment in New York were Ossie Davis and Ruby Dee, as well as Lorraine Hansberry, Maya Angelou, Rosa Guy, Sarah Wright, John Oliver Killens, Julian Mayfield, and John Henrik Clarke, all of whom were involved in either the Cultural Association for Women of African Heritage or the Harlem Writers Guild, or both. They were all artists and writers frustrated with a civil rights leader (referring to Martin Luther King Jr.) who "turn[ed] out to have heavy feet of clay," as the longtime civil rights activist Ella Baker put it in 1960. They were not afraid to criticize King and other leaders who cautiously steered the Civil Rights Movement in the context of Cold War politics and distanced themselves from independent Black dissent and Third World resistance elsewhere that challenged the status quo. Meanwhile, they found in their close friend Malcolm X key ingredients that could radicalize the existing Civil Rights Movement and especially modern politics, although they knew that Malcolm was constrained, as a faithful of the Nation of Islam, from throwing in his lot with these community activists and artists to further energize racial militancy. In search of an alternative, the political acquaintances of Roach and Lincoln refused to structure the debate over the directions of the Black freedom movement along the bipolar politics of integrationism and separatism that placed these positions as diametrically opposed to each other. Rather than foreclosing the challenge of the Black radical force that carried forward, in tandem, the torch of Malcolm X's radical politics, the impetus of the nonviolent Black youth movement spreading across the Jim

Crow South, the waves of decolonization worldwide, and the jubilee of the Cuban Revolution, their *Freedom Now Suite* helped usher in a new ethos.[53]

The case of the grassroots organizing activity of John Henrik Clarke, Mae Mallory, and Julian Mayfield in 1960–1961 best illustrates this link between the power of music and the formation of critical consciousness among individuals enmeshed in historical Black struggles. The work of Clarke, Mallory, and Mayfield represented the dynamic process out of which aesthetics and politics linked up, and one could almost hear their concrete political engagement musically in "Freedom Day," one of the tracks on *We Insist!*. The combination of the interweaving solos of Julian Priester (trombone), Walter Benton (tenor saxophone), and Booker Little (trumpet); James Schenck's steady bass line; Max Roach's drumming; and Abbey Lincoln's singing dramatized the moment of Black self-emancipation in 1863 that was at once jubilant and redeeming but also characterized by political uncertainty and anxiety. Such a sound of "the slave sublime," as Gilroy calls it, or an antiphon of self-fashioning—an urge to constitute independently of dominant available political options to achieve a total human liberation through ceaseless strivings—was, among Black activists and artists surrounding the *We Insist!* project, the incubator producing the Black radical force.[54]

Mayfield, Clarke, and Mallory, for instance, spearheaded a fundraising campaign, called the Coordinating Committee for Southern Relief, to provide material support to working-class Blacks in Monroe, North Carolina, where Williams, in his capacity as a local branch president of the NAACP, rallied members to take the position of armed self-defense to counter the repeated violent campaigns of white terror. Malcolm X also came on board to help Williams's cause.[55] Meanwhile, Mayfield and Clarke, along with Williams, became active in an organization that was tied to the Old Left, called the Fair Play for Cuba Committee. Williams had come to play a key role, traveling across the country to communicate the link between the Cuban Revolution and Black liberation and the position of nonalignment to present Cuba as a viable political alternative in the international community, which was rigidly shaped by the bipolar politics of the Cold War. In July 1960, both Clarke and Mayfield traveled to Cuba along with artists tied to the Harlem Writers Guild, such as Sarah Wright, LeRoi Jones (later Amiri Baraka), and Harold Cruse, to join Williams to witness the work of the Cuban Revolution and its commitment to eradicate the vestiges of racial discrimination. This movement in a racial groove via "the Cuban challenge," as Mayfield called it, pulled him and others closer toward the tradition of Roach and Lincoln's sounds, which in turn enabled them to reach a conclusion that "social change need not wait on the patient education of the bigot and reactionary."[56]

Ultimately, this force was what guided those who took part in the skirmishes inside the United Nations and a street protest and rally on First Avenue in February 1961 to denounce the political assassination of Congo's Patrice Lumumba and the complicity of the United States and the Western world. Thoroughly cognizant of the expressive power of these protestors' commitment to make palpable in the everyday the "unsayable claims to truth" that were often rendered irrelevant or muffled, John Henrik Clarke explained the symbolic significance of their act of defiance in this way:

> The demonstrators in the United Nations gallery interpreted the murder of Lumumba as the international lynching of a Black man on the altar of colonialism and white supremacy. Suddenly, to them at least, Lumumba became Emmett Till and all of the other black victims of lynch law and the mob. The plight of the Africans still fighting to throw off the yoke of colonialism and the plight of the Afro-Americans, still waiting for a rich, strong and boastful nation to redeem the promise of freedom and citizenship became one and the same.[57]

Although Mayfield was not present, his friends who shared a similar politics, such as Jones and Mallory, along with community activists associated with the Liberation Committee for Africa, On Guard, the African American Nationalist Pioneer Movement, and the Cultural Association for Women of African Heritage, were all there in the UN gallery and beyond, and endorsements came from James Baldwin and Lorraine Hansberry, both publicly, and Malcolm X privately.[58]

The insurgent spirit of Black artists and activists who orbited around Roach's *We Insist!*, eager to widen the circle of the culture of the emergent Black liberation movement, helped fashion the discourse and praxis of what Clarke called "the New Afro-American nationalism."

They reminded each other and the world at large that " 'Negroes' were now 'Afro-Americans.' " This category of collective self-identification, as Kevin Gaines explains so eloquently, "promised the achievement of a unity through which black and African people might know themselves and each other and imagine a world transformed by their action on that knowledge."[59] The members of *Kokujin Kenkyu no Kai*, as they prepared the publication of *Amerika Kokujin Kaiho Undo*, were in dialogue with Williams, Clarke, and Mayfield, intellectual-activists who were intimately involved with the "new Afro-American" political projects that articulated the Afrodiasporic expressions of dignity and hope. This transpacific coeval transfer of the Black radical tradition was further facilitated by Nakajima Yoriko, an interlocutor translating the culture of Black internationalism and seeking to establish the context for Black collaboration with the political acquaintances of Williams so that Japanese intellectuals could link up with the currents of Black radicalism and internationalism.

## How Nakajima Yoriko Raised the Banner of "Colored-Internationalism"

At the time of Nakajima Yoriko's first encounter with Robert F. Williams in January 1961, she was an international graduate student in political science in her third and final year at the University of Michigan, coming from Doshisha University in Kyoto, where she had earned her master of arts degree. At Michigan, she achieved acute analytical and theoretical advances as her research on the relationship between the Black freedom struggle and the future of American politics began to take shape. It was in the midst of this intellectual maturity that she encountered Williams. He was on a speaking tour in the Midwest on behalf of the Fair Play for Cuba Committee, and Nakajima heard Williams's lecture titled "Cuba and Negroes in the American South" in Ann Arbor in January 1961. His speech transformed her vision, and soon after she visited Williams and his family in Monroe on her way to Atlanta, Georgia, to conduct fieldwork for her dissertation during the last months of her sojourn. The friendship she struck up with Williams then ultimately led to a letter from him in Cuba—in December 1961—by way of Ann Arbor and Atlanta, encouraging her, now back in Japan, to come witness the work of the Cuban Revolution, a microcosm of revolutions in Africa and China, as Williams framed it. The implications of the Cuban Revolution were transnational, William argued, and such that the racial politics of these Third World revolutions would transform the Black American struggle for freedom. Williams and Nakajima shared these thoughts on race, transnational politics, and revolution first in Monroe and continued their dialogue in Cuba in the summer of 1962 and thereafter through correspondence.[60]

When read with the knowledge of Nakajima's deep ties with Williams, the essay that Nakajima contributed to the *Kokujin Kenkyu no Kai* anthology, titled "The Cuban Revolution and the Negro People of the American South," and her translation of Julian Mayfield's "Challenge to Negro Leadership: The Case of Robert Williams" together represented the tendency coming out of the community of solidarity not only aiding Williams's armed self-defense activity but also listening to Max Roach and Abbey Lincoln's *Freedom Now Suite*. In her essay, Nakajima chronicled the backstory of how she became a collaborator in Williams's political world, which was constituted at the intersection of the Cuban Revolution and the Black liberation movement, beginning with her first encounter in early 1961 through their reunion in the summer of 1962 and ending with the up-to-date status of Williams in 1964, one year before he departed Cuba for Hanoi for good and eventually settled in Mao's China. What emerged from her narration was her firm grasp of Williams's political outlook. While Nakajima's own piece centered on circumstances leading up to Williams's life in exile and his subsequent emergence as a Black radical internationalist operating out of Cuba, Mayfield's article was an eyewitness account of the making of Williams's political leadership as the local president of the NAACP and the central role he played in Monroe working-class Blacks' armed self-defense resistance to white supremacy. Throughout, Mayfield discussed how all of this became an affront to Black bourgeois leadership within the national NAACP office and a counterpoint to the King-led and King-centric Civil Rights Movement. Although Nakajima deliberately framed her own essay as a sequel to Mayfield's account, not detailed were just how both Mayfield and Nakajima were in close proximity at a critical juncture in Williams's life.[61]

Nakajima visited Williams in Monroe in March 1961, during a period when Mayfield, along with Clarke and Mallory, were in contact with Williams and his associates, a period that ran through the first eight months of 1961. Through the work of the Coordinating Committee for Southern Relief, Mayfield, Clarke, and Mallory shuttled back and forth between Harlem and Monroe to deliver food, clothes, and guns (supplied by LeRoi Jones, who had connections with New Jersey gangsters) to aid and reinforce the Monroe Blacks' armed self-defense struggle until August, a fateful month in which Williams and his wife, Mabel, and two children, together with Mallory and Mayfield, were forced to leave Monroe, stealthily at night, in the face of mounting white violence that threatened their lives. The cause of the intensification of white mob action was a contingent of the Civil Rights Movement, the group of Freedom Riders that came to Monroe to demonstrate the efficacy of nonviolence. Their escape to the North ultimately ended with the Williams family's political exile in Cuba in September; Mayfield's fugitive life via Canada and London, which led to exile, with his family, in Ghana in December; and Mallory's arrest and subsequent imprisonment. In the midst of this sequence of life-changing events that swallowed these activists, Nakajima prepared to return to Japan, and she eventually did in late October by sea. But she did not depart unscathed, for FBI agents came after her as well in Ann Arbor, soon after the news of Williams's escape and federal kidnapping charges against Williams became known, suspecting she might be hiding Williams. As Nakajima aptly described, although she and Mayfield missed each other in Monroe, they had been like "two moons orbiting around Williams." Their bonds became stronger upon her return to Japan via preparation for the publication of *Amerika Kokujin Kaiho Undo*.[62]

Nakajima and Mayfield had come to be joined at the hip on the grounds of their shared opposition to Cold War racial liberalism. Their belief was that the Cold War–induced directive for racial integration, endorsed by white liberals in the government and Black civil rights leaders, did more harm than good for Black working-class masses seeking racial justice and equality. For Nakajima, Williams, and Mayfield, Cold War racial liberalism was a subterfuge that would simultaneously create the euphoria of the universalistic aspiration of American democracy and conceal the fact that this ideology of American exceptionalism was the driving force behind American hegemony, which severely narrowed the life chances and political options for working-class Black Americans and darker nations and peoples emerging out of colonialism in the Cold War era.[63] Mayfield's diagnosis of the bankruptcy of racial liberalism in the United States, translated by Nakajima and collected in the *Kokujin Kenkyu no Kai* anthology, was a clear illustration of his repudiation of the American conception of democracy and his complete break with the Black bourgeoisie, which catered to white liberal America to gain social acceptance and political freedom:

> These are the great masses of the unskilled, who belong to no labor unions or civil organizations, whose churches are more concerned with leading their flocks to heaven than to a fuller share of democracy on earth, whose only fraternity is that of the millions of neglected and untrained who have nothing to barter in the labor market but their willingness to work. Only yesterday the man of this class could pick the cotton, run the elevator, pack the crate, but now the machine can do it better and displaces him. Government statistics hardly suggest how great his number is, much less what he is feeling and thinking, but we know he is everywhere. . . . A casual walk through any colored section of [a] Southern town or city will reveal him, standing on the corner, lounging near the bar, slouched on the doorstep, staring into the uncertainty that is his future. The "they" in his life, those who make decisions that vitally affect him, are not only the governments, federal, state, and local, the captains of industry and finance, but even the Negro middle class and the striking students, all of whom seem to be going someplace without him.[64]

Nakajima was in agreement with Mayfield's assessment of the widening gulf between the reality of the impoverishment of Black working-class masses and civil rights leaders and students. His criticism was that "the Negro middle class and the striking students" who pursued nonviolence and legal means to change U.S. race relations operated with a blind spot, denying and vilifying the potential of uncompromising opposition to white supremacy to overthrow this system. This uncompromising position was best represented by Williams's tactics and actions, which came out of the self-organization of the Black working class. With the bourgeois elements fixated on the righteousness of their own political orientation and trapped inside the calculated nature of pragmatism, Mayfield believed that they suffered from a case of woe-fully underdeveloped political imagination. Nakajima was certainly not interested in "going someplace" without the Black masses.[65]

Following the tracks that Williams and Mayfield laid, Nakajima headed straight into what Mary Dudziak calls "Cold War civil rights," which Nakajima categorized as the Achilles' heel of domestic and international politics. She sought to make the grounds for local, trans-national, and global resistance fertile to transcend this nexus of Cold War foreign policy and dominant civil rights reform initiatives that were "purely legalistic" and fixated on the omnipotence of nonviolence. The international system of competitive nation-states structured by the bipolar politics of the Cold War was an enabler. Since the United States was so wedded to its self-image as a beacon of democracy against communism, the constant exposure of the repeated patterns of white-supremacist institutional practices and exercises of power in the Amer-ican liberal democratic state and international institutions could actu-ally help make acute advances in the movement for human liberation. Both Williams and Mayfield felt certain that the U.S. federal govern-ment would "act only under strong pressure" to try to rescue besieged American democracy. Explaining the unintended consequence result-ing from the globalized crisis of racial liberalism, Mayfield wrote, "Without the cold war and the competition between the colossi of West and East, it seems doubtful that the many African nations could have gained independence so rapidly." Endorsing Williams's racial militancy, which he called "armed self-reliance," Mayfield insisted on the impera-tive of challenging the Cold War status quo on the home front "by a more militant assertion of [Blacks'] rights—including 'meeting vio-lence with violence.'"[66]

Nakajima also acknowledged the efficacy of activists pushing for a more militant position, at the risk of being labeled "communists," to exceed the hegemonic category of "Cold War civil rights." For her, this realization came during her six-month sojourn in the Jim Crow South from March to September 1961. She moved through the segregated Black world in Monroe, North Carolina, and Atlanta and the country-side of Georgia, meeting with working-class Blacks who spoke frankly about politically "taboo" subjects, as Nakajima put it. The case in point was the topic of the atomic bombings of Hiroshima and Nagasaki.

While Nakajima was at the University of Michigan, whenever this topic came up, her white, liberal American peers always justified the action of the United States, which brought unspeakable human and environmental calamities. They reminded her of the Japanese attack on Pearl Harbor and argued that it was a "good war" waged in opposition to fascism to "liberate" the Japanese. The nature of the discussion was qualitatively different with working-class southern Blacks, however. They would first ask her why the United States did not drop atomic bombs in Nazi Germany but in Japan and then in the next breath tell her that it had everything to do with race. Far from being dismissive of such a race-based worldview, she measured seriously this tendency to break existing categories of perceptions and interpretations, defining it as a force to be reckoned with.[67]

For her, this Black worldliness helped clear the path and broaden the horizon of political expectation. What she gleaned from conversations with working-class Black men and women, who expressed a strong cultural conviction that "the era of white prosperity had withered" while acknowledging with alarm that white resistance to desegregation had become increasingly violent and unbound, was a certain kind of vernacular moral and political authority, or what Clyde Woods has called "the blues tradition," a passionate, emotive, and expressive power rooted in slave culture. In sharp contrast to the officials of the NAACP, CORE, and the Southern Christian Leadership Conference (SCLC) whom she interviewed for her research and who separated African anticolonial nationalism and the Cuban Revolution from their own causes, these working-class Blacks rejoiced with the anticipation of better days ahead as the currents of Third World liberation movements intensified. Nakajima felt the pulse of Black radicalism and internationalism in all-Black towns and segregated urban neighborhoods in the South, an outlook that decisively exceeded the national boundaries, and she concluded that working-class Blacks presented a far more mature political understanding about the world they inhabited than did the leaders of the mainstream Civil Rights Movement.[68]

Nakajima aligned with these Black masses and intellectual-activists, who had concluded, Mayfield wrote, "that the only way to win the revolution is to be a revolutionary."[69] And she certainly did live up to that ideal. Yet, in doing so, she paid a high price, for at least seven years after

returning to Japan in late 1961, her repudiation of American exceptionalism via her association with Williams crippled her academic career.
While Williams and Mayfield paid the price of their dissent in the form
of political exile, Nakajima suffered from a serious case of isolation,
which was compounded by gender-based job discrimination within
the academy. Throughout these years, she "tried to get [a] teaching or
research job," but as she wrote to Robert and Mabel Williams in June
1964, "all of these seemingly run away from me because of my visiting
to Cuba, my writing on Cuba." She continued,

> Some colleges and universities [do not] even care of my observation on
> Negro movement in the USA, which they are worried may effect on their
> exchange programs with USA university or funds given from the USA.
> They were earger [sic] to hear about Cuba and Cubans, but not earger
> [sic] to have me when I express my interest to be employed as teacher
> or research. I did [not] know for long [time] I am listed on the black list
> at the American Embassy in Tokyo, but I have recently learned Japanese
> government does the same to me. I am furious about it and try not to
> be defeated.[70]

Despite political marginalization and repression, Nakajima was resilient, and her resolve to stay committed came out of her theoretical and
methodological approach to the study of race, seeing this concept as the
political category of struggle. In the process, she came to realize that
talking about the political vision of Williams and Mayfield in Japan,
through the practice of translation and participation in *Kokujin Kenkyu
no Kai*, was a matter of cultivating the culture of liberation and inventing the discourse of Black radicalism and internationalism anew. If, for
Williams and Mayfield, their respective sites of exile were considered
to be "an external vantage point that enabled critical insight into U.S.
overseas propaganda and the nation's relationship to the world . . . [and
gave] tangible meaning to pan-Africanism," as Kevin Gaines argues,
for Nakajima, *Kokujin Kenkyu no Kai*'s collectivity helped give form to
the new political language of Black radicalism and internationalism.
Indeed, the outcome of Nakajima's transpacific infusion of the Black
radical tradition was etched in the caption of the featured photographs
of Robert Williams in the anthology *Amerika Kokujin Kaiho Undo*, one

of them taken with his wife, Mabel, and showing Robert shaking hands with Mao on the occasion of their first visit in China in October 1963: the caption read, "Colored-Internationalism."[71]

*Kokujin Kenkyu no Kai*'s formulation of "colored-internationalism" was a testament to its engagement with the transpacific project of internationalizing Black radicalism both in theory and in practice. Not a mere translator or a participant-observer, Nakajima played a central role in transpacific strivings as a "Black" collaborator, working closely with such radical Black internationalists as Williams, Mayfield, and a host of artists associated with the world of Roach and Lincoln's *Freedom Now Suite*. Crossing boundaries, both in language and in transnational political struggles, she helped *Kokujin Kenkyu no Kai* find the ideological orientation of "colored-internationalism." With a strong, clear vision and leadership, she guided its members to use this newly developed language not necessarily to reproduce the Black radical tradition but rather to create the rhythms of a new "theme song," the soul of Williams's radicalism and internationalism, in harmony with the tradition of historical Black struggles.[72]

One of the marvelous outcomes of Nakajima's invention of the language of "colored-internationalism" and its praxis came later, independently of *Kokujin Kenkyu no Kai*, in the early 1970s. In response to Williams's legal battle against extradition to North Carolina for trumped-up kidnapping charges, which were visited on him shortly after his return from political exile in China, Nakajima and another principal coordinator, Takahashi Toru, helped constitute a transpacific collective, called the Japanese Committee for Defense of the Life and Fundamental Human Rights of Robert F. Williams, to aid his legal defense campaign in the United States. Even as Williams distanced himself from the vilified Black militancy by cutting his ties with the Republic of New Afrika, in which he was deeply enmeshed as a leader and a living legend—in 1969, ironically, at the height of the Black Power movement—he could not extricate himself from his own celebrated existence as long as he faced this legal battle. But Nakajima and Takahashi stayed with him during this transitional period in his life because Williams turned to them for support. Between 1970 and 1975, the group of progressive Japanese intellectuals found ways to make a scandal of this case of extradition through a combination of community organizing and strategic media-outreach activity. The Japanese Committee not only managed to enlist moral and political support from some of the leading intellectuals and political leaders in Japan but also carried out a successful petition campaign that resulted in amassing over ten thousand signatures from concerned ordinary Japanese citizens.[73]

Writing in 1993, some thirty years after joining *Kokujin Kenkyu no Kai* and no longer as actively involved in its activity as in the past, Nakajima recounted one of the comical yet revealing exchanges she had with Furukawa Hiromi. By the invitation of Nukina Yoshitaka, she delivered, on May 26, 1962, a talk titled *"Atolanta no Niguro-taun"* (The Negro Town of Atlanta) before the audience of *Kokujin Kenkyu no Kai.* She discussed the differing conceptions of "politics"—which she deliberately placed in quotation marks in her publication—between the Black intelligentsia and masses to address how the latter broke with the former and expressed a yearning to pursue an independent course of political action.[74] After the talk, Furukawa asked her a question:

> "Ms. Nakajima, your talk did not mention that famous organization of his [W. E. B. Du Bois] called 'Nasupu.' Have you heard of it?"
> "'Nasupu'? I have never heard of it. How do you spell it?"
> "It's N-A-A-C-P."
> "Oh, that's referred to as 'N-double-A-C-P.'"

Possibly, Furukawa turned to the following two points of reference to pronounce NAACP as *Nasupu:* (1) the pronunciations of two pre-war proletarian cultural organizations in Japan that went by the acronyms NAPF and KOPF (pronounced *nappu* and *koppu,* respectively), which Nukina orbited around and Furukawa was probably aware of; and (2) the pronunciation of the commonly known acronym WASP (White Anglo-Saxon Protestant). Regardless, Furukawa continued to play a word-association game of sorts thereafter, which appeared in the December 1963 and March 1964 issues of *Kokujin Kenkyu.* In the form of a tiny insert titled "NAACP," Furukawa introduced variations of the "N-double-A-C-P" appellation that appeared in Lorraine Hansberry's *A Raisin in the Sun: A Drama in Three Acts* (1959) and John Oliver Killens's novel *And Then We Heard the Thunder* (1962). Interestingly, these two writers were closely associated with the Harlem Writers Guild, the

*Freedomways* collective, and the political activism of the "new Afro-American nationalism," which was tightly bound up with the musical activism of Roach's *We Insist!* Where all of these associations' artistic and political directions met, the articulation of a counterpoint to the NAACP appeared most sharply. But equally striking was the clarity with which *Kokujin Kenkyu no Kai's* Black radical tradition manifested itself through this politics of identification.[75]

Indeed, Furukawa's exploration of "NAACP" was not simply evidence of his thirst for knowledge; it animated his *Burakku he no Tabiji* (A Journey toward Blackness), as he titled the three-volume collection of his own writings and essays, which chronicled the many routes he took into Black worldliness. Central to this journey were two governing principles that helped to make Black radicalism and internationalism anew in Japan, *michikusa* (dawdling) and *honyaku* (translation) —the titles for volumes 1 and 3 of *Burakku he no Tabiji*. Both of these principles facilitated *Kokujin Kenkyu no Kai's* attempts to make an inroad into the culture of liberation and to transform this culture into a discursive space for the articulation of new forms of politics in Japan, albeit at times taking detours through the ideologically heterogeneous arenas informed by the Marxian debate on the "Negro Question," the progressive wing of the Esperanto movement, and "the New Afro-American nationalism." What came out of this racial formation and transformation, nonetheless, was a shared ethos of transpacific strivings.[76] The next chapter carries this story of the dynamics of multiple border crossing underpinning the formation of *Kokujin Kenkyu no Kai* to occupied Okinawa in the late 1960s and early 1970s, where diverse constituents involved in the antiwar, antibase, antireversion, antiracist, and Third World liberation struggles moved toward each other to link up in solidarity.

# 4

## The Presence of (Black) Liberation in Occupied Okinawa

For Okinawans, 1969 was supposed to mark a realization of their dream. Since 1960, the Okinawa Prefecture Council for Reversion to the Home Country, called *Fukkikyo*—an umbrella organization for the reversion movement consisting of the Okinawa Teachers' Association, the Okinawa Prefecture Youth Group Council, the Council for the Okinawa Public Office Workers' Union, and progressive political parties—sought to unite Japanese-flag-waving Okinawans. *Fukkikyo*'s goal was to bring an end to U.S. occupation so that Okinawa's Japanese prefectural status would be fully restored. After being detached from mainland Japan and placed under the U.S. occupation authority called the U.S. Civil Administration of the Ryukyu Islands (USCAR) in 1952, Okinawa acquired a liminal territorial status, neither a part of the United States nor a part of Japan, and its inhabitants were categorically rendered stateless.

The genesis of this ambiguous arrangement was the 1951 Treaty of Peace with Japan, which officially marked the end of the Second World

War. While this peace treaty ended U.S. occupation in mainland Japan, Okinawa experienced the reverse. John Foster Dulles, the architect of Article 3 of this treaty, stated that the United States would have absolute power over Okinawa while preparing to place it under United Nations trusteeship (which never happened) and that Japan would only have "residual sovereignty" over Okinawa. Okinawa's status remained pending on purpose until the 1971 Okinawa Reversion Treaty set the timetable for Okinawa's return to Japan in 1972.[1]

Yet reversion supporters, once regarded as communists because they called into question the legitimacy of U.S. colonial and military rule, did not celebrate the Sato-Nixon joint communiqué in November 1969 that led to the Okinawa Reversion Treaty. This shift in Okinawans' attitude caught the leaders, officials, and policymakers on both sides of the Pacific by surprise.[2] Rather than looking forward to the prospect of becoming Japanese, local people took to the streets and headed straight to the military bases. They mobilized an islandwide opposition to the U.S. occupation authority and called for the abrogation of this bilateral agreement, demanding the immediate and unconditional removal of military personnel, bases, and weapons of mass destruction.[3]

The surge of antireversionism was not an abrupt change of sentiment. Antireversionism acquired support in the final years of the occupation period because of the escalation of and furor about the U.S. war in Vietnam. As the strategic importance of bases in Okinawa increased after 1965, local people were drawn into the vortex of this war. B-52s departed from the U.S. Air Force's Kadena Air Base, the largest in the Far East, to conduct air campaigns to plunder villages and people in Southeast Asia; the Marines constantly trained on the ground, in the mountains, and in the sea, thereby disrupting local people's everyday activities; rapes and crimes committed by GIs increased and threatened the lives of local people, especially women and children; and the troops used the island as a place not only for rest and recreation but also to store poisonous gases and nuclear weapons. Local people's rejection of the terms of reversion had to do with the realization that their twin aims, reversion to Japan and opposition to the Vietnam War, were incompatible. Japan was one of the key allies supporting the U.S. war in Southeast Asia, and U.S. military bases in Okinawa would remain intact to buttress U.S. global hegemony and aggressive militarism, even after the island returned to Japan. It meant that Okinawa would continue to function as a highly militarized colonial outpost.[4]

From this vantage point, Okinawans saw "no contradiction between the reversion movement and the protest movement now," as Koji Taira, an Okinawan scholar and economist based in the United States, explained in his letter to the *New York Times* in 1972. The central objective of the reversion movement had always been ending the American occupation, which meant (1) the removal of all bases and weapons of mass destruction and (2) integration into the Japanese nation through its constitutional framework of antimilitarism and pacifism, commonly known as Article 9 of the Japanese Constitution. However, the Reversion Treaty merely proposed a "one-third autonomy" rather than "the fullest possible autonomy under the Constitution" of Japan. Far from realizing the goals of ushering in a basefree society and rehabilitation as full members of the Japanese nation, Taira explained, "Okinawans saw themselves involved in two-pronged struggles against the military dictatorship at home and against the corruption of the meaning of reversion in the hands of Tokyo conservatives." They had to contend with two imperial powers that were committed to maintaining a large military buildup on the islands, which would make their efforts to achieve lasting peace impossible.[5]

While Taira presented the antiwar position of the reversion movement, which carried forward the spirit of resistance in the final years of the U.S. occupation period, there also emerged a new insurgent sentiment that was even more far-reaching. A handful of intellectuals, writers, and student activists, certain that nothing would change upon their return to Japan, began calling for the rejection of the whole idea of reversion. Most prominent among them was the *Okinawa Times* journalist and critic Arakawa Akira, who was also known as a nonconformist poet who detested and resisted all manifestations of orthodoxies, including those coming out of the progressive movement. These critics challenged the uncritical acceptance of "Okinawans' sameness with the 'Japanese,'" which structured the existing reversion movement. They argued that Okinawa's full autonomy would never be realized by integrating into the Japanese nation. Arakawa and other antireversionists insisted that Okinawans' demand for reversion, in fact, fueled the Japanese and U.S. nation-states' imperative to continuously dominate and exploit subjects who were historically regarded and treated as racially different and inferior. Their main criticism was that Okinawans' reincorporation as Japanese national subjects would merely reinscribe their racialized otherness, thereby strengthening the power of the state over every aspect of how Okinawans lived and related to the mainland Japanese.[6]

Cognizant of this irony of integration, these Okinawan critics highlighted the logic of the nation-state, which would co-opt the politics of reversion and make the architecture of colonial rule anew in Okinawa. Repudiating the commonly accepted idea that entering into a social contract with the nation-state was a political objective worth pursuing, Arakawa declared that Okinawans had to categorically reject "Japaneseness," which resided within "all political thinking on both the left and the right in Okinawa," and reach out for a new ontological category. He and other intellectuals theorized the emancipatory potential of Okinawans' distinct ethos, identity, history, and experience, calling them to find a mode of belonging other than the one provided by the U.S. and Japanese nation-states and the reversion movement itself. They were interested in articulating a new form of identification. As Miyume Tanji writes, "The crux of [their] anti-reversionism is that the Okinawans' struggle against the state could be sustained only by recognizing the 'alien' status within the nation-state."[7]

On the eve of Okinawa reversion in the late 1960s and early 1970s, these antireversionists were not alone in occupied Okinawa in their struggle to transcend "the false idea that nation-state is the sole arbiter of universal values and legitimate political aims," as Nikhil Pal Singh nicely puts it. While the protest movements of the 1960s splintered in different directions in the United States and elsewhere by late in the decade and amplified the general sense of crisis in radical political thought and activity, a shared sense of commitment to justice in occupied Okinawa did not falter in many instances. In fact, at the grassroots, this commitment was still salient, not at all passé, as activists from around the world converged and began fashioning themselves as internationalists in occupied Okinawa. The pacifists from the United States and mainland Japan, for instance, came to realize, by way of opposing the U.S. war in Southeast Asia, that occupied Okinawa was a strategic site for the struggle against U.S. and Japanese imperialism. Some GIs stationed in Okinawa also stepped into the space of anti-imperialism because they had become repulsed by aggressive militarism and its manifestations in their daily lives. In particular, buoyed by the growing strength of the Black Power and Third World liberation movements, Black GIs and some antiracist white GIs made this space of resistance productive by way of making connections between the Vietnam War, the violence of militarism, the ascent of neocolonialism, and the persistence of white racism at home and in the military. White feminists also made a critical inroad into this space by pointing out the problem of white heteropatriarchy. And above all, facing the prospects of indefinite U.S. military domination and reannexation by the Japanese government, Okinawans took a stance against reversion and searchingly headed toward a politics capable of generating a new identity and revolutionary consciousness.[8]

All of these diverse constituents of social movements moved from strength to strength. Coming together in localized projects and building relations across difference through multiracial organizing work, they took giant steps to carve out communities of solidarities through transnational, anti-imperialist, and antiracist struggles. Their struggles to create what Angela Davis calls "unpredictable coalitions" through transpacific strivings enabled them to imagine "the world not yet born" and to find an alternative mode of racial belonging, or "the future in the present." This chapter unearths this dynamism of social identities in occupied Okinawa, especially the manner in which the discourse of race helped incite among participants of multiracial coalition work the "ever present flame of hope" or "rugged sense of somebodyness," as Martin Luther King Jr. once put it, thereby making the culture of liberation productive for the articulation of a new kind of revolution, politics, and collectivity.[9]

## In Pursuit of Soul

In the end, what the participants of progressive, multiracial coalition-building projects tried to change during the era of Okinawa reversion did not change. To this day, Okinawa remains the keystone of the militarized international security system controlled by the United States and Japan and a host to over thirty military bases and installations. In fact, 75 percent of all the military bases and facilities in Japan are still concentrated in Okinawa prefecture, although it is the smallest and poorest one in Japan. Most recently, initially animated by the campaign promise of Prime Minister Hatoyama Yukio, of the Democratic Party of Japan, to relocate the U.S. Marine Corps Futenma Air Station out of Okinawa, Okinawans, pushing their political demand with high hope and urgency, galvanized an islandwide antibase mass struggle. Yet Hatoyama's bold pronouncement simultaneously indexed his fall from political power, a fall that was just as dramatic as his party's over-throw of the fifty-year dominance of Liberal Democratic Party leader-ship. In the end, unable to break through the walls of the realpolitik of regional security, he reached a compromise with President Barack Obama, announcing that the Futenma base would be relocated to the less crowded north side of the island rather than moved off the island. The potential of transpacific, cross-racial Obama-Hatoyama Demo-cratic Party coalition building was nowhere to be found, despite the unexpected news of President Obama winning the Nobel Peace Prize, which became known in the midst of this battle over Okinawa in Octo-ber 2009. Japan ended up reaffirming its junior-partner status in its relations with the United States, so as to continue U.S.-Japan military domination and colonial arrangement in Okinawa. Ultimately, the impending no-confidence vote forced Hatoyama to resign in June 2010, ending his mere nine-month tenure as prime minister.[10]

The point in reminding readers of this unfulfilled contemporary political challenge is not to highlight the absence of progressive Afro-Asian policymaking across the Pacific, nor is it to make a case that localized social struggles, then and now, as far as the quest for creating a basefree society in Okinawa is concerned, are futile in the face of real-politik. Rather, throughout this chapter, I emphasize the shape of hope, what activists and intellectuals in occupied Okinawa dreamed as they entered the transpacific culture of liberation. During the late 1960s and early 1970s, engaging politically in opposition to racism, militarism, sexism, and imperialism and developing the social networks of identi-fications and affiliations in Okinawa, mainland Japanese and American peace activists, Black Power GIs, antiwar and antiracist white GIs, radi-cal feminists, and local people changed their outlook—the way they feel and see, imagine, relate to others, and live. What emerged was an intense creative and collective activity that unleashed their capacities to produce new knowledge and praxis.

In *Freedom Dreams*, Robin D. G. Kelley refers to this rarely acknowledged presence of an alternative paradigm for change in the everyday as "the poetics of struggle." Defiantly arguing against those who think about change in purely political terms and dismiss the idea that expressive traditions and cultural products can become a catalyst in the service of revolution, Kelley assigns utmost confidence in poets-in-the-making, activists and intellectuals who are "bold enough to still dream" to usher in "the future in the present." As he explains, "Revolutionary dreams erupt out of political engagement; collective social movements are incubators of new knowledge." As contemporary Okinawa still faces the intractable problem of aggressive militarism, the story of the multiracial struggle for freedom during the era of Okinawa reversion in the late 1960s and early 1970s—how activists and intellectuals underwent radicalization and articulated transpacific forms of resistance to white supremacy—can have a bearing on contemporary challenges to creating a basefree society. It has the potential to have a conversation-changing function in the present.[11]

The poet Adrienne Rich has described the nature of the human mind's most creative capacities to produce new knowledge and praxis as "a kind of a gated, landscaped neighborhood—or a river, sometimes clogged and polluted, carrying many kinds of traffic including pollen and contraband, but in movement: the always-regenerating impulse toward an always-beginning future." In occupied Okinawa, the dynamic of the freedom struggle was such that myriad clusters of activists engaging in political activism struggled to reach such a terrain where they themselves would become the currents of a new movement.[12] Among these activists, the key to this breakthrough at the levels of epistemology and social practice was the manner in which they began performing the task of racial formation and transformation, considering what it would take to manifest a critical insight that the category of race had everything to do with the politics of identification.

Specialist 4 Quinton T. Allen II of the U.S. Army, who went by the name "Saint," was one of the activists who found "the future in the present" in Okinawa through concrete engagement in the solidarity project that demanded moving in a racial groove.[13] On April 15, 1973, Allen was among a group of Black GIs that went to the base movie theater to watch the action-packed blaxploitation film *Slaughter* (1972), starring Jim Brown as a former Green Beret. With anticipation, Black GIs walked into the theater in pursuit of pleasure. But what was expected to be a night out for them, away from all the rigidity, repressiveness, and racism in the military, ended rather quickly. The theater was heavily garrisoned. Surrounding them were a dozen MP officers, Criminal Investigation Division agents, and several uniformed high-ranking officers. When the images of the Capitol, the White House, and the American flag moved across the movie screen as the national anthem played in the background, all GIs, except one, stood to show their loyalty to the nation. Allen alone refused. He sat silent with his head down and ignored Lieutenant Corporal A. R. Gonzalez's order to stand. After the national anthem concluded, Allen was escorted out of the theater. He was later charged with disobedience and violation of a general regulation in the military. Allen was the twenty-seven-year-old son of a career military father and, formerly, an active member of the Denver chapter of the Black Panther Party for Self-Defense. He knew he was right about his refusal to stand and pledge allegiance to the American flag. "I'm going to stand up for it when the time arrives," he said resolutely.[14]

Although Allen's commander offered him nonjudicial punishment, which could have given him a lenient sentence, most likely a fine of no more than $200 and a demotion in rank, Allen demanded a court-martial. The right to seek a court-martial was guaranteed in the Code of Military Justice, but such action carried risks, of which he was, of course, aware. His defense team, which consisted of William Schaap, a white volunteer civilian lawyer sponsored by the National Lawyers Guild's Military Law Project, and several other white American peace activists who were enmeshed in the GI movement in Okinawa, had already apprised him of the consequences. In his case, if convicted, he would not only be locked up in jail for at least six months but also receive a dishonorable discharge and fines of over $1,000.[15]

On June 1, 1973, Allen sat through an Army Special Court-Martial held at Fort Buckner, Okinawa, and listened to A. R. Gonzalez's testimony, portraying himself as a reformer who helped improve race relations in the Army in Okinawa. As director of the Army's Special Services, whose responsibilities included planning and overseeing educational, cultural, and recreational events and activities, he claimed that he had contributed to the military's effort to achieve "racial harmony" among the ranks and as a result had seen, as he testified, "a significant decrease in the rowdy, abusive, undisciplined behavior of minority groups." To him, thus, Allen's behavior was reprehensible and out of line with what he claimed as the military's efforts to eradicate racial antagonism within the ranks to achieve integration in the military.[16]

Gonzalez's reaction was characteristic of contemporary observers' and critics' attitudes toward revolutionary Black masculinity. Since the 1965 Watts rebellion and the defiance of the Black Panther Party against myriad forms of institutional violence and structural inequality, such as police brutality, poverty, and permanent unemployment, Black masculinity had become the target of police and government repression, the focus of public policies, the subject of social science research and sensational journalism, and the primary source of white backlash and paranoia. These contemporaries, both liberals and conservatives, saw Black men as either a case of a social crisis that needed to be reformed or a threat to the American institution that had to be altogether rooted out.[17]

For instance, FBI director J. Edgar Hoover spearheaded the bureau's counterintelligence program, commonly known as COINTELPRO, to crush revolutionary Black nationalist organizations that mobilized around the image of militant Black men. Others, influenced by Daniel Patrick Moynihan's report *The Negro Family: The Case for National Action*, popularized cultural explanations for the problems of structural inequality and insisted that the cultivation of personal responsibility and work ethic among African American men and women was the key to the realization of a truly integrated society in America. These liberals contended that the restoration of Black patriarchy could mitigate many of the problems in inner-city Black communities, including poverty, joblessness among African American men, growing welfare dependency among African American women, and the high rate of illegitimate births. Other liberals saw growing Black male militancy as a major roadblock to the efforts to construct the image of respectable Black manhood. Black civil rights leaders and white liberals, thus, criticized revolutionary Black nationalism as "racism in reverse."[18]

Allen's masculine dissent, contrary to these claims, represented Black GIs' pursuit of a sense of community, or perhaps "soul," an idiom and an aesthetic that helped shape the Black political imagination in the late 1960s and early 1970s. For Allen and others, "soul" was not simply a tool for racial identification, pride, and solidarity. It was something emotive and intuitive, as well as a matter of survival and resistance. It was, as Kelley explains, "a discourse through which African Americans, at a particular historical moment, claimed ownership of the symbols and practices of their own imagined community." Black GIs' masculine dissent produced a language to communicate oppressed people's lived experience and desire for another world. It engendered a "poetic language" that had the capacity "to find expressive forms where [they were] supposed to shut up," as Adrienne Rich writes. In other words, Allen's testimony was a visceral acknowledgment of a shared commitment to create and inhabit a new world, and his poetic articulation emerged as what Rich refers to as an "autonomous terrain apart from the ripped-off or colonized languages of daily life." About standing for the national anthem, Allen declared, "I don't feel I have the right to do it when my people are oppressed. Blacks and whites, [I]ndians, [P]uerto [R]icans and [C]hicanos. I'm really worried about it, and that's what I'm feeling, and it's not just myself. Because if it was just me, I could just forget everything and say I don't care and go paint somewhere, like a hermit or something. But I'm not that kind of person; I'm emotional about my people." He understood the following philosophical foundation of human liberation summarized by King in *Where Do We Go from Here*: " 'I' cannot reach fulfillment without 'thou.' The self cannot be self without other selves."[19]

For this reason, to characterize Allen's masculine dissent as a mere case of an emergent Third World internationalism would be inadequate. Such an interpretation would miss the significance of what he did. The work of constructing a new identity and forging solidarity was "literally the labor of creating art in everyday life," as Kelley writes. Allen and other dissenting GIs and peace activists created art by challenging head-on "a society fraught with official lying . . . [and] contrived obsolescence of words" so that a new community and subjectivity could be imagined and reinvented. When Allen testified and said, "I feel deep for my people, real deep," his supporters and friends—Black and white GIs, as well as Okinawan and white activists in the GI movement—understood what he meant. They connected with each other. Such a moment of solidarity at the court-martial was further sharpened when the lies told by Gonzalez were laid bare. Although Allen never said a word throughout the confrontation with Gonzalez, and three witnesses confirmed it, Gonzalez accused him of making "several verbal denials." His testimony did not stand. Everyone, including the judge, knew he lied under oath. Allen's friends and activists were exulted when the truth made this court-martial a mockery of justice. Allen ended up with a simple fine of $50 for failure to follow the regulation.[20]

Seeing identity formation and multiracial coalition building as the work of creating art is useful in making sense of how diverse constituents of protest movements linked up in the context of social movement mobilization in occupied Okinawa. The freedom struggle in Okinawa contained multiple nodes, and when linked, they revealed a new form of human activity and life. These nodes were strategies of resistance and aspirations of activists that "emerg[ed] here, [and] then there, building up gradually in confined spaces, then erupting on a global level."[21] These nodes can be described as the "winged seeds" of the freedom struggle, and they moved through, behind, above, and below the United States, Japan, and Okinawa, circulated across the Pacific, and returned to all three locales in a whirlwind before burying under the soil, ready to grow into the dream of a basefree society, GI resistance, Black Power, Third World liberation, and women's liberation. In the process, these seeds sprouted a striving to create a world other than the one structured by the values and truths upheld by those in the position of power.[22]

Indeed, Chinese American activist and philosopher Grace Lee Boggs, who has devoted her life to the cause of Black liberation, along with her husband, African American activist and writer James Boggs, has observed that the process of Martin Luther King Jr.'s coming into being as a revolutionary leader in his final years offers a key insight. Boggs explains, "King had a vision of people at the grassroots and community level participating in creating the new values, truths, relationships, and infrastructures as the foundation of a new society." Delivering his speech at a Riverside Church meeting sponsored by Clergy and Laymen Concerned about Vietnam in New York City on April 4, 1967, King explained his own distinct conception of world revolution and the pedagogy of human liberation in this way: "I am convinced that if we are to get on the right side of the world revolution, we as a nation must undergo a radical revolution of values. We must rapidly begin the shift from a 'thing-oriented' society to a 'person-oriented' society. When machines and computers, profit motives and property rights are considered more important than people, the giant triplets of racism, materialism, and militarism are incapable of being conquered." The participants of the freedom struggle in Okinawa underwent what King called "a radical revolution of values," and like King, they had already made up their minds that they would go on living beyond "Vietnam," that is to say, go on constructing "the future in the present."[23]

A white American peace activist, William Schaap of the National Lawyers Guild's Military Law Project, clearly recognized how this "idea of the revolution of the mind," which was so central to King's conception of liberation from "the giant triplets of racism, materialism, and militarism," transformed the GI movement in Okinawa.[24] Working as a civilian lawyer representing GIs struggling against injustices in the military, Schaap commented that "much of the direction [in the movement] is coming from the blacks." Unlike the dominant orientation within the GI movement in mainland Japan, where activists and participants operated with the belief that "only blacks can organize blacks and only whites can organize whites," Schaap saw something different in Okinawa. The space of antiracism, antimilitarism, and anti-imperialism had become productive precisely because dissenting Black and white GIs, as well as local Okinawan supporters and white activists who operated out of the headquarters of the GI movement in Okinawa, called the People's House, did not organize separately. Rather, they recognized that Black GIs' self-activity and their masculine dissent transformed the movement space. He explained, "We have some white GI's here who are much more racist than most politically active whites. . . . If there are GI's who can't relate to a place where blacks come too, then they don't come back, or else they learn to begin to deal with those problems." He reported, for instance, that Black and white GIs in the brig, "brought together by . . . similar experiences, and who know each other from the People's House, . . . have been working together to organize other prisoners."[25]

Specialist 5 Melvin McIntosh of the U.S. Army was one of the few white men who took part in "organizing the whole stockade" with Black GIs. With Specialist 5 King, a Black soldier, McIntosh and other prisoners in the stockade carried out a creative act of disobedience. On

October 9, 1972, they collectively refused to eat dinner. What appeared to be an odd behavior, however, turned out to be highly symbolic. They explained their action as a decision to honor the fifth anniversary of the death of Che Guevara, hoping "that their meal would be donated to a needy CIA agent . . . [and] that he might choke on it."[26]

In another case, a white GI named Edgar K. Eldridge, of the U.S. Navy, had crossed over into this space of resistance that was informed by the antiracist conception of world revolution, by struggling to sever his ties with "a fascist dictatorship which calls for an unthinking machine." He tried everything in his power to emancipate himself from this machine. He applied for conscientious objector status but was denied. He sought resignation for good service, but that, too, was rejected. He then submitted a request for a discharge, but that did not come through. Ultimately, exhausting all the means by which to cut his connections with the military, he simply quit. On November 9, 1972, he wrote a letter to the commander of U.S. Naval Mobile Construction Battalion Five to explain his action: "I consider myself no longer a part of the military service." "If you wish to speak to me," he said, "I will be in my room during working hours or at least somewhere on the base, devoting my time to writing and thinking. . . . I have resigned, quit." Eldridge no longer wanted to be associated with, as he explained, "an organization which forces a man to be a racist."[27] In the most succinct and poetic language, John B. Spearman, a Black GI stationed with the 2nd Battalion, 9th Marine Regiment, at Camp Schwab in Okinawa, explained the political orientation of these dissenting GIs, both Blacks and whites, who "look[ed] at the world" and saw "nothing but misery": "Misery is a six-letter word that means war; misery is a six-letter word that means poverty; institutionalized racism; the denial of human rights; police brutality; and dope. What it boils down to is that misery is nothing but a lot of unnecessary suffering and shame, creating problems brought upon us by . . . racialized institutions."[28]

The grounds for these antiracist, antiwar, and anti-imperialist GIs' poetic articulations were moving toward the end of revolutionary praxis, and the manifestation of this ethos of liberation as dissent within the armed forces became widespread by the late 1960s and early 1970s. American combat soldiers could no longer reconcile what they were doing in Vietnam and what the U.S. government and military claimed they were setting out to achieve. Their personal, moral, and political struggles transformed into what the surrealist writer Pierre Mabille once described as "the struggle of freedom itself against everything that holds it back or tries to destroy or weaken it." Military aggression, imperial arrogance, the brutal reality of war, especially the colossal scale of violence and destruction that these GIs wrought and witnessed, disillusioned and enraged them. Questioning America's rationale fundamentally, they began to make certain choices and adjustments. Some, for instance, detached themselves from the war mentally, while others resorted to more aggression. Drug usage increased. Some defied orders to kill or killed their officers. By the early 1970s, AWOL (absent without leave) cases increased, and organized resistance against the war within the military threatened to undermine the very foundation and morale of the armed forces.[29]

For Black GIs, however, their politicization also involved coming to grips with the structural and global dimensions of racism. As Black leaders such as Martin Luther King Jr., Muhammad Ali, James Baldwin, Stokely Carmichael, and Huey P. Newton, to name just a few, began denouncing the war as racist and imperialist in the mid-1960s, the political consciousness of Black soldiers and veterans sharpened and eventually caught up with these leaders' outlook.[30] Black journalist Wallace Terry's study on changing attitudes of Black and white soldiers and their radicalization is particularly revealing. While working as a correspondent for *Time* magazine for more than two years in Vietnam in the late 1960s, Terry circulated some 833 questionnaires and conducted interviews with respondents between May and September 1969. His study showed that while many of the Black soldiers he interviewed in 1967 "roundly criticized" antiwar Black leaders, by 1970, they had altered their opinion completely. The Black critics of the war had come to "stand highest in their esteem." Becoming aware of what King called "the giant triplets of racism, materialism, and militarism," especially how this interconnected system of domination hindered poor people's pursuit of happiness and freedom at home and abroad, was the first step toward Black soldiers' radicalization.[31]

Just as King could not remain "silent in the face of such cruel manipulation of the poor," many of the Black soldiers spoke out in opposition to the U.S. war in Southeast Asia. They contended that young Black men were sent to the war to subdue the poor people of the Third World and were being killed at higher rates than whites in the name of American democracy, while their loved ones and friends at home faced a tough reality of poverty, joblessness, crime, police brutality, inadequate public schools, and shrinking life chances. According to Terry, "A large majority of the black enlisted men agreed that black people should not fight in Vietnam because they have problems of discrimination to deal with at home, a striking contrast with the typical attitude of the Black soldiers I talked with in 1967." For them, as James Baldwin once explained, "The American idea of freedom, and still more, the way this freedom is imposed, have made America the most terrifying nation in the world." Writing from Istanbul, Turkey, in 1967, Baldwin's indictment against a racist and imperialist nation rang true to many of the Black soldiers: "A racist society can't but fight a racist war—this is the bitter truth. The assumptions acted on at home are also acted on abroad, and every American Negro knows this, for he, after the American Indian, was the first 'Viet Cong' victim."[32]

Yet there was something specific about how Black GIs underwent radicalization and articulated their masculine dissent in occupied Okinawa. The place mattered as much as these GIs' experience in the military and war and the influence of the Black Power movement. Historically, Black soldiers' participation in U.S. wars in Asia, such as the Philippine-American War and the Korean War, contributed to the formation of critical consciousness. For instance, the figuration of Asians as subhumans not worthy of life—made explicit by the sheer violence that the U.S. military unleashed at a genocidal rate against Filipinos during the Philippine-American War and beyond, as Filipinos fought the war of liberation—compelled some Black soldiers, most notably Corporal David Fagen, to demonstrate their solidarity with anticolonial insurgent activity. Moreover, during the Korean War in the early 1950s, the Black press, such as the *Baltimore Afro-American* and the *California Eagle*, took a clear stance against yet another war to defend *herrenvolk democracy* and presented a sharp critique of "the U.S.-led [United Nations] intervention as a colonial crusade" designed to carry on the racial subordination of darker nations and peoples, which included, as one Black writer put it, "the dark Korean people." These wars in Asia had a way of linking up Black soldiers' personal experience with racism with the macro-dynamics of U.S. imperialism and colonialism, thereby creating discourse that could not only shatter prevailing explanatory constructions about race and democracy but also shape an insurgent form of racial identity and a more expansive notion of racial politics among Black soldiers.[33]

In the context of social struggles in occupied Okinawa, this work of linking up ensued as well, specifically at the intersection of Black Power GIs' antiracism and anti-imperialism and Okinawan and white American peace activists' opposition to U.S. occupation and aggressive militarism. It engendered a new politics that was capable of organizing a dynamic network of identifications. Learning from each other, the diverse constituents of the freedom struggle in Okinawa articulated a broader notion of what it meant to be free and human. For Black Power GIs in Okinawa, for instance, even as they asserted their Blackness to demand their rights and to defend their manhood, their efforts to act in unity were not exclusively defined in relation to the experiences of people of African descent. Approaching the category of race as a lever of internationalism to link up with others in the freedom struggle in the United States, Vietnam, Okinawa, and elsewhere, they sought to forge connections with others to give form to an emergent multiracial political alliance. For local Okinawan activists and transnational white American peace activists, Black GIs' masculine dissent produced an ideological language that helped them affirm their commitment to carve out liberated spaces where they could learn to assert the power of human dignity in their own political projects. These activists' identification with Blackness, in other words, was a political choice. It was not informed by fetishism, an act of soul-stealing. Likewise, Black GIs transformed as they came into contact with white American peace activists involved in the GI movement in Okinawa, as well as dissenting Okinawans who rose up in opposition to Okinawa reversion and the U.S. occupation authority's arrogance and violence. Such a condition of reciprocity was what made the practice of transpacific strivings an incubator of utopian aspirations, revolutionary commitment, and multiracial coalition building during the era of Okinawa reversion in the late 1960s and early 1970s.

## Living in the Era of Liberation

Shortly after completing Peace Corps work in Ivory Coast in 1969, Barbara Bye, daughter of a Quaker family in Pennsylvania, returned to the United States. Soon she began to assume a new identity as an internationalist and a committed activist, fighting in solidarity with Okinawans and antiracist and anti-imperialist GIs. Like other white Americans who entered the protest movements of the 1960s, she devoted her time and energy in the struggle for social justice, peace, and the liberation of the oppressed. However, unlike countless New Left adherents who became disillusioned or dropped out of radical politics by the late 1960s, she remained confident in the ability to create a new society. While remaining close to the spirit of resistance that transformed the consciousness of 1960s activists, she staked out a new space of resistance as the Students for a Democratic Society disintegrated and the pace of Black militancy quickened. Bye operated in concert with the assertion of Staughton Lynd, who stood front and center in the 1960s New Left: "If none of our experiments has yet been successful, one day soon it will be otherwise." Bye did not measure change and the success of activist movements according to gains made in electoral politics and courtrooms. Reflecting on the significance of the later writings of Simone Weil, a French philosopher and political activist, Lynd concluded, "A small piece of *good work*, for instance, a single life well lived, makes a difference. . . . The first step in advancing toward our end is to desire it greatly." Bye did take that step.[34]

Bye learned about occupied Okinawa, U.S. imperialism in Asia, and the growing strength of the GI movement in Japan when she participated in one of the largest antiwar demonstrations in American history in Washington, D.C., in November 1969. Among half a million concerned citizens and activists who gathered on the Mall was Oda Makoto, a writer, critic, and antiwar activist from Japan. Just before the announcement of the Sato-Nixon joint communiqué, the Committee of Concerned Asian Scholars invited Oda to be part of a cross-country lecture tour to educate activists about colonialism in Okinawa and security imperialism in Asia. Bye's encounter with Oda in Washington, D.C., marked the beginning of her involvement in the freedom struggle in Okinawa. She learned a great deal about America's imperialist thrust in Asia and a people's movement to challenge this global system of domination. She later told a reporter, "I came to realize how essential Japan was to America's Pacific-rim policy. . . . I decided to go to Japan for about two or three months and to see what makes the country tick. I . . . wanted to familiarize myself with the Japanese antiwar groups and with the American pressure."[35] Oda showed her the road to reach this space of resistance created by the culture of liberation.

By 1969, Oda had become the voice of a new generation critical of the underlying imperialism of American and Japanese Cold War democracy. The author of one of the most notable books published in Japan in the 1960s, *Nandemo Mite Yaro* (I Want to See It All), which he wrote after backpacking across Europe and Asia penniless, Oda exposed everything he saw—living legacies of imperialism, colonialism, and wars, the presence of fascism in the everyday, and realities of racial discrimination not just in Japan and the United States but throughout the world. It was such audacity that led him and Japan's leading critics, such as Tsurumi Shunsuke, Tsurumi Yoshiyuki, Muto Ichiyo, Yoshikawa Yuichi, Iida Momo, and Oe Kenzaburo, to organize an antiwar movement when the American bombing campaign in North Vietnam began in early 1965. By April 1965, Oda emerged as the icon of this movement, which called itself <*Betonamu ni Heiwa o!*> *Shimin Rengo* (Japan "Peace for Vietnam!" Committee) and was commonly known as Beheiren.[36]

Beheiren was conceived as a network of protest groups, and members came from diverse occupational, social, and political backgrounds. Some were intellectuals and critics, while the majority were citizens concerned with the escalation of the Vietnam War and the Japanese involvement. Writers, composers, artists, professors, housewives, students, businessmen, foreigners in Japan, shopkeepers, and the elderly founded local chapters in their neighborhoods and operated without dues at the grassroots level. The members led petition campaigns and teach-ins and wrote and distributed pamphlets and flyers near U.S. military bases and installations. They also organized fund-raising to place advertisements in major U.S. newspapers (the *New York Times* and the *Washington Post*) and wrote letters to local and national newspapers and elected officials. They were always present at demonstrations and rallies, and at times, some of them participated in underground activities by offering American deserters safety and shelter. Iida Momo regarded Beheiren as "a catalyst to introduce fluidity into the too rigidly organized, and severely divided traditional movement." She explained that it emphasized the "voluntary action of every individual" and mobilized around the following principles: "Peace for Vietnam," "Vietnam for the Vietnamese," and "Against Japan's Collaboration."[37]

Many of the movement's participants, including Barbara Bye, were attracted to Beheiren precisely because it did not affiliate with a progressive political party or participate in sectarian struggles. It operated independently of the politics of the Left. The leaders of Beheiren stressed that the movement offered a space where individuals concerned with war, militarism, and violence could learn about self, community, and freedom through practical activity. Historian Thomas R. H. Havens explained the philosophy of Beheiren's activism in this way: "The aim was self-awareness as a step toward helping one another build a society of democratic individualism. The purpose of joining a demonstration was not to merge with the mass of protesters but to achieve self-consciousness as an individual participant."[38]

Beheiren offered such a space for individuals to experience radicalization. It helped instill revolutionary commitment in members "to work against all inhumanity and barbarism, including [those] that [reside] within" each individual. Its slogan—*Korosuna!* (Stop the Killing!)—asked people to come to grips with their own role as a killer and to break away from this existence, especially in terms of their social contract with the coercive state. It encouraged them to transform their identities and to help establish the necessary foundation to create a new polity, something other than the existing polity that buttressed the expansion of global systems of aggressive militarism and racial and colonial domination. Oda regarded the principle of civil disobedience as a political right, which needed to be exercised and practiced to "resist compulsion by the state."[39]

The members of Beheiren applied this right to veto—a refusal to be an accomplice to the coercive power of the state—as the basis for building an international solidarity struggle. From the movement's inception, it showed solidarity with the Vietnamese liberation struggle. It also sought to strengthen solidarity with participants of the Black freedom struggle and peace movement. The leaders of Beheiren, for instance, linked up with activists of Students for a Democratic Society,

Oda Makoto speaking at a rally in Washington, D.C., in November 1969, protesting the
Sato-Nixon joint communiqué (Beheiren, ed., *Beheiren News Shuksatsu Ban, 1964–1974*
[Tokyo: Beheiren <Betonamu ni heiwa wo!> Shimin Rengo, 1974])

the Student Nonviolent Coordinating Committee, the Black Panther
Party for Self-Defense, and numerous peace groups. They were in contact with David Dellinger, A. J. Muste, Noam Chomsky, Jean-Paul Sar-
tre, Howard Zinn, Ralph Featherstone, Stokely Carmichael, Eldridge
Cleaver, and Katherine Cleaver. Beheiren was committed to promoting
internationalism in solidarity with people mobilizing resistance against
imperialism, white supremacy, and the rampant pursuit of wealth. It
supported the emancipation of the self from the militarized totalitarian
state through grassroots organizing, doing small things with the understanding that the implications of individual acts could reach beyond
national boundaries.

Oda's call for action to create what George Lipsitz calls "movement
spaces" caught Bye's attention in the fall of 1969.[40] It stirred her instinctual striving toward a total human liberation. She heard Oda speak either
at the U.S. Imperialism and the Pacific Rim conference on November 13
and 14 or at demonstrations against a Nixon-Sato talk on November 17
and 19 or at both events. The conference attracted progressive groups

working around antiwar, Black Power, youth activism, and Third World issues, and it coincided with the Nixon-Sato talk on November 20, aimed at reaching a bilateral agreement on Okinawa reversion. A day before the demonstration outside the White House, Oda, along with conference participants stayed up all night to make a large puppet that represented a "monster." The head of the monster depicted Uncle Sam, and its tail, Sato. The monster and street performers showcased skits, chanting in Japanese, *Ampo Funsai!* (Scrap the Treaty), *Okinawa Kaiho!* (Okinawa Liberation), and *Betonamu ni Heiwa!* (Peace in Vietnam). Some twenty people, including nine women, performed acts of civil disobedience in front of the White House and were consequently arrested by the police. The Pacific Rim Coalition, which consisted of antiracist, antiwar, and anti-imperialist activists, intellectuals, and scholars and which organized the conference and demonstration, issued the following statement to express their commitment to a transnational people's movement against what they called "a racist rule of U.S. military colonialism" in Okinawa:

> This week Sato and Nixon will strike a deal on Okinawa, a deal wherein the U.S. will return Okinawa to Japan, but not until 1972 and four more years of murder in Vietnam—and the bases will be left in Okinawa indefinitely. By thus agreeing to the actual reversion of Okinawa, they hope to undercut the struggle to crush the Security Treaty in 1970. It is a trick. But it won't work, because the people will not be deceived. They will continue their militant struggle in Okinawa and the mainland to drive the U.S. from Okinawa, to end the Security Treaty, to stop Japanese rearmament, and to crush the Sato government.[41]

Several months after Bye first encountered the radical possibility of anti-imperialist coalition building among people of color and antiracist whites in Washington, D.C., she found her own way to join the peace movement and Beheiren in Japan. By the summer of 1970, Beheiren had already garnered strong citizen support. In particular, it had responded to repeated patterns of GI desertions from U.S. military bases in mainland Japan and organized around these deserters and other dissenting GIs. By the late 1960s, American GIs in Vietnam, the United States, South Korea, the Philippines, Hong Kong, West Germany, mainland

Japan, and Okinawa began to voice their opposition to American foreign policy and rebelled against the legitimacy of military authority.
Many of them took the risk of dishonorable discharge, outright imprisonment, and transfer to isolated posts or battlefields.[42]

In mainland Japan and Okinawa, GI organizing required crossing
barriers that separated diverse constituents of protest movements. The
key to the success of the GI movement in Asia was not just civilian support but also organizing across differences in language, politics, culture,
and race. Around early 1969, a coalition of civilian groups in mainland
Japan and Okinawa enlisted the critical support of transnational peace
activists from the United States to begin working with dissenting GIs
to build a solidarity project against aggressive militarism. The activists
involved in the emergent GI movement organized rallies and sit-ins,
interacted with servicemen through counseling activity, documented
their war experiences, participated in a collaborative project to publish
underground newspapers, and disseminated radical literature coming out of the Black and women's liberation movements. Bye arrived
in Japan in the midst of this successful coalition-building campaign.
Throughout the summer of 1970, she immersed herself in this organizing activity by taking part in the work of not just Beheiren but also the
Pacific Counseling Service (PCS).[43]

The PCS was an American civilian organization that worked closely
with dissenting GIs, who demanded justice under military law. Like
the Central Committee for Conscientious Objectors (CCCO), a well-
established organization that had been providing support to American
servicemen since 1948, the PCS provided vital services assisting individuals to make decisions about their participation in war. The PCS was
founded by Sidney Peterman, a veteran white civil rights activist and a
gay minister. The first office opened near Fort Ord in Monterey, California, in May 1968. Under Peterman's leadership, the PCS expanded
its activities at home and abroad. During its first six months, it came
into contact with over seven hundred GIs and handled their cases. In
October and November 1969, the PCS expanded by opening new offices
in San Francisco, Oakland, and San Diego and hiring an additional
thirteen paid staff members. Many of the paid and voluntary counselors were former veterans, women, Catholic and Protestant clergymen,
and concerned citizens. These offices handled approximately 150 GIs'

complaints a week. In early 1970, the PCS branched out its operation across the Pacific. Sid Peterman himself went to Japan and established a PCS office next to Beheiren's Tokyo office in June 1970. By the end of 1972, the PCS had opened offices in the following locations across Asia: Balibago, Angel City, and Olongapo City (all in the Philippines); Tokyo, Iwakuni, Misawa, and Yokota (all in Japan); Honolulu; Hong Kong; and Okinawa. PCS's ties with Beheiren, especially support from concerned citizens and those living in communities surrounding U.S. bases and installations, contributed to the expanded role of military counseling in mainland Japan and Okinawa.[44]

Peterman was one of the most influential transnational activists in the Japanese peace movement in the early 1970s. For two years, until the PSC halted its operations in Japan in April 1972, he steered the direction of antiwar resistance in Japan and left an indelible mark in the memories of Beheiren movement participants. Primarily responsible for changing the tactics of Beheiren's antiwar activity, he helped galvanize the GI movement in mainland Japan and Okinawa. Movement participants learned from Peterman that both the survival of political GIs within the military and solidarity struggles with these GIs were key to stopping the war machine. After working with Peterman, Japanese peace activists no longer assisted GIs in deserting to Sweden or kept them in hiding just for the sake of helping them. He trained these activists to "put dissident GIs in touch with one another." To this end, he instructed that "counselors can continue to aid GI organizers by providing advice, funneling new GIs who come in for counseling into the group, providing the group with literature, organizing support groups, encouraging and aiding political responses to counseling problems, and setting up off-base centers for organizing activities." The National Lawyers Guild, an organization that collaborated with the PCS, explained the radical aim of military counseling in this way: "Reliance must be placed on the people themselves and on efforts to raise their consciousness, convince them of their strength and help them organize their struggle. Legal assistance can complement political organizing, and can attract potential GI activists to a service they need. Once the assistance is given the real work begins."[45] Unlike mainstream GI counseling services, such as the CCCO, the PCS operated with a strong conviction that a "purely legal approach will not work in the long run" and that the promise of liberation ultimately ought to be placed in GIs' self-activity, especially their practice of collective self-reliance and instinctive strivings to resist the coercive power of the U.S. military by struggling within the "belly of the beast."[46]

Throughout the summer and fall of 1970, Bye participated in this emerging GI movement and matured intellectually and politically. At the Iwakuni Marine Air Station in Yamaguchi prefecture in mainland Japan, she passed out antiwar handbills and copies of the underground GI newspaper called *Semper Fi*. She spoke at rallies and showed solidarity with GIs across the barbed-wire fences. Most of her time was spent talking with servicemen in coffeehouses, noodle shops, and bars. She not only counseled those seeking to oppose the Vietnam War but also exchanged perspectives on war and militarism with both GIs and the Japanese. She came into contact with some one hundred GIs and shared information about the procedures for conscientious objector status. Some of them seriously considered taking the administrative discharge option.

Through the work of the PCS and Beheiren, Bye sharpened her perspective on institutional violence and structural inequality, connecting her GI organizing work in Iwakuni to her own experience as a health extension worker for the Peace Corps in Ivory Coast in 1967–1969. In the GI movement in Japan, she achieved cognitive clarity. What Nikhil Pal Singh calls "the geopolitics of images," which linked realities of challenges to decolonization in Africa, the forces of state-sanctioned violence on a global scale, and white resistance to the movement toward Black inclusion and citizenship in the United States, gave her a sense of categorical unity.[47] The work of coalition building that she was doing at the grassroots in Japan changed her antiracist concept of world revolution from an intellectual concept to everyday life activity enmeshed with human existence. In short, she began to link race, neocolonialism, militarism, and imperialism through her concrete political engagements, and she herself became the change that she wanted to see in the existing society, which was built on the subordination of darker nations and peoples. She told a reporter, "I guess my Quaker religion was what originally propelled me into the antiwar, civil rights, and third world liberation movements, . . . but I became secularized by my experience in the Peace Corps." She continued, "In the end . . . I realized that the wells, the latrines, the purified water—all that I had been doing—was insignificant. These countries need a much more profound change in the nature and structure of their government and system. I began to see the Peace Corps as an extension of American foreign policy, as something hindering social progress and supporting the status quo."[48]

Bye acknowledged that she identified herself with "the left wing of Quakerism," but what she ultimately advocated was the self-activity of people struggling against the global system of domination. Her commitment to work toward revolutionary change, especially socialism, was not defined in terms of Maoism or Marxist-Leninism. Her approach to a revolutionary movement was informed by the conviction that the "ultimate trust of human beings must be based on the lives and hopes of people—not on the often self-serving interests of 'great men.'"[49] Meanwhile, like Bye, many of the activists who participated in coalition work during the era of Okinawa reversion also found "movement spaces," through which they resisted the coercive power of the state, which protected the legitimacy of bases, aggressive militarism, and white supremacy in Okinawa.

Bye entered occupied Okinawa in the aftermath of a rebellion against U.S. domination in Koza (known today as Okinawa City) on December 20, 1970, and quickly started to work with Okinawans, antiwar white and Black GIs, and transnational peace activists.[50] The incident that triggered the revolt was a car accident involving a local Okinawan worker and a vehicle driven by an American serviceman. A Military Police Corps member (MP) hastily tried to clean up the scene of the accident, while local people surrounded the scene and protested. The MP fired into the air to quiet the crowd. But the local residents of Koza remained resilient. In response to the MP's display of power and violence, local people overturned and set fire to his car. The urgency of the Koza rebellion spread quickly throughout the base town, and thousands of people joined this anti-imperialist struggle. They set American personnel vehicles on fire one after another and battled against MPs, U.S. armed forces, and Ryukyu police for nearly six hours. In the aftermath of the rebellion, the mayor of Koza, Oyama Asatsune, captured the sentiments of the masses in this way: "Fire was not set by local people in Koza; it was set as a result of the explosion of people's opposition to twenty-five years of U.S. domination. Since fire was burning inside of ordinary people, it could not be put off by water."[51]

Two days later, a group of Black GIs from the Kadena Air Base issued a dramatic appeal to express their solidarity with local people's defiance against the U.S. occupation authority. The statement was printed in both Japanese and English at the local printing shop and distributed widely by the local chapter of Beheiren and other antibase and antiwar civilian groups. Black GIs stressed the process through which they were radicalized during the course of the escalating U.S. war in Vietnam and argued that they were "trying to become a part of the solution, not the problem." The statement read,

> Black people have been fighting for Liberation for a long time. So have the Okinawa[ns]. Who can stop you from having what is rightfully yours? No One. . . . Black people have been discriminated against for over 400 years, and it hasn't stopped yet. The same with Okinawans; they've been discriminated against also. So you see we both are in the same situation. . . . The Black GIs are willing to help and talk to Okinawans in order to form much better relations between the oppressed groups, because we have so much in common. So why not get our heads together and come up with a solution to destroy the problem. The Black GIs are aware of the situation that brought about the riot, and this was truly a RIGHT-ON-MOVE. That's the only way [the U.S. will] bend.[52]

The appeal of dissenting Black GIs to Okinawans was an effort to base their own liberation struggle within the localized project of the internationalist, anti-imperialist, antiracist, and anticolonial struggle in Okinawa. The liberation of Okinawa was linked to the liberation of Blacks and the Third World, as well as to the liberation of working-class GIs, both whites and Blacks, from the repressive military.

Working alongside these dissenting Black GIs were Jan Eakes and Dianne (Annie) Durst, young, white radicals from California. They were the co-conspirators behind the antiracist and anti-imperialist solidarity project in Okinawa. Like many white college students, Eakes underwent radicalization when he became deeply involved in 1960s protest movements on a university campus. The pace of his political education was quickened as a result of touring South Vietnam in the summer of 1967, as well as his participation in campus politics as the president of the Associated Students of Sacramento State College. In this capacity, he helped bring Martin Luther King Jr. to campus in October 1967. King delivered a speech titled "The Future of the Civil Rights Movement," a variation of his penetrating "Beyond Vietnam" address that linked the escalation of the Vietnam War to the consequences of the fight for Black equality on the home front. The impact of this event was significant, for it emboldened student activists to further cultivate and nurture the space of resistance to war, militarism, and white supremacy on the Sacramento State campus. Meanwhile, Eakes immersed himself in expanding antiwar and draft resistance in California. Faced with the possibility of being drafted, he ultimately chose the path of political exile. He decided to become active in overseas resistance projects. Upon his graduation from Sacramento State College, he took a flight to Japan to meet up with his then girlfriend, Dianne Durst, in the summer of 1969. Durst was also a Sacramento State student. She was in the midst of a sojourn across Asia after completing a study-abroad program in Asian studies in Taiwan. Together, Eakes and Durst came into contact with Beheiren activists in Tokyo and began participating in the GI movement not just in Japan but also in Hong Kong and Okinawa in the years between 1969 and 1971.[53]

Eakes was convinced that race-based activism involving militant Black Power GIs, antiracist white GIs, Okinawans, and peace activists, each group working on its own to achieve its own aims and sometimes converging around a specific issue to fashion a "coalition politics," held a key to engendering a revolutionary outcome in occupied Okinawa. He was interested in inciting a movement in a racial groove in Japan, for through this experience, as he once declared, individuals would become radical on local and global scales and learn to link up with myriad antiracist projects. Critical of the Japanese New Left, which was slow to acknowledge the centrality of mobilizing around race-based activism in Japan, he issued a call for a synthesis in revolutionary thought and activity. He challenged Japanese intellectuals and activists to see immigrant workers from the Philippines, Indonesia, and Malaysia as "Japan's 'Mexican Americans,'" or Korean and Chinese residents in Japan whose parents were brought to Japan as colonial subjects as "Japan's Black people," or opposition to the system of immigration restriction in Japan as the equivalent of the Civil Rights Movement in the United States, or the struggles on behalf of the Ainu or the oppressed caste group called *Buraku* as central to the Japanese conceptualization of liberation. He was confident that the efforts to develop the GI movement across Asia to resist the machineries of war and aggressive militarism had the potential to link up the global and local currents of antiracism that were leading toward a total human liberation.[54]

As Eakes's sojourn in Asia extended and the FBI moved closer to arresting him, he more openly began to show disappointment and frustration toward the Japanese New Left's inability to recognize its major blind spot, as far as its position on Okinawa was concerned. Among those associated with the Japanese New Left, the widely accepted position was that the Okinawan reversion movement was a progressive cause. Eakes disagreed with such an ideological orientation fundamentally. Like the antireversion Okinawan activists, he considered the nationalist orientation of mainland Japanese progressives, who uncritically endorsed the reversion movement as a cause to celebrate and support, as a major obstacle blocking Okinawans' path to human liberation. Drawing an analogy with white progressives' relationship with the Black Power movement, he believed that acute advances in revolutionary thought and activity could only materialize if Japanese intellectuals and activists became cognizant of the logic of the nation-state underpinning their own uncritical acceptance of Okinawa's reversion to Japan and ultimately repudiated this logic by acknowledging that the interests of Okinawans and their vision of the future were not the same as those of the mainland Japanese. Just as he categorically defined race-based autonomous action led by militant Black activists and organizations as fundamentally progressive in its scope and nature, even when it stirred anger and disappointment among white progressives committed to racial integration and interracialism, he regarded the movement led by and for Okinawans as having the ability to become a revolutionary force within the sphere of the Japanese New Left.[55]

Although Eakes was unable to immerse himself in resistance projects in various parts of Japan for a long period of time because of his uphill battles with the Japanese immigration authority and the encroachment of the U.S. government, he nonetheless began developing working relationships, particularly in Okinawa, with dissenting GIs, both Blacks and whites, and local antiwar and antibase activists. During his short visits in October–November 1969 and March 1970, he laid the groundwork. At last, during the summer of 1970, from June to September, Eakes and Durst found a short-term residence and began organizing in a sustained way. Focusing their organizing work around the Kadena Air Base, especially in the Black GI district of the base town of Koza, called Teruya (also known as Four Corners), they decided to screen the Black Panther Party's recruiting film, *Off the Pig*. It brought a large crowd, including some Black GIs whom Eakes had come into contact with during his visits several months before. Soon they began brainstorming some concrete actions. Most of them were Black airmen and eager to be a part of the movement. Some of them decided to work with Durst on the project of publishing their own GI underground newspaper, while others led reading groups to discuss radical literature at Eakes's residence or held rallies on the street corners of Koza.[56]

Eakes and Durst found the radical possibility of coalition politics among Blacks, Okinawans, and antiwar activists. Their efforts culminated in the publication of the antiwar Kadena Air Base underground newspaper *Demand for Freedom*, put together by Black GIs and edited by Durst. The first issue, appearing in October 1970, covered stories of repeated race-based patterns of harassment, discrimination, and mistreatment in the military. It opened with the following statement: "We don't belong in this military; we have nothing to defend over here. All of you who go around and kiss this pig's ass are just the ones that are holding back our liberation from this racist, capitalist society. Whoever it is who reads this should remember one thing—it's the TRUTH." Eakes, for his part, was increasingly playing the role of a one-man GI counseling and legal service to empower GIs with all aspects of military law so that they could better defend their rights as soldiers and fight discrimination and mistreatment. He even lent his support to represent a Black GI involved in a court-martial, on the pretense of being a civilian lawyer of the Center for Constitutional Rights (based in New York).[57]

Although Eakes and Durst's nascent organizing work did crack open a space of resistance to allow a small group of Okinawan activists and Black GIs to come together, albeit intermittently, the majority of Okinawans found Black GIs' masculine dissent a nuisance. They often singled out Black GIs for provoking racial conflicts with white GIs and the Military Police and for endangering the lives of local people, even though whites were responsible for instigating fights just as much as Blacks were. Residents in and around Teruya were especially infuriated by what they saw as Blacks' recklessness and gross negligence, as there were reports of numerous violent and property crimes, such as robberies, rapes, thefts, and burglaries. Certainly, repeated instances of military and sexual violence perpetuated the mainstream perceptions of Black men as predators and prone to criminal activities. Some Okinawan business owners in Teruya detested that their businesses had come to be situated in the so-called slum and associated with Blackness. It was not uncommon for them to blame their financial woes on the presence of Black GIs. Following the protocols of the Jim Crow system of U.S. racial rule, taxi drivers, bar and restaurant owners, hotel managers, hostesses, and prostitutes in base towns across Okinawa often denied services to Black GIs and chose to do their business only with white GIs.[58]

Such repeated patterns of Okinawans' anti-Black racism angered Black GIs and propelled them to take action to demand respect. On August 17, 1971, for instance, a series of Black-Okinawan conflicts created a highly volatile situation in Koza. When three Black Power GIs walked into one of the bars in Koza that denied them services and one of them started breaking glasses, Okinawans ganged up on them. Managers, waiters, and customers punched and kicked a Black man repeatedly until he was subdued. After these GIs were kicked out of the bar, they returned with some thirty fellow Black GIs and demonstrated outside. At first, local people watched them from afar, but soon fights broke out. The scene of a Black-Okinawan conflict attracted more than one hundred spectators; Black GIs were totally cornered. As the growing and rancorous crowd shouted *"Kuronbo, Korose!"* (Kill the Niggers!), the GIs fled. Meanwhile, the spectacle created gawker traffic, causing a car accident involving vehicles driven by an Okinawan and a Black GI. Immediately, MPs were sent to the scene of the car accident, while the crowd of more than a thousand yelled and jeered. Outnumbered, a Black GI and MPs sought safety in the local police station. The crowd threw stones at the station, breaking windows and injuring police officers.[59]

Moreover, in a rather revealing interview with Barbara Bye in November 1970, then under arrest at the Haneda airport hotel in Tokyo for violating tourist-visa provisions by working under false pretenses (which meant that she participated in "political" activities), an Okinawan activist involved in antiwar resistance, Miyagijima Akira, blatantly reinforced the anti-Black stereotypes, particularly emphasizing Black GIs' alleged criminality. Pointing out the growing racial antagonism between Black and white GIs in and around base towns in Okinawa in recent months, Miyagijima commented that Bye, as a white woman, might well become the target of assaults by militant Black GIs if she were to return to Okinawa to participate in organizing work again. Bye, who had worked closely with support efforts for race-based political action around the struggle for Black GIs' self-determination alongside Durst and other PCS activists, was quick to reject Miyagijima's poverty of racial thinking. She presented a sharp racial analysis by questioning not only the way he equated Black GIs' racial militancy with a threat to white womanhood but also the failure on his part to point out the unchecked white-supremacist campaigns that were rampant within the military and in the battlefields across Southeast Asia. Bye said, "What concerns me the most right now are those whites who have absolutely no regard for humanity."[60]

The work of building a political coalition among the oppressed remained challenging, for some of the Black GIs in Okinawa believed that local people who exhibited anti-Black sentiments were "disillusioned." Referring to the racism of Okinawan taxi drivers specifically, one of the Black Power GIs of the Kadena Air Base, writing in *Demand for Freedom*, explained, "Some of these drivers have been led to believe obscene tales of Black people, and their dispositions. Some have . . . recklessly broadened their dislikes and hatred toward Black people as a whole." A Black GI writer claimed that these Okinawans had uncritically accepted the myth of Black male criminality, even though Okinawans themselves were victims of the white power structure. He emphasized, "Just as the man has washed other countries and groups other than whites, he is doing the same on Okinawa."[61]

However, these Black GIs generally failed to acknowledge that structural racism limited Okinawans' options for social mobility, asset accumulation, and political development. More important, at the center of such a globalized system of inequality was the exploitation of women, for they were forced to satisfy everyday needs of military personnel as maids, laundresses, tailors, waitresses, and sex workers. The livelihood of local residents—men and women—was dependent on the service sector and the prosperity of bars and brothels. During the Vietnam War, sex work in base towns thrived since a large number of American soldiers either moved through Okinawa on their way to Southeast Asia or returned to Okinawa for rest and recreation. The base commanders joined local authorities and base-town business owners to make prostitution an industry. As feminist critic Cynthia Enloe writes, "There were institutional decisions, there were elaborate calculations, there were organizational strategies, there were profits."[62]

However, the truth was that none of these tertiary jobs actually improved the living standard of Okinawan men and women. Many remained poor, reinforcing their dependency on the U.S. occupation authority, which stood in as a patriarchal, sexist, paternal, and racist guardian. Arguing that the "tertiary sectors have expanded wholly out of proportion with the rest of the Ryukyuan economy," Okinawan economist Koji Taira commented that the colonial system "deepened the dependence of the Ryukyuans upon the military bases." The occupation authority was "an absolutist government in its relations with the Ryukyuan native population whose freedom tends to be merely the freedom to obey." Moreover, one of the Okinawan male observers involved in the prostitution business said, "These Black GIs tend to complain about how they were victims of racism, but the truth is we are the ones who are racially discriminated [against]." He continued, "I do this line of work not because I enjoy it. I had no choice after losing a large plot of land for U.S. military bases; I had to eat and live."[63]

Yet both Okinawans and Blacks GIs occupied a highly complex place within the racist rule of the U.S. colonial authority in occupied Okinawa. Both groups struggled over identity, place, and the meanings of these categories. Some Okinawan observers, for instance, showed deep understanding toward Black GIs' struggles with racism. Characterizing Teruya as a "soul town," an Okinawan male taxi driver commented, "Although I get mad whenever I encounter violence on the streets [between Black and white GIs], they [Blacks] do what they do, I think, because of whites. . . . They did not carve out an area of their own voluntarily. Rather, they did not have a place to go other than Four Corners; they were forced out of other GI districts in Koza by whites. They know that this is a place where they will be treated equally. They can drink without being harassed and humiliated by whites, and they can talk with their brothers."[64] This taxi driver interpreted Teruya as a place where Black GIs healed wounded Black masculinity.

The racialized, gendered, and sexualized dynamics in the base town also reminded the taxi driver of his own experience, especially his sense of being powerless and a victim as an Okinawan man. He explained, "Like Blacks, there is no government that can represent us [Okinawans]; there are no laws that protect the lives of Okinawan people. All that we have are inequalities, as well as regulations and laws that protect the legitimacy of bases. They deny the rights of local people. In this regard, we are worse off than Blacks."[65] In this specific setting in Okinawa, Black GIs and local men fraternized. Certainly, their unresolved struggles with the systems of domination brought them closer, but what strengthened the bonds of affection between these men was masculine dissent. At the height of the Black Power period and during the era of Okinawa reversion in the late 1960s and early 1970s, the Black male conception of freedom functioned as a mode of identification in the context of local struggles against imperialism, racism, and militarism.

One Okinawan writer, Takamine Tomokazu, then a young journalist for *Ryukyu Shimpo*, indeed recognized how masculine Black dissent functioned as a modality to make sense of racial tragedies. Takamine was impressed with the politically conscious Black soldiers' group called Bush Masters, which had as many as one hundred members in 1969–1970. The members of Bush Masters often rented space at a bar and organized workshops to read, study, and discuss Black Panther Party literature, as well as other works on revolutionary politics, movements, and philosophy, especially Maoism. They also participated in various aspects of community organizing in and around Teruya. Countless times, Bush Masters aided white GIs to find their way out of the Black district when they mistakenly roamed into the area, so as to avoid racial confrontation. Moreover, when local residents of Teruya could not acquire adequate medical attention in local hospitals, Bush Masters took them to military base hospitals. They organized a blood drive when a local resident underwent major surgery. Some members of Bush Masters were concerned that Black GIs committed both petty and violent crimes in Teruya and threatened residents' welfare and security, so members often policed and patrolled the area. When Black GIs left restaurants, bars, or retail stores without paying, for instance, Bush Masters made sure they paid. If they did not have enough money, members helped to pay these bills.[66]

According to Takamine, during the era of Okinawa reversion, Black soldiers' groups representing a wide range of political opinions, such as Bush Masters, Black Hawk, Sons of Malcolm X, Mau Mau, Afro-American Society, People's Foundation, and Zulu, were formed to demonstrate their opposition to the escalation of the Vietnam War and the persistence of racial discrimination in the military. These groups were deeply influenced by the Black Power movement. The Black Power aesthetics—Afro hairstyle, embroideries, hand slaps, finger snaps, clothing, dancing, and soul music—abounded and enabled the space of Teruya, the Black district in Koza, to become productive for new formations in terms of both identity and community building.[67] Takamine later recorded these Black GIs' militant dissent in a memoir titled *Shirarezaru Okinawa no Beihei* (The Unknown American GIs of Okinawa). In this book, Takamine presented the method by which to forge solidarity in a space of heterogeneity and multiplicity by mapping two historical and political developments—the Vietnam War and Okinawans' struggle for reversion—as perpendicular to each other. Where these two developments intersected, occupied Okinawa stood. He argued that the lives of Okinawans, dissenting American GIs (both Blacks and whites), and peace activists from the United States overlapped, despite differences in race, culture, class, and politics, emphasizing that they all struggled to make sense of themselves and cultural realities in the face of the violence, terror, and destruction of the U.S. war in Vietnam and the occupation of Okinawa. He noted in passing in the epilogue that he had intended to call his memoir *Machikado no Betonamu Senso* (The Vietnam War on the Street Corner). What he had in mind was a conceptualization of occupied Okinawa as a microcosm of the world system, where racism, war, and imperialism uprooted and transformed the lives of diverse people, while at the same time providing opportunities to ascribe new meanings to their identities and solidarity projects at the local level.[68]

As Takamine crossed over into the realm of Black freedom to frat-
ernize with these Black GIs, he had come to interpret both Blacks and
Okinawans as witnesses to the violence of militarism and racism. One
day in early 1970, he was in the bathroom of a bar in Teruya that Bush
Masters often frequented. He saw an engraving of one of the Bush Masters' signatures, probably penned during his farewell party before he
was sent to the front line to fight. It was scratched with a jack knife onto
the wall, which was covered with drawings of female nudity, depictions
of sexual intercourse, and other graffiti.

GOOD BY BROTHER
I GO TO VIETNAM.
J.B.
A MEMBER OF BUSH MASTER[S][69]

Embodied in this signature, Takamine later wrote, was an expression
of young Black GIs' anger, pain, and sorrow. He expressed an affinity
toward them and stepped into the realm of masculine Black dissent. He
was aware of the fact that Black men were sent on dangerous missions
and died in the combat zone more than their white counterparts did
and that the majority of them came from a working-class background
and entered military service because they could not find decent jobs
after graduating from high school. He also knew that they enlisted, and
often reenlisted, to support their loved ones and families, to provide for
aging mothers, or to assist their sisters through college and that they
did not have access to resources to secure exemptions, as many white,
middle-class college students did. He was told that Black GIs had to
deal with daily humiliation in the military and that they encountered
numerous cases of a racist double standard. For instance, while visible white-supremacist political activities remained unpunished, Black
Power GIs' cultural practices and expressions were subjected to puni-
tive policies.[70]

Takamine underwent the process of identification with a poetic
language that could bring to the fore sensuous human activity at the
core of the work of human liberation and the solidarity project. Maria
Damon contends that such was a defining characteristic of "micropoetries," or "poetries that fly beneath the radar of accepted poetic practice."

They often appear as "ephemera" or "gnomic thought-bytes and lyrical bullets," as she calls them, and provide categorical unity within a complex and highly uneven terrain of social practices. The following poem, which appeared in the second issue of *Demand for Freedom* in November 1970, also exhibited the capacity of Black GIs' micropoetries to make readers want to pursue prospects for another world, a more humane and just one, as Takamine experienced. This poem could be interpreted as one of the cases of what Damon calls "clairaudient visitations with a hermeneutic spin."

> *Lifers (Black)*
> Cool-slick-fly,
> A whole generation of
> Mistaken identities
> March by.
> A whole generation of
>    unidentified
> Persons
> Who fear the uncertainty
>    of truth,
> Who know the sheer
>    hypocrisy
> Their lives,
> Who have sold themselves
> To the Sandman![71]

Takamine showed utmost sensitivity toward the workings of Black GIs' masculine dissent, recognizing that Black GIs transformed the male-centered definition of Blackness in a generative and enabling way. Based on his encounters and interactions with them, he concluded that their masculine dissent did not appear exclusionary. Nor did the group simply define Blackness in terms of racial pride or cultural nationalism alone. These men reached across differences searchingly, while negotiating the imbalances of social power in local projects to coalesce around the expansive notion of Blackness. Masculine Blackness was a flexible modality that animated such identifications and alliances toward human liberation.[72] One of the dissenting Black GIs of the Kadena Air

Base, writing in *Demand for Freedom*, ruminated on what it meant to be Black and to express manhood: "What makes a man a man? Money? Security? A good job? A good woman?" He explained, "For being Black is the ability to understand and relate to people."[73]

During the era of Okinawa reversion, some local people, especially students, intellectuals, and those affiliated with the GI movement, recognized the imperative of pursuing a different path to forge a new community. They embraced their unsettling identity and projected their deep desire to claim a new mode of belonging. Like Takamine, one of the writers for the *Okinawa Times* accurately reported that "the GI movement in bases grew out of Black GIs' struggle for freedom and became a model of activism for other dissenting American GIs. This was made possible as a result of people's belief that there existed something sensuous beyond differences in 'color' or 'class.'" At the same time, revolutionary Black masculinity also served as an important point of reference for Okinawans, for it confirmed, according to this writer, a desire on their part to "materialize the ideals of '*Hansen*' [antiwar] and '*Jichi*' [autonomy or self-governance] to transform Okinawan identity."[74] At the point of antiracist, anti-imperialist, and gendered identifications between these two groups, an alternative (Black) conception of political rights and human agency crystallized and emerged as a generative force at the local level.

## The Future in the Present

Although dissenting Black GIs defined Blackness in various ways as power, resistance, and Third World solidarity and emphasized coalition building, they were still unable to fully recognize themselves as agents of U.S. imperialism and sexual aggressors. Since many of them, especially those involved with the publication of *Demand for Freedom*, placed an emphasis on combating emasculation, the direct outcome of white racism, their expressions of masculine dissent had become, as Black feminist critic bell hooks writes, "a discursive practice . . . that link[ed] Black male liberation with gaining the right to participate fully within patriarchy."[75] Implied in the way they discussed the denial of Black manhood, in other words, was their desire to regain control of female sexuality. They did not recognize that their assertion and performance of Blackness did not "exist outside gender and sexuality"; it was "constituted by both," as legal scholar Devon W. Carbado emphasizes.[76] The result was the privileging of the Black male experience with racism over other oppressed people's experiences, positioning Black masculinity as a model of resistance, even though militarized prostitution, rapes, male aggression, and voyeuristic and sadistic spectacles were integral to war making, military occupation, and the institutionalization of white supremacy on a global scale.[77] Such a heterosexist conception of Black radicalism rendered invisible military violence against Okinawan women and women's human agency. It was unable to fashion a critique that would expose the heteronormative imperative for domination that underpinned the whole racist and sexist project of the American occupation in Okinawa and the American imperial war in Vietnam.

Missing from these men's critique was an understanding that as men and members of the U.S. armed forces, they possessed a wide range of privileges—class, gender, sexuality, and nation—in their relations with Okinawan men and women. First, they presided over Okinawans as representative men responsible for educating politically backward masses, especially Okinawan men, to show them how to overcome racial oppression. Second, they failed to point out the function of prostitution in maintaining the basic structure of globalized white supremacy built on heteronormative imperatives. As Black feminist scholar Rose Brewer comments, "These are complex social relations involving multiple sites of oppression, occurring in conjunctive, disjunctive, and contradictory ways to generate a system of race, color, gender, sexual, and class oppression."[78] They remained uncritical of the implication of their desire to recuperate manhood through the control and exploitation of women's bodies. An Okinawan male observer brought up the issue in this way: "Black GIs say that Okinawan male managers and female hostesses discriminate against them. But have they ever considered what it would be like for Okinawan women to sell their bodies to live?"[79]

In an appeal written to Okinawans and the Japanese to forge solidarity, a Black GI writer emphasized that all of them faced a common enemy, "Amerik-ka." He continued, "You are not alone. You have 200 million people of color to depend on if everyone unites. POWER TO THE THIRD WORLD! POWER TO THE PEOPLE!"[80] Yet, throughout this

narrative of defiance and solidarity, the writer repeatedly cast Okinawans as students in need of tutelage by Black men. A strain of colonial
paternalism ran throughout this narrative. Although the writer recognized that U.S. imperialism in Asia was responsible for the underde-
velopment of Okinawa, he criticized Okinawans' uncritical acceptance
of existing unequal power relations, seeing them as too accommodat-
ing. He wrote, "True, it gives many jobs, but now you're dependent on
Amerik-ka. Amerik-ka is the one gaining because you're working your
ass off for low wages, but yet to you it's fair or good."[81] Okinawan subordination, however, did not mean that ordinary people lacked initiative
to change their unequal status. The manner in which the writer offered
political advice to Okinawans reinforced the privileged political position he occupied.

Moreover, the Black GI's critique of Okinawa's dependency to
"Amerik-ka" had little to say about one of the cornerstones of the base
political economy, military prostitution. It failed to discuss the crucial role it played in maintaining the basic structure of white supremacy. He wrote, "Now Okinawa depends on its American visitors for
income. Amerik-ka legalized prostitution in Okinawa for its soldiers.
. . . Why legal here? To keep the Americans happy, or what? Now Okinawa depends on prostitution for a big income. Amerik-ka has made
Okinawans, your friends, into viscious [sic] businessmen. They value
the dollars more so than their fellow brothers and sisters."[82] Rather
than pointing out the interconnectedness of white supremacy, capitalism, and heteropatriarchy, the writer turned to a criticism of base-
town business interests, highlighting how these key establishments
within the base-town political economy chose greed over the struggle
for liberation.

The outcome of this limited antiracist and anti-imperialist discourse
was that it glossed over the state of Okinawan women's subordination
and struggle. Although the Black GI writer understood the problems
of militarism, racism, and capitalism, he did not, as Cynthia Enloe
emphasizes, "think about violence against women in general."[83] The
limitation of Black GIs' anticolonial nationalist thought was that it did
not ground its vision of struggle within radical feminism. Takamine
was acutely aware of the limited conception of masculine Black dissent.
In the end, despite the effort by a small group of committed Black GIs

to build a solidarity struggle with Okinawans, Takamine emphasized that conflicts between Okinawans and Black GIs, racial antagonisms between Black and white GIs, and above all violence against women impeded the progress of coalition work. Such a political limitation also reinforced the ideological and political project of criminalizing and demonizing Black men.[84]

However, a handful of white American feminists, peace activists, enlisted men's wives, women in the military, and local women started to explore creative ways to address the intersection of racism and sexism. While the majority of male activists and dissenting GIs held narrowly conceived ideas about methods by which to establish the foundation for revolutionary change, the multiracial women's group in Okinawa, composed mostly of whites but with some Okinawan and Black women also, insisted that the issues of race and gender were "as fundamental as those of class."[85] Their politics was similar to that of a revolutionary Black, lesbian, feminist group called the Combahee River Collective, which was formed in Boston in 1974. In "A Black Feminist Statement" (1977), Barbara Smith, Beverly Smith, and Demita Frazier explained their political position: "We are not convinced . . . that a socialist revolution that is not also a feminist and antiracist revolution will guarantee our liberation."[86] At least twice a week, these feminist activists in Okinawa met to discuss how women could forge a cultural identity by organizing around issues of health care, domestic violence, military violence against women, and rape. What started out as a fledgling women's group within the GI movement in Okinawa had transformed itself into a far-reaching project in the struggle against war, imperialism, racism, and sexism. It was called the Women's House project.

In October 1972, the Women's House was established as "a center for living, rapping, examining history and problems, forming actions and solutions to problems." It provided educational, medical, and legal resources, as well as a space for "solidarity to grow among women." Although its primary constituents were women connected with the military, especially some twenty-five thousand dependents (wives and daughters), it also reached out to members of the Women's Army Corps (WACs), women musicians of the U.S. Air Force band (WAFs), and local women. Moreover, the activists of the Women's House saw themselves operating in a broader context of self-determination not just for

American women but also for all oppressed people, including Blacks and Okinawans. "By providing opportunities for relationships between American and Asian women," the activists wrote, the Women's House functioned as "a channel for greater understanding of the particular forms of oppression faced by different people, and the needs for self-determination for all people."[87]

Sharon Danaan, one of the white American peace activists and a founding member of the Women's House, matured politically and personally through political engagements in Okinawa in the early 1970s. She described what she experienced as a "whole chain of realizations." She wrote, "once there was that initial eye-opening to Okinawa and its struggles—of course, there was the racism against Okinawans to get through first in many cases since the military laid that on super thick —also there was a whole lot of energy that came off of responding to the strikes or other struggles . . . and rapping with [local] people. . . . There was a whole lot for all of us to learn." Before coming to Okinawa, she lived in Tokyo for a year. Her Japanese-language proficiency proved useful in organizing activities, enabling her to crisscross cultural and racial boundaries with ease. She fraternized and developed relationships with local men and women, while working alongside William Schaap of the National Lawyers Guild, Takamine Tomokazu of *Ryukyu Shimpo*, and a host of other transnational peace activists associated with Beheiren and the PCS, such as Barbara Bye and Dianne Durst. She explained that "the context of being in Okinawa is a big factor in the changes people go through."[88]

Danaan always followed what moved her. Her self-awareness of how to forge a political identity and to build the movement for revolutionary change was clear. Sometimes she heard other activists say, "You're not in touch with your anger as a woman" or "Your focus on women comes from your petty bourgeois background." She detested such a prescribed method of becoming political. She called it "women's-consciousness-guilt trips or class-consciousness-guilt trips." She once said, "fuck calling each other politically incorrect." For her, enabling the space to become political was "not one of those resolvable issues where we can figure out that it's correct or incorrect for certain reasons." Politics was necessarily messy, and she seemed to embrace the messiness of struggle.[89]

In one of Danaan's ruminations on "images of women" in Okinawa, she described her conversation with an Okinawan sex worker that challenged her thinking. One day, through a chance encounter, she and an Okinawan woman started debating how the institution of marriage affected women. As a feminist, she regarded marriage as a regulatory device to maintain the heterosexist system of subordination of women, and her opinion had appeared in one of the featured articles in the local newspaper, titled "I Wouldn't Think of Getting Married." Having read the interview in the paper recently, an Okinawan woman started talking to Danaan while other sex workers surrounded them. "How come you not get married? Maybe next time you find boyfriend, you get married," she said. Danaan tried to explain her feelings about marriage to the woman, but "there was something very serious in her manner." While other Okinawan women teased and laughed during the exchange between the two, this one sex worker, described as "the woman with the blond wig," kept a straight face. Danaan later wrote, "there was something urgent in her attempt to communicate with me." As an activist in Okinawa, Danaan was in motion, groping toward something poetic. She said, "I'm for figuring out a real synthesis."[90]

A pursuit of "a real synthesis" underpinned some of the projects that Danaan participated in through the Women's House, which reflected a kind of synthesis that the Black, lesbian feminists of the Combahee River Collective later developed "to combat the manifold and simultaneous oppressions that all women of color face." Danaan and other feminist activists were in search of "integrated analysis and practice" that would enable women in Okinawa to effect the change that they wanted to see in a society structured by racism, patriarchy, misogyny, sexual exploitation and violence, and aggressive militarism.[91]

For instance, collaborating with two Black activists—a registered nurse and her husband, a doctor who worked for the military hospital on the base—Danaan and her fellow activists in the Women's House took part in an effort to establish a free health center for women. Before the Women's House came into existence, these Black medical professionals had attempted to open a free clinic, especially to provide treatment and medications for people with sickle-cell anemia, but they "were stopped from renting space and carrying it out on their own." One thing that they had come to recognize as they worked in the base hospital was that the care that women received was inadequate. Believing that health care was a right not a privilege, these Black activists sought to expand care in the areas of women's health, family planning, pregnancy, and venereal disease treatment and to provide these services for free to all women, including sex workers who were afflicted with various types of sexually transmitted diseases. They played a key role during the nascent years of the Women's House project.[92]

Although the dynamic antiracist and radical feminist organizing tradition existed alongside Black GIs' antiracist, antiwar, and anti-imperialist activism in Okinawa, it did not intersect with their political engagements. In what could be described as political myopia, the limitation of Black GIs' radical politics hindered the development of a broader conception of solidarity and a more concrete articulation of a multiracial coalition politics that could bring an end to gender and sexual normativity.[93] Although Black GIs' masculine dissent served as a catalyst in the struggle for revolutionary change, enabling diverse peace activists and Okinawans to participate in the political process, feminists' approach to human liberation, especially how they resisted the interlocking system of a wide range of oppressions, did not come to the fore. This oversight, ultimately, had to do with how human liberation was envisioned. The marginalization of radical feminist political projects was, to borrow from Robin D. G. Kelley's critique, "less a matter of deliberate exclusion than *conception*."[94] Absent in the Black GIs' vision of liberation was understanding that the interests and lives of Blacks and other oppressed people were being defined, shaped, and contested through multiple sites of oppression. Indeed, as Rose Brewer insists, "It is within this conceptual frame of multiplicity that the continuation of Black exclusion, economic exploitation, and state violence must be understood."[95]

Yet small-scale multiracial organizing efforts in occupied Okinawa in the late 1960s and 1970s forever transformed the political consciousness and identity of activists. A decade after reversion, Barbara Bye, reuniting with Takamine Tomokazu in Oakland, California, in 1982, told him that solidarity struggles among Okinawans and dissenting GIs incited many of her colleagues to link up, including her mother, Mary Bye, a Quaker, who was then active in the antiwar coalition group called the Concerned Citizens of Bucks Country and the Peace Committee of the Society of Friends in Pennsylvania. Taking a position much like that of the Okinawan antireversionists, as discussed in the opening of this chapter, both mother and daughter began to see the "reversion question" in occupied Okinawa as a politics of identity leading to total human liberation, and through concrete political engagement, they emerged as internationalists committed to a transnational people's movement. Not afraid of being characterized as utopian or idealist, they carried the voice of antireversionists to the Senate Foreign Relations Committee, chaired by Senator J. William Fulbright of Arkansas, to communicate the poetics of liberation.[96]

Writing from Koza, Barbara Bye demanded that the Senate committee secure Okinawans' political representation and stated what was obvious to practitioners of representative democracy, albeit glaringly absent. To dare America to halt Okinawa's reversion, she asked a probing question: "Clearly, with more than fifty per cent of the Okinawan people opposed to the current reversion agreement, how can the American Senate condone approving the reversion agreement without first consulting representatives of the Okinawan people?"[97] Mary Bye, writing from Doylestown, Pennsylvania, also echoed her daughter's larger point. She reminded the senators that "moral bankruptcy leads to total bankruptcy," and the current policy toward Okinawa was a case in point. With ironic tenacity, she presented her stance: "Had the Okinawans been included in the discussions of this matter so vital to their interest, they would have endorsed reversion," but of a qualitatively different kind. It would have been "a special kind of reversion free from military occupation, free from polluting industry. They want a return to their peacetime economy, largely farming and fishing, both impossible as long as their farmlands were covered with military bases and their fishing areas with oil spills."[98] Although the mother and daughter were physically apart, they nonetheless moved together across, below, above, and behind nation-states during the era of Okinawa reversion and the Vietnam War. Without missing a beat of this movement for peace and racial justice, they joined transpacific strivings and learned to cross over into the culture of liberation.

In occupied Okinawa, this culture of liberation emboldened activists such as Mary and Barbara Bye to push boundaries of all kinds to expand multiracial social networks on a local and global scale, so as to link up with the diverse constituents of social movements. During the Senate Committee on Foreign Relations sessions to discuss the Okinawa Reversion Treaty, held from October 27 to 29, 1971, the letters they sent to Senator Fulbright appeared as an annex to the hearings. Far from being mere statements of grievances, their articulation of the ethos surrounding the projects of multiracial organizing possessed resonance and specificity in the struggle. Their poetics communicated not the basis for shared identity among the diverse constituents of struggles in occupied Okinawa but rather activists' multivalent journeys through the challenging terrain of antiracist and anti-imperialist organizing activity, marked by unequal power relations that recalled and renewed what Ralph Ellison referred to as "an identity of passions" as foundational to their social practices. Guided by the conviction that to change and ultimately to go beyond "America" was to repudiate white supremacy, militarism, and imperialism, both within oneself and in society at large, just as King had made it known in his statement of opposition to the Vietnam War, the participants of transpacific strivings pursued this audacity to make the world anew, doing all that needed to be done to keep the horizon of history open.[99]

# Conclusion

## We Who Become Together

Toni Morrison's meditation on the writer's craft can be read as a serious challenge. Morrison explains,

> I have wanted always to develop a way of writing that was irrevocably black. I don't have the resources of a musician, but I thought that if it was truly black literature, it would not be black because I was, it would not even be black because of its subject matter. It would be something intrinsic, indigenous, something in the way it was put together—the sentences, the structure, texture, and tone—so that anyone who read it would realize [it].[1]

Her effort to enunciate "Blackness"—its infinite variety and complexity—in language without being overcome by the corruption of race is intended to be paradigmatic. And it is to this bold call for reworking that has helped chart, in this book, the analysis of variations of transpacific strivings in Black America, Japan, and Okinawa. The work of animating Afro-Asian solidarity mirrors the challenge of creating art that Toni Morrison describes.

Following Morrison's insight, this book has argued that the diverse participants of Afro-Asian solidarity projects in Black America, Japan, and Okinawa in the twentieth century found ways to link up through imagination and social practice, and this process of identification was irrevocably racial. Yet it had little to do with the color of participants of Afro-Asian solidarities. Nor did it have to do with how Black and white American, Japanese, and Okinawan intellectual-activists tapped into the tradition of the historical Black struggle, although that was one of the essential vectors that quickened the transpacific currents of resistance. The loci of their struggles appeared in opposition to war, militarism, imperialism, and colonialism, and the texture of these struggles was characterized by a variety of acts of coming together. It followed both familiar and unlikely routes, from Marxism to Esperanto and pacifism. It also took forms that brought together seeming opposites. Black intellectual-activists with Marxist groundings, for instance, saw the symbolic significance of Japan's race-conscious defiance within the international system of competitive nation-states and took a pro-Japan position, although they were keenly cognizant of the fact that Japan was an imperialist power and a colonizer in Asia, no champion of darker nations and peoples. Moving in a racial groove, they reworked their rhetorical stance and sharpened their strategic practices of criticism. Dissenting Black GIs in occupied Okinawa also drew inspiration from the revolutionary ferment on the eve of reversion to searchingly carve out a new terrain of struggle alongside Okinawa liberation, even when their sense of righteousness against racial injustices did not neatly translate into shared contempt for American imperial hubris and instead clashed with Okinawans' anti-Black racism.

In other words, the challenge of recalibrating the optics of race, as Morrison conceived it, demanded an understanding of the intrinsic yet contingent, as well as animating yet antagonistic, qualities of transpacific identification. The dynamism of myriad efforts by the participants of Afro-Asian solidarities to put together an ensemble was such that it engendered a culture of liberation that could transmit the heartbeat of freedom, the ceaseless struggle of freedom. An emphasis was placed on certain kinds of tones that were restless and affirming and

that governed transpacific social practices, for it was this musical quality that helped make this culture of crossover productive for the formation of new racial subjects and Afro-Asian solidarities in Black America, Japan, and Okinawa.

What ultimately pushed my inquiry in this direction to consider the
fluid yet layered transpacific formations of the culture of liberation was
a dynamic learning collaborative in which I took part as an instruc-
tor of Black studies at Borough of Manhattan Community College of
the City University of New York (BMCC/CUNY). At the end of each
semester, I felt that students and I discovered how to dwell in a space
that could be characterized as the next-closest place to utopia. Perhaps
this community of solidarity was something resembling the commons,
where our needs and desires to usher in a new form of thinking that is
just, democratic, and poetic would come to be manifest. Yet that was
not at all my pedagogical intent. There was an element of unpredict-
ability and creativity, combined with the always already antagonistic
and contingent nature of politics. This was not at all easy work when
the enormity of differences in identity, background, and politics had to
be confronted head-on. Despite this historical weight of difference, created through domination, and its perpetuation in the present, we would
begin assembling a new domain. Learning how to imagine a new possibility without compromising heterogeneity, which is so central to the
community of solidarity in the classroom, the condition of our social
existence slowly metamorphosed through this process of identification.
If this is what it means to become truly *diasporic*, then it was. This community of solidarity called diaspora emerged as "a place where traditions operate but are not closed, where the black experience is historically and culturally distinctive but is not the same as it was before," to
borrow Stuart Hall's definition.[2]

Each semester, taking my courses in Black studies were African
Americans, Puerto Ricans, Dominicans, and West Indians from Ja-
maica, Trinidad, Antigua, and Barbados, recent immigrants and children of immigrants, whose lives and identities were always on the move.
A few white American students, along with international students from
five continents—Africa, Asia, Europe, and North and South America
—also trickled in. Some of them were superb students; they could write
and speak with tremendous eloquence, depth, authority, and sensitivity.

Self-evident was their love of reading. While these students had a keen sense of human drama and the importance of craft, others struggle to transform their inchoate ideas into an academic voice of confidence. Making their flashes of revelation legible was challenging at best, and the horizon of their learning was so vast that they had to steer clear of the overwhelming sense of expectation and the crushing power of disappointment and self-doubt. But something elemental and possessing universal appeal, such as the enduring strength of human dignity in the midst of suffering, struck a chord when they surveyed the tradition of the historical Black struggle. It had necessary resonance to help them locate the mainspring of sustenance, in the discourses of both the past and the present. This emotive and intuitive specificity was not tightly wrapped up in Black vindicationism, however. It had the capacity for self-fashioning. Whereas at the outset they could not yet see themselves as "subjects of a possible discourse," an emergent culture of liberation in the classroom allowed them to "take in a bit of the other, as well as being what they themselves are," as Hall explains, and become something else, or something qualitatively new, which they so much desired in the present. Such was the defining feature of this learning collaborative at BMCC/CUNY.[3]

A catalyst responsible for making this culture of liberation generative and enabling was friction engendered by the very fact that the figure of authority in the classroom was an Asian. Upon entering and seeing my face on the first day, students could not hide their surprise, amusement, and confusion. Others were more frank. They showed their discontent since the promise of occupying a space to affirm their Blackness was foreclosed. Those who identified as Afrocentrists were first to challenge the legitimacy of this Asian presence. Doubting my ability to relate to the Black historical experience, they listened to everything I said closely, often correcting how I framed the movement of Black history. If I placed an emphasis on the human agency of Africans and people of African descent, for instance, they reminded me of the unspeakable scale of violence unleashed by the Atlantic slave trade, colonialism, slavery, and Jim Crow segregation and their living legacies. However, if I placed more than usual emphasis on what the white-supremacist system and oppressors did to Black people, then they accurately pointed out the resilience of the Black freedom struggle. Also if I failed to mention such crucial information as the African roots of Western civilization and the rich histories of ancient African civilizations, they drew from their local knowledge by referring to the writings of John Henrik Clarke and Yosef Ben-Jochannan and encouraged everyone to consult their work.

We sustained our dialectical thinking in this way, moving recursively through the currents of domination and resistance, both in the past and in the present, rising above and going under and taking forward what was left to engage with something new. Along the way, we made this quality foundational to our experience of race. Moving in a racial groove, while stretching and redefining the boundaries of Blackness, we intensified this movement. Ever more cognizant of our own complex subjectivity, we pursued the impulse to translate difference, allowing the supple workings of race to make our identities more expansive. While this struggle of freedom never ceased, we did acknowledge with the overtones and undertones of our ecumenical search for a committed human life that Afro-Asian solidarity has the potential to rework the ontological totality of Blackness fundamentally and thus to give categorical unity to the African-inflected idea of solidarity—"we who become together"—that is at once race specific and racefree.[4] However small-scale and localized our Afro-Asian exchanges and entanglements were in the classroom, there was "something in the way it was put together," as Morrison frames it, that suggested that this practice of freedom would unleash a new set of values to quicken the movement toward total human liberation. Contained in this experience was a tale of utopian potential.

# NOTES

## NOTES TO THE INTRODUCTION

1. W. E. B. Du Bois, "Forum of Fact and Opinion," *Pittsburgh Courier*, 20 March 1937, in *Newspaper Columns by W. E. B. Du Bois*, ed. Herbert Aptheker (White Plains, NY: Kraus-Thompson, 1986), 2:181–182. Not mentioned in Du Bois's remark about the presence of Black sailors in Perry's expedition to Japan is an important subplot. Perhaps Du Bois knew of the presence of minstrels who stole Black humanity since some of the prints of this expedition did capture their performance, or maybe he was unaware of it altogether. Regardless, at the center of Perry's landing and this dazzling display of the arsenal of American democracy was blackface minstrelsy performed by white sailors aboard the USSF *Powhatan*, calling themselves the "Ethiopian Band of the *Powhatan*, who style themselves as 'Japanese [Olio] Minstrels.' " As Lieutenant George H. Preble, who was part of this expedition, described, the Japanese envoy "enjoyed the imitations of the negro, and laughed very heartily, [going] so far as to put his arms around the Commodore's neck and embrace him." How would Du Bois's thinking have changed if he had heard the Japanese envoy's laughter as he told Perry in a "drunken embrace" that "Nippon and America [shared] the same heart"? Such is an irony of transpacific race contact. See George Henry Preble, *The Opening of Japan: A Diary of Discovery in the Far East, 1853–1856*, ed. Boleslaw Szczesniak (Norman: University of Oklahoma Press, 1962), 152–153; Victor Fell Yellin, "Mrs. Belmont, Matthew Perry, and the 'Japanese Minstrels,' " *American Music* 14:3 (Fall 1996): 257–275; Matthew C. Perry, *The Japan Expedition, 1852–1854: The Personal Journal of Commodore Matthew C. Perry*, ed. Roger Pineau (Washington, DC: Smithsonian Institute Press, 1968), 189.

2. W. E. B. Du Bois, *Dusk of Dawn: An Essay toward an Autobiography of a Race Concept*, in *Writings* (New York: Library of America, 1986), 591.

3. Howard Winant, *The World Is a Ghetto: Race and Democracy since World War II* (New York: Basic Books, 2001), xiv; W. E. B. Du Bois, "Atlanta University," in *From Servitude to Service* (Boston: American Unitarian Association, 1905), 197; W. E. B. Du Bois, *John Brown*, ed. and introd. David Roediger (Philadelphia: G. W. Jacobs, 1909; reprint, New York: Modern Library, 2001), 231 (page cites refer to the reprint edition).

4. The Negro Commission, C.P., U.S.A., "Japanese 'Law and Order' in Manchuria,"

in *A Documentary History of the Negro People in the United States, 1933–1945*, ed. Herbert Aptheker (Secaucus, NJ: Citadel, 1974), 311–314; Henry L. Stimson to W. E. B. Du Bois, 24 January 1940, in *The Correspondence of W. E. B. Du Bois*, ed. Herbert Aptheker (Amherst: University of Massachusetts Press, 1976), 2:205–206; Manning Marable, *W. E. B. Du Bois: Black Radical Democrat* (Boston: Twayne, 1986), 153–154; David Levering Lewis, *W. E. B. Du Bois: The Fight for Equality and the American Century, 1919–1963* (New York: Holt, 2000), 387–421; Reginald Kearney, *African American Views of the Japanese: Solidarity or Sedition?* (Albany: SUNY Press, 1998), 152; Ernest Allen Jr., "Waiting for Tojo: The Pro-Japan Vigil of Black Missourians, 1932–1943," *Gateway Heritage* 15 (Fall 1995): 51; Gerald Horne, *Race War! White Supremacy and the Japanese Attack on the British Empire* (New York: NYU Press, 2004), 43–59; John W. Dower, *War without Mercy: Race and Power in the Pacific War* (New York: Pantheon Books, 1986), 173–178; Kenneth C. Barnes, "Inspiration from the East: Black Arkansans Look to Japan," *Arkansas Historical Quarterly* 69:3 (Autumn 2010): 203–217.

5. C. L. R. James, "The Historical Development of the Negroes in American Society," in *C. L. R. James on the "Negro Question*," ed. and introd. Scott McLemee (Jackson: University Press of Mississippi, 1996), 82–83; C. L. R. James, "The Revolutionary Answer to the Negro Problem in the United States," in ibid., 139.

6. Robin D. G. Kelley, introduction to *A History of Pan-African Revolt*, by C. L. R. James (Chicago: Kerr, 1995), 15–18; C. James, "The Historical Development of the Negroes in American Society," 87; C. James, "The Revolutionary Answer to the Negro Problem in the United States," 139. Also see Paul Buhle, *C. L. R. James: The Artist as Revolutionary* (New York: Verso, 1988); Ken Worcester, *C. L. R. James: A Political Biography* (Albany: SUNY Press, 1996); Cedric J. Robinson, *Black Marxism: The Making of the Black Radical Tradition* (Chapel Hill: University of North Carolina Press, 2000), 241–286; Sundiata Keita Cha-Jua, "C. L. R. James, Blackness, and the Making of a Neo-Marxist Disporan Historiography," *Nature, Society & Thought* 11 (Spring 1998): 53–89; Anthony Bogues, *Caliban's Freedom: The Early Political Thought of C. L. R. James* (London: Pluto, 1997).

7. Nikhil Pal Singh, *Black Is a Country: Race and the Unfinished Struggle for Democracy* (Cambridge: Harvard University Press, 2004), 65; Angela Davis, "Reflections on Race, Class, and Gender in the USA," in *The Politics of Culture in the Shadow of Capital*, ed. Lisa Lowe and David Lloyd (Durham: Duke University Press, 1997), 322.

8. W. E. B. Du Bois, "The Winds of Time," *Chicago Defender*, 25 August 1945, in Aptheker, *Newspaper Columns*, 2:650.

9. George Katsiaficas, *The Imagination of the New Left: A Global Analysis of 1968* (Boston: South End, 1987), 10; David Howard-Pitney, ed., *Martin Luther King Jr., Malcolm X, and the Civil Rights Struggle of the 1950s and 1960s: A Brief History with Documents* (Boston: Bedford/St. Martin's, 2004), 145.

10. Robinson, *Black Marxism*, xxxii.

11. On the notion of *Afro-Asia*, see Fred Ho and Bill V. Mullen, eds., *Afro Asia:*

*Revolutionary Political and Cultural Connections between African Americans and Asian Americans* (Durham: Duke University Press, 2008), 5; Vijay Prashad, "Bandung Is Done: Passages in AfroAsian Epistemology," in *AfroAsian Encounters: Culture, History, Politics*, ed. Heike Raphael-Hernandez and Shannon Steen (New York: NYU Press, 2006), xi–xxiii; Robin D. G. Kelley, *Freedom Dreams: The Black Radical Imagination* (Boston: Beacon, 2002), 60–109.

12. Singh, *Black Is a Country*, 44. See Nakajima Yoriko, *Kokujin no Seijisanka to Daisanseiki America no Shupatsu* (Tokyo: Chuo Daigaku Shutpan, 1989).

13. Kelley, *Freedom Dreams*, 9–11; W. E. B. Du Bois, "The Position of the Negro in the American Social Order: Where Do We Go from Here?," in *Writings by W. E. B. Du Bois in Periodicals Edited by Others*, ed. Herbert Aptheker (Millwood, NY: Kraus-Thompson, 1982), 79; Paul Gilroy, *The Black Atlantic: Modernity and Double Consciousness* (Cambridge: Harvard University Press, 1993), 36. Grace Lee Boggs's discussion of "futuring" helped sharpen this argument. See Grace Lee Boggs, *Living for Change: An Autobiography* (Minneapolis: University of Minnesota Press, 1998), 253–254.

14. Gilroy, *The Black Atlantic*, 36.

15. Ibid. I am indebted to H. L. T. Quan's assessment of Cedric Robinson's *Black Marxism*. H. L. T. Quan, "Geniuses of Resistance: Feminist Consciousness and the Black Radical Tradition," *Race & Class* 47:2 (2005): 39–53; Du Bois, *Dusk of Dawn*, 640; Charles W. Mills, *The Racial Contract* (Ithaca: Cornell University Press, 1997), 119.

16. Roderick A. Ferguson, "'W. E. B. Du Bois': Biography of a Discourse," in *Next to the Color Line: Gender, Sexuality, and W. E. B. Du Bois*, ed. Susan Gillman and Alys Eve Weinbaum (Minneapolis: University of Minnesota Press, 2007), 278, 286.

17. Prashad, "Bandung Is Done," xvi; Vijay Prashad, *Everybody Was Kung-Fu Fighting: Afro-Asian Connections and the Myth of Cultural Purity* (Boston: Beacon, 2001); Bill V. Mullen, *Afro-Orientalism* (Minneapolis: University of Minnesota Press, 2004); Ho and Mullen, *Afro Asia*. Also important are David Haekwon Kim, "The Meaning of Her Majesty's Madness: *Dark Princess* and Afro-Asian Anarchy" (unpublished paper, 2002); George Lipsitz, "'Frantic to Join . . . the Japanese Army': The Asia Pacific War in the Lives of African American Soldiers and Civilians," in Lowe and Lloyd, *The Politics of Culture in the Shadow of Capital*, 324–353. On the study of the Black America–Japan nexus, see especially Ernest Allen Jr., "When Japan Was 'Champion of the Darker Races': Satokata Takahashi and the Flowering of Black Messianic Nationalism," *Black Scholar* 24 (Winter 1994): 23–46; Allen, "Waiting for Tojo"; Kearney, *African American Views of the Japanese*; Marc Gallicchio, *The African American Encounter with Japan and China: Black Internationalism in Asia, 1895–1945* (Chapel Hill: University of North Carolina Press, 2000); Yukiko Koshiro, "Beyond an Alliance of Color: The African American Impact on Modern Japan," *positions: east asia cultures critique* 11 (Spring 2003): 183–215; Furukawa Hiromi and Furukawa Tetsushi, *Nihonjin*

to *Afurikakei Amerikajin: Nichibei Kankeishi ni okeru sono Shoso* (Tokyo: Akashi Shoten, 2004).

18. Stuart Hall, "Subjects in History: Making Diasporic Identities," in *The House That Race Built: Black Americans, U.S. Terrain,* ed. and introd. Wahneema Lubiano (New York: Pantheon Books, 1997), 291–294. On the insight into the autonomy of race as grounds for resistance, see Brent Hayes Edwards, "Introduction: The 'Autonomy' of Black Radicalism," *Social Text* 19:2 (Summer 2001): 1–13.

19. Hall, "Subjects in History," 291, 292, 294.

20. Sterling Stuckey, " 'I Want to Be African': Paul Robeson and the Ends of Nationalist Theory and Practice, 1914–1945," *Massachusetts Review* 17:1 (Spring 1976): 81–137; Sterling Stuckey, *Slave Culture: Nationalist Theory and the Foundations of Black America* (New York: Oxford University Press, 1987), 303–358; Philip S. Foner, ed., *Paul Robeson Speaks: Writings, Speeches, and Interviews, 1918–1974* (New York: Brunner/Mazel, 1978); Royal Hartigan with Fred Ho, "The American Drum Set: Black Musicians and Chinese Opera along the Mississippi River," in Ho and Mullen, *Afro Asia,* 285–290; Penny M. Von Eschen, *Race against Empire: Black Americans and Anticolonialism, 1937–1957* (Ithaca: Cornell University Press, 1997).

21. Quoted in Stuckey, *Slave Culture,* 321.

22. Ibid., 348, 351; on the notion of "wails" as an insight into the culture of liberation, see Singh, *Black Is a Country,* 45–46; David R. Roediger, *Working toward Whiteness: How America's Immigrants Became White* (New York: Basic Books, 2005), 93–110.

23. Clyde Woods, *Development Arrested: The Blues and Plantation Power in the Mississippi Delta* (New York: Verso, 1998); Robinson, *Black Marxism,* 171; Gilroy, *The Black Atlantic,* 37, 200.

24. Toni Morrison, "Home," in Lubiano, *The House That Race Built,* 9. See David R. Roediger, *Towards the Abolition of Whiteness: Essays on Race, Politics, and Working-Class History* (New York: Verso, 1994); David Roediger, *History against Misery* (Chicago: Kerr, 2006), 131–180.

NOTES TO CHAPTER 1

1. Harry Haywood, *Black Bolshevik: Autobiography of an Afro-American Communist* (Chicago: Liberator, 1978), 72.

2. Ibid., 83.

3. V. P. Franklin, *Living Our Stories, Telling Our Truths: Autobiography and the Making of the African-American Intellectual Tradition* (New York: Scribner, 1995), 144–147; Haywood, *Black Bolshevik,* 83; Chad L. Williams, "Vanguards of the New Negro: African American Veterans and Post–World War I Racial Militancy," *Journal of African American History* 92:3 (Summer 2007): 347; Mark Solomon, *The Cry Was Unity: Communists and African Americans, 1917–1936* (Jackson: University Press of Mississippi, 1998); Mark Naison, *Communists in Harlem during the Depression* (New York: Grove, 1983); Robert A. Hill, "Introduction: Racial

and Radical: Cyril V. Briggs, The CRUSADER Magazine, and the African Blood Brotherhood, 1918-1922," in *The Crusader*, vol. 1, ed. Robert A. Hill (New York: Garland, 1987), v–lxxiii; Winston James, *Holding Aloft the Banner of Ethiopia: Caribbean Radicalism in Early Twentieth-Century America* (New York: Verso, 1998), 157–184; Philip S. Foner, *American Socialism and Black Americans: From the Age of Jackson to World War II* (Westport, CT: Greenwood, 1977), 309–311.

4. Williams, "Vanguards of the New Negro," 348; V. P. Franklin, *Black Self-Determination: A Cultural History of African-American Resistance* (Brooklyn, NY: Lawrence Hill Books, 1992), 6.

5. Minkah Makalani, "For the Liberation of Black People Everywhere: The African Blood Brotherhood, Black Radicalism, and Pan-African Liberation in the New Negro Movement, 1917–1936" (Ph.D. diss., University of Illinois at Urbana-Champaign, 2004), 75–82; Minkah Makalani, *In the Cause of Freedom: Radical Black Internationalism from Harlem to London, 1917–1939* (Chapel Hill: University of North Carolina Press, 2011); Jeffrey B. Perry, *Hubert Harrison: The Voice of Harlem Radicalism, 1883–1918* (New York: Columbia University Press, 2009), 299.

6. Stephen R. Fox, *The Guardian of Boston: William Monroe Trotter* (New York: Atheneum, 1970), 217.

7. Perry, *Hubert Harrison*, 230; W. James, *Holding Aloft the Banner of Ethiopia*, 185–194.

8. Perry, *Hubert Harrison*, 373–385. See Harrison's invocation of unity across the sea in "The White War and the Colored World," published in the *Voice* in August 1917: "We look for a free India and an independent Egypt; *for nationalities in Africa flying their own flags and dictating their own internal and foreign policies.* This is what we understand by 'making the world safe for democracy.' Anything less than this will fail to establish peace on earth and good will toward men. For the majority of races cannot be eternally coerced into accepting the sovereignty of the white race. They are willing to live in a world which is the equal possession of all people—white, black, brown and yellow." Hubert Harrison, "The White War and the Colored World," in *A Hubert Harrison Reader*, ed. Jeffrey B. Perry (Middletown, CT: Wesleyan University Press, 2001), 203.

9. Perry, *Hubert Harrison*, 5 (Randolph quote), 141–239, 266–268, 273, 314.

10. Ibid., 282; Ernest Allen Jr., "The New Negro: Explorations in Identity and Social Consciousness, 1910–1922," in *1915, The Cultural Moment: The New Politics, the New Women, the New Psychology, the New Art and the New Theatre in America*, ed. Adele Heller and Lois Rudnick (New Brunswick: Rutgers University Press, 1991), 48–68. Also see Barbara Foley, *Spectres of 1919: Class and Nation in the Making of the New Negro* (Urbana: University of Illinois Press, 2003), 1–69; Franklin, *Living Our Stories, Telling Our Truths*, 122–125, 147–158.

11. Naoko Shimazu, *Japan, Race and Equality: The Racial Equality Proposal of 1919* (London: Routledge, 1998), 55.

12. Margaret Macmillan, *Paris 1919: Six Months That Changed the World* (New York: Random House, 2001), 312–316; Shimazu, *Japan, Race and Equality*, 51–53.

13. Shimazu, *Japan, Race and Equality*, 17; Marc Gallicchio, *The African American Encounter with Japan and China: Black Internationalism in Asia, 1895–1945* (Chapel Hill: University of North Carolina Press, 2000), 21–24.

14. Shimazu, *Japan, Race and Equality*, 20.

15. Ibid., 20–21, 23–28; Walter LaFeber, *The Clash: A History of U.S.-Japan Relations* (New York: Norton, 1997), 122–124; Gallicchio, *The African American Encounter with Japan and China*, 24.

16. Shimazu, *Japan, Race and Equality*, 30; Gallicchio, *The African American Encounter with Japan and China*, 24.

17. Shimazu, *Japan, Race and Equality*, 30.

18. Quoted in Gerald Horne, *Race War! White Supremacy and the Japanese Attack on the British Empire* (New York: NYU Press, 2004), 36–37.

19. "The Negro—A Menace to Radicalism," *Messenger*, May–June 1919, 20.

20. Hubert Harrison, "When Might Makes Right," in *A Hubert Harrison Reader*, 215. On the construction of white justice and rights, see especially Charles W. Mills, *The Racial Contract* (Ithaca: Cornell University Press, 1997); Charles W. Mills, *Blackness Visible: Essays on Philosophy and Race* (Ithaca: Cornell University Press, 1998).

21. Jonathan D. Spence, *The Gate of Heavenly Peace: The Chinese and Their Revolution, 1895–1980* (New York: Penguin Books, 1981), 154–159.

22. David Levering Lewis, *W. E. B. Du Bois: The Biography of Race, 1868–1919* (New York: Holt, 1993), 567–569, 576–578; Clarence G. Contee, "Du Bois, the NAACP, and the Pan-African Congress of 1919," *Journal of Negro History* 57 (January 1972): 13–28; Manning Marable, "The Pan-Africanism of W. E. B. Du Bois," in *W. E. B. Du Bois on Race and Culture: Philosophy, Politics, and Poetics*, ed. Bernard W. Bell, Emily Grosholz, and James B. Stewart (New York: Routledge, 1996), 199–202; W. E. B. Du Bois, "Negro in Paris," in *Writings by W. E. B. Du Bois in Periodicals Edited by Others*, ed. Herbert Aptheker (Millwood, NY: Kraus-Thompson, 1982), 127–129; W. E. B. Du Bois, *The World and Africa: An Inquiry into the Part Which Africa Has Played in World History*, enlarged ed. (1945; reprint, New York: International, 1996), 6–13.

23. Hubert Harrison, "Africa at the Peace Table," in *A Hubert Harrison Reader*, 211–212.

24. Perry, *Hubert Harrison*, 278; Hubert Harrison, "Race Consciousness," in *A Hubert Harrison Reader*, 116–117.

25. Hubert Harrison, "The Line-Up on the Color Line," in *A Hubert Harrison Reader*, 219.

26. Marcus Garvey, "Race Discrimination Must Go," *Negro World*, 30 November 1918, in *The Marcus Garvey and Universal Negro Improvement Association Papers*, vol. 1, ed. Robert A. Hill (Berkeley: University of California Press, 1983), 305; Paul Gordon Lauren, *Power and Prejudice: The Politics and Diplomacy of Racial Discrimination* (Boulder, CO: Westview, 1998), 79.

27. Cyril V. Briggs, "Negroes of the World Unite in Demanding a Free Africa,"

*Crusader*, December 1918, in Hill, *The Crusader*, 113; Hubert Harrison, "Two Negro Radicalisms," in *A Hubert Harrison Reader*, 103.

28. Maj. W. H. Loving to the Director, Military Intelligence Division, in Hill, *The Marcus Garvey and Universal Negro Improvement Association Papers*, 338.

29. This notion of an "invading new society" is derived from C. L. R. James's invocation of "the invading socialist society." See C. L. R. James, *A New Notion: Two Works by C. L. R. James*, ed. and introd. Noel Ignatiev (Oakland, CA: PM, 2010).

30. Marcus Garvey, "Advice of the Negro to Peace Conference," in Hill, *The Marcus Garvey and Universal Negro Improvement Association Papers*, 302–304; "Bureau of Investigation Reports," in ibid., 288; "Announcement in the *New York Call*," in ibid., 284; Allen, "The New Negro," 54; A'Lelia Bundles, *On Her Own Ground: The Life and Times of Madam C. J. Walker* (New York: Scribner, 2002), 254–256.

31. Bundles, *On Her Own Ground*, 253–254.

32. "Bureau of Investigation Reports," 305–306; David Levering Lewis, *W. E. B. Du Bois: The Fight for Equality and the American Century, 1919–1963* (New York: Holt, 2000), 59; Fox, *The Guardian of Boston*, 223–224.

33. For an overview of the International League of Darker Peoples, see Bundles, *On Her Own Ground*, 257–265.

34. "Maj. W. H. Loving to the Director, Military Intelligence Division," in Hill, *The Marcus Garvey and Universal Negro Improvement Association Papers*, 344–346.

35. "Internationalism," *Messenger*, August 1919, 5–6. Also see "Peace Terms," *Messenger*, March 1919, 11.

36. "Bureau of Investigation Reports," 305–306.

37. Garvey, "Race Discrimination Must Go," 304.

38. Ibid., 304. Also see "Bureau of Investigation Reports," 309–310.

39. Kearney, *African American Views of the Japanese*, 59 (Bruce quote); Horne, *Race War!*, 46–49; Perry, *Hubert Harrison*, 70–72.

40. Bundles, *On Her Own Ground*, 255, 258.

41. New York State Legislature, *Revolutionary Radicalism: A Report of the Joint Legislative Committee of New York Investigating Seditious Activities*, vol. 2 (Albany, NY: J. B. Lyon, 1920), 1517.

42. Ula Y. Taylor, "Intellectual Pan-African Feminists: Amy Ashwood-Garvey and Amy Jacques-Garvey," in *Time Longer than Rope: A Century of Black American Activism, 1850–1950*, ed. Charles M. Payne and Adam Green (New York: NYU Press, 2003); Ula Y. Taylor, " 'Negro Women Are Great Thinkers as Well as Doers': Amy Jacques-Garvey and Community Feminism in the United States, 1924–1927," *Journal of Women's History* 12 (Summer 2000): 104–126; Ula Y. Taylor, *The Veiled Garvey: The Life and Times of Amy Jacques-Garvey* (Chapel Hill: University of North Carolina Press, 2002).

43. W. James, *Holding Aloft the Banner of Ethiopia*, 174–175; Perry, *Hubert Harrison*, 458n. 11. On the relationship between Hubert Harrison and the Socialist Party, read Perry's *Hubert Harrison* in its entirety.

44. On Campbell, see W. James, *Holding Aloft the Banner of Ethiopia*, 174–177;

Makalani, "For the Liberation of Black People Everywhere," 120–130; Solomon, *The Cry Was Unity*, 4.

45. W. James, *Holding Aloft the Banner of Ethiopia*, 177.

46. Michelle Rief, "Thinking Locally, Acting Globally: The International Agenda of Black American Clubwomen, 1880–1940," *Journal of African American History* 89 (Summer 2004): 215–216.

47. Kelley, *Freedom Dreams*, 27.

48. Jessie Fauset, "Letter to the Editor," *Survey*, 8 August 1917, 448.

49. Jane Kuenz, "The Face of America: Performing Race and Nation in Jessie Fauset's *There Is Confusion*," *Yale Journal of Criticism* 12 (Spring 1999): 89–111; Deborah E. McDowell, "The Neglected Dimension of Jessie Redmond Fauset," *Afro-Americans in New York Life and History* 5 (July 1981): 33–49.

50. W. E. B. Du Bois, "The Souls of White Folk," in *Black on White: Black Writers on What It Means to Be White*, ed. and introd. David R. Roediger (New York: Schocken Books, 1998), 186.

51. Harrison, "Two Negro Radicalisms," 103.

52. "Peace Conference," *Messenger*, March 1919, 5.

53. Amy Kaplan, *The Anarchy of Empire in the Making of American Culture* (Cambridge: Harvard University Press, 2002), 196. For the analysis of how W. E. B. Du Bois developed the discourse of anticolonialism in *Darkwater*, see ibid., 190–197.

54. Ibid., 180–181.

55. "Peace Conference," 5.

56. "Japan and the Race Issue," *Messenger*, May–June 1919, 6.

57. "Japan on American Lynching," *Messenger*, August 1921, 225.

58. Harrison, "Africa at the Peace Table," 211.

59. Hubert Harrison, "The Washington Conference," in *A Hubert Harrison Reader*, 230–231.

60. Hubert Harrison, "Disarmament and the Darker Races," in *A Hubert Harrison Reader*, 233.

61. Perry, *Hubert Harrison*, 233–239, 278, 294–296, 337–339; Allen, "The New Negro," 58–59.

62. LaFeber, *The Clash*, 128–143.

63. Ikuhiko Hata, "Continental Expansion, 1905–1941," trans. Alvin D. Cox, in *The Cambridge History of Japan*, vol. 6, ed. Peter Duus (New York: Cambridge University Press, 1988), 283; Akira Iriye, *After Imperialism: The Search for a New Order in the Far East, 1921–1931* (Cambridge: Harvard University Press, 1965), 13–21; LaFeber, *The Clash*, 128–143.

64. Harrison, "Disarmament and the Darker Races," 234.

65. Andrea Razaf[in]keriefo, "The Reason," *Crusader*, January–February 1922, in Hill, *The Crusader*, 6:1358.

66. Harrison, "The White War and the Colored World," 202–203; Perry, *Hubert Harrison*, 230–231.

67. Perry, *Hubert Harrison*, 352–353, 392–395.

68. Ibid., 251–256.
69. Andrea Razaf[in]keriefo, "Disarmament," *Crusader*, January–February 1922, in Hill, *The Crusader*, 6:1358.
70. Lawrence W. Levine, *Black Culture and Black Consciousness: Afro-American Folk Thought from Slavery to Freedom* (New York: Oxford University Press, 1977), 195–196.
71. Ibid., 320.
72. Kelley, *Freedom Dreams*.
73. "The Disarmament Conference," *Messenger*, December 1921, 298.
74. Ibid.
75. "Labor and Disarmament," *Messenger*, February 1922, 352.
76. Chandler Owen, "Disarmament," *Messenger*, November 1921, 279–280; Harrison, "Disarmament and the Darker Races," 232.
77. Cyril V. Briggs, "Liberating Africa," *Crusader*, August 1921, in Hill, *The Crusader*, 3:1208.
78. W. James, *Holding Aloft the Banner of Ethiopia*, 164; Cyril V. Briggs, "The Gathering War Clouds," *Crusader*, December 1920, in Hill, *The Crusader*, 3:942.
79. Hill, "Introduction," v–lxxiii; W. James, *Holding Aloft the Banner of Ethiopia*, 157–184; Foner, *American Socialism and Black Americans*, 309–311.
80. Briggs, "The Gathering War Clouds," 942.
81. Briggs, "Liberating Africa," 1208.
82. Cyril V. Briggs, "The Conference for White Supremacy in the Pacific," *Crusader*, November 1921, in Hill, *The Crusader*, 5:1277; Cyril V. Briggs, "Need for Another 'Arms Conference,'" *Crusader*, November 1921, in ibid., 5:1315.
83. Perry, *Hubert Harrison*, 121–123, 443; Harrison, "The White War and the Colored World," 203; Theodore W. Allen, *The Invention of the White Race*, vol. 1, *Racial Oppression and Social Control* (New York: Verso, 1994); Theodore W. Allen, *The Invention of the White Race*, vol. 2, *The Origin of Racial Oppression in Anglo-America* (New York: Verso, 1997).
84. Andrea Razaf[in]keriefo, "Civilization," *Crusader*, October 1921, in Hill, *The Crusader*, 5:1254.
85. Makalani, "For the Liberation of Black People Everywhere," 121–123; Kevin K. Gaines, *Uplifting the Race: Black Leadership, Politics, and Culture in the Twentieth Century* (Chapel Hill: University of North Carolina Press, 1996), 243–245.
86. "The Japanese Problem," *Messenger*, November 1920, 143–144; Solomon, *The Cry Was Unity*, 3–21.
87. Daryl Scott, "'Immigrant Indigestion': A. Philip Randolph: Radical and Restrictionist," Center for Immigration Studies, June 1999, http://cis.org/AfricanAmericanAttitudesImmigration-APhilipRandolph.
88. "Immigration and Japan," *Messenger*, August 1924, 247.
89. Shimazu, *Japan, Race and Equality*, 164–188.
90. Perry, *Hubert Harrison*, 171, 365, 366–395; Horne, *Race War!*, 345; W. E. B. Du Bois, "Listen, Japan and China," in *W. E. B. Du Bois on Asia: Crossing the World*

*Color Line*, ed. Bill V. Mullen and Cathryn Watson (Jackson: University Press of Mississippi, 2005), 74.

## NOTES TO CHAPTER 2

1. W. E. B. Du Bois, "Forum of Fact and Opinion," *Pittsburgh Courier*, 10 April 1937, in *Newspaper Columns by W. E. B. Du Bois*, ed. Herbert Aptheker (White Plains, NY: Kraus-Thompson, 1986), 1:186.
2. W. E. B. Du Bois, "The Clash of Colour: Indians and American Negroes," in *W. E. B. Du Bois on Asia: Crossing the World Color Line*, ed. Bill V. Mullen and Cathryn Watson (Jackson: University Press of Mississippi, 2005), 72.
3. Characterized as a "history subjected to theory" by the Black radical scholar Cedric J. Robinson, *Black Reconstruction in America* mounted a rigorous critique of the structure of modern political thought, which consistently suppressed the fact of Black humanity, and outlined the contemporary political implication of knowing Black Americans' role in making anew the nation's insurgent democratic tradition during and after the Civil War. See Cedric J. Robinson, *Black Marxism: The Making of the Black Radical Tradition* (Chapel Hill: University of North Carolina Press, 2000), 195; W. E. B. Du Bois, *Black Reconstruction: An Essay toward a History of the Part Which Black Folk Played in the Attempt to Reconstruct Democracy, 1860–1880* (New York: Atheneum, 1935).
4. Robinson, *Black Marxism*.
5. David Scott, *Conscripts of Modernity: The Tragedy of Colonial Enlightenment* (Durham: Duke University Press, 2004), 7, 22, 40.
6. Harry Harootunian, *Overcome by Modernity: History, Culture, and Community in Interwar Japan* (Princeton: Princeton University Press, 2000), 218, 384.
7. Cemil Aydin, *The Politics of Anti-Westernism in Asia: Visions of World Order in Pan-Islamic and Pan-Asian Thought* (New York: Columbia University Press, 2007), 161–189; David Scott, *Refashioning Futures: Criticism after Postcoloniality* (Princeton: Princeton University Press, 1999), 3.
8. Scott, *Refashioning Futures*, 7.
9. W. E. B. Du Bois to Alfred Harcourt, 11 February 1937, in *The Correspondence of W. E. B. Du Bois*, ed. Herbert Aptheker (Amherst: University of Massachusetts Press, 1976), 2:137.
10. Thomas C. Holt, "The Political Uses of Alienation: W. E. B. Du Bois on Politics, Race and Culture, 1903–1940," *American Quarterly* 42:2 (June 1990): 310; W. E. B. Du Bois, *Dusk of Dawn: An Essay toward an Autobiography of a Race Concept*, in *Writings* (New York: Library of America, 1986), 765.
11. Du Bois, *Dusk of Dawn*, 766, 770; Du Bois, "Postscript," *Crisis* 41 (April 1934): 117.
12. Du Bois, *Dusk of Dawn*, 761.
13. Joe William Trotter, "From a Raw Deal to a New Deal," in *To Make Our World Anew: A History of African Americans*, ed. Earl Lewis and Robin D. G. Kelley (New York: Oxford University Press, 2000), 409–444; Philip F. Rubio, *A History of Affirmative Action, 1619–2000* (Jackson: University Press of Mississippi, 2001),

92–93, 102–104; Harvard Sitkoff, *A New Deal for Blacks: The Emergence of Civil Rights as a National Issue* (New York: Oxford University Press, 1978), 45–57.

14. Du Bois, "Postscript," 115–116; Du Bois, *Dusk of Dawn*, 770–771. Also see W. E. B. Du Bois, "Color Caste in the United States," *Crisis* 40 (March 1933): 59–60, 70; Trotter, "From a Raw Deal to a New Deal," 414–416; Bruce Nelson, *Divided We Stand: American Workers and the Struggle for Black Equality* (Princeton: Princeton University Press, 2001).

15. Nikhil Pal Singh, *Black Is a Country: Race and the Unfinished Struggle for Democracy* (Cambridge: Harvard University Press, 2004), 86; David Roediger, "Carry It On: Du Bois's *Black Reconstruction* in the New Millennium," in *History against Misery* (Chicago: Kerr, 2006), 93–94.

16. Du Bois, "Postscript," 116.

17. W. E. B. Du Bois, "Postscript," *Crisis* 40 (April 1933): 94; Du Bois, *Dusk of Dawn*, 771.

18. W. E. B. Du Bois, "Pan-Africa and New Racial Philosophy," *Crisis* 40 (November 1933): 247; Sterling Stuckey, *Slave Culture: Nationalist Theory and the Foundations of Black America* (New York: Oxford University Press, 1987), 290–297.

19. Du Bois, *Black Reconstruction*, 700, 704.

20. Ralph J. Bunche, "The Programs of Organizations Devoted to the Improvement of the Status of the American Negro," *Journal of Negro Education* 8 (July 1939): 542, 546; Singh, *Black Is a Country*, 81–83.

21. Bunche, "The Programs," 548.

22. Ibid., 539.

23. Ibid., 548.

24. Ibid., 549.

25. Ibid.

26. W. E. B. Du Bois, "The Position of the Negro in the American Social Order: Where Do We Go from Here?," in *Writings by W. E. B. Du Bois in Periodicals Edited by Others*, ed. Herbert Aptheker (Millwood, NY: Kraus-Thompson, 1982), 75.

27. Ibid., 78–79.

28. Ibid., 79.

29. Du Bois, "The Union of Colour," in *W. E. B. Du Bois on Asia*, 66.

30. Herbert Marcuse, "The Foundations of Historical Materialism," in *Studies in Critical Philosophy*, trans. J. de Bres (London: New Left Books, 1972), 23, 25, 34–35; Stuckey, *Slave Culture*, 286–289.

31. Du Bois, "The Clash of Colour," 73.

32. Marcuse, "The Foundations of Historical Materialism," 35.

33. Du Bois, "The Clash of Colour," 73.

34. Du Bois, *Black Reconstruction*, 182, 577, 711–712, 714.

35. Robinson, *Black Marxism*, 186–187, 203–204; Du Bois, *Black Reconstruction*, 714.

36. Du Bois, *Black Reconstruction*, 708.

37. Ibid., 57, 708, 727; David R. Roediger, *The Wages of Whiteness: Race and the*

*Making of the American Working Class* (New York: Verso, 1991), 174; Singh, *Black Is a Country*, 92–97; David Roediger, "Emancipation: The Biggest Story in U.S. Labor History," in *History against Misery* (Chicago: Kerr, 2006), 121–122.

38. Stuckey, *Slave Culture*, 284.

39. W. E. B. Du Bois, "Forum of Fact and Opinion," *Pittsburgh Courier*, 5 June 1937, in *Newspaper Columns*, 1:207.

40. Du Bois, *Dusk of Dawn*, 679–680.

41. Du Bois, *Black Reconstruction*, 124; Robin D. G. Kelley, *Freedom Dreams: The Black Radical Imagination* (Boston: Beacon, 2002), 157–194.

42. Du Bois, *Black Reconstruction*, 123–124; Singh, *Black Is a Country*, 93.

43. Stuckey, *Slave Culture*, 253–255; Sterling Stuckey, "'Ironic Tenacity': Frederick Douglass's Seizure of the Dialectic," in *Going through the Storm: The Influence of African Art in History* (New York: Oxford University Press, 1994), 45.

44. Karl Marx, *Economic and Philosophic Manuscripts of 1844*, in *The Marx-Engels Reader*, ed. Robert C. Tucker (New York: Norton, 1978), 116.

45. Singh, *Black Is a Country*, 122.

46. Du Bois, *Black Reconstruction*, 708, 727.

47. W. E. B. Du Bois, "Forum of Fact and Opinion," *Pittsburgh Courier*, 27 March 1937. This column was curiously omitted from Herbert Aptheker's edited volume of Du Bois's newspaper columns, but now it appears in a collection of Du Bois's writings on Asia that Bill V. Mullen and Cathryn Watson edited. See W. E. B. Du Bois, "What Japan Has Done," in *W. E. B. Du Bois on Asia*, 78–82.

48. Harootunian, *Overcome by Modernity*, 359, 361, 363. I am deeply indebted to historian Paul Barclay for sharing with me this key insight on the differences in the conception of nation between Black America and Japan. It allowed me to develop a critique of Du Bois's Afro-Asian philosophy of world history.

49. *Osaka Mainichi Shimbun*, 3 December 1936.

50. Alys Eve Weinbaum, "Reproducing Racial Globality: W. E. B. Du Bois and the Sexual Politics of Black Internationalism," *Social Text* 19 (Summer 2001): 1–41; Dana Nelson, *National Manhood: Capitalist Citizenship and the Imagined Fraternity of White Men* (Durham: Duke University Press, 1998); Roderick A. Ferguson, "'W. E. B. Du Bois': Biography of a Discourse," in *Next to the Color Line: Gender, Sexuality, and W. E. B. Du Bois*, ed. Susan Gillman and Alys Eve Weinbaum (Minneapolis: University of Minnesota Press, 2007), 274, 286–287.

51. *Tokyo Nichi-Nichi Shimbun*, 3 December 1936; *Osaka Mainishi Shimbun*, 3 December 1936.

52. "Color Prejudice Recent Product, Says Dr. Du Bois," *Manchuria Daily News*, 21 November 1936. I thank historian David Tucker for sharing with me this crucial piece of evidence that he unearthed while doing research on the Japanese colonial project in Manchuria. On nonwhiteness, see David R. Roediger, *Colored White: Transcending the Racial Past* (Berkeley: University of California Press, 2002), 14–18.

53. David Vance Tucker, "Building 'Our Manchukuo': Japanese City Planning,

Architecture, and Nation-Building in Occupied Northeast China, 1931–1945"
(Ph.D. diss., University of Iowa, 1999); Prasenjit Duara, *Sovereignty and Authen-
ticity: Manchukuo and the East Asian Modern* (Lanham, MD: Rowman and
Littlefield, 2003), 48, 61–79; David Levering Lewis, *W. E. B. Du Bois: The Fight for
Equality and the American Century, 1919–1963* (New York: Holt, 2000), 408–412.

54. Harootunian, *Overcome by Modernity*; Duara, *Sovereignty and Authenticity*.

55. Eri Hotta, *Pan-Asianism and Japan's War, 1931–1945* (New York: Palgrave Macmillan, 2007), 123–125, 147.

56. Duara, *Sovereignty and Authenticity*, 62–63; Hotta, *Pan-Asianism and Japan's War*,
124.

57. "Color Prejudice Recent Product."

58. David R. Roediger, "A Reply to Eric Kaufmann," *Ethnicities* 6:2 (2006): 258.

59. "Color Prejudice Recent Product."

60. Ibid.

61. Roediger, "A Reply to Eric Kaufmann," 259; Cheryl I. Harris, "Whiteness as
Property," *Harvard Law Review* 106 (June 1993): 1707–1791; David R. Roediger,
*How Race Survived U.S. History: From Settlement and Slavery to the Obama Phe-
nomenon* (New York: Verso, 2008).

62. David R. Roediger, "Du Bois, Race, and Italian Americans," in *Are Italians White?
How Race Is Made in America*, ed. Jennifer Guglielmo and Salvatore Salerno
(New York: Routledge, 2003), 262; David R. Roediger, *Working toward White-
ness: How America's Immigrants Became White* (New York: Basic Books, 2005), 94.
Amoja Three Rivers said, "White people have not always been 'white,' nor will
they always be 'white.' It is a political alliance. Things will change." Quoted in
David R. Roediger, *The Wages of Whiteness: Race and the Making of the American
Working Class*, rev. ed. (New York: Verso, 1999), 186.

63. "Color Prejudice Recent Product," 8; Roediger, "A Reply to Eric Kaufmann," 259.

64. Roediger, "Du Bois, Race, and Italian Americans," 259–263; Roediger, *Working
toward Whiteness*, 93–110.

65. Roediger, "A Reply to Eric Kaufmann," 259.

66. Alys Eve Weinbaum, "Interracial Romance and Black Internationalism," in Gillman and Weinbaum, *Next to the Color Line*, 100–101, 116.

67. Alvin D. Cox, "The Pacific War," in *The Cambridge History of Japan: The Twentieth
Century*, vol. 6, ed. Peter Duus (New York: Cambridge University Press, 1999),
323–324; Lewis, *W. E. B. Du Bois: The Fight*, 410–411.

68. W. E. B. Du Bois, "As the Crow Flies," *Amsterdam News*, 30 March 1940, in *Newspaper Columns*, 1:291–292.

69. Wahneema Lubiano, "Mapping the Interstices between Afro-American Cultural
Discourse and Cultural Studies: A Prolegomenon," *Callaloo* 19:1 (Winter 1996):
72; Du Bois, "Forum of Fact and Opinion," *Pittsburgh Courier*, 13 February 1937,
in *Newspaper Columns*, 1:166–167.

70. Scott, *Conscripts of Modernity*, 71; Paul Gilroy, *The Black Atlantic: Modernity and
Double Consciousness* (Cambridge: Harvard University Press, 1993), 35.

71. Du Bois, "Forum of Fact and Opinion," 13 February 1937, 1:167.

72. Ibid., 1:166.

73. Ferguson, "W. E. B. Du Bois," 277; W. E. B. Du Bois, "The Conservation of Races," in *W. E. B. Du Bois: A Reader*, ed. David Levering Lewis (New York: Holt, 1995), 21, 23, 24–26; Stuckey, *Slave Culture*, 264; Du Bois, *The Souls of Black Folk*, 365. See Anthony Appiah, "The Uncompleted Argument," in *W. E. B. Du Bois on Race and Culture*, ed. Bernard W. Bell, Emily R. Grosholz, and James B. Stewart (New York: Routledge, 1996); Lucius Outlaw, " 'Conserve' Races? In Defense of W. E. B. Du Bois," in ibid.; and Robert Gooding-Williams, "Outlaw, Appiah, and Du Bois's 'The Conservation of Races,' " in ibid.

74. Du Bois, "Forum of Fact and Opinion," 13 February 1937, 1:167.

75. Weinbaum, "Reproducing Racial Globality," 19.

76. Du Bois, *The Souls of Black Folk*, 539, also quoted in Stuckey, *Slave Culture*, 248; Weinbaum, "Reproducing Racial Globality," 25.

77. W. E. B. Du Bois to Alfred Harcourt, 11 February 1937, in *The Correspondence of W. E. B. Du Bois*, 2:137–138.

78. Ibid.

79. Ibid.; Kevin K. Gaines, *Uplifting the Race: Black Leadership, Politics, and Culture in the Twentieth Century* (Chapel Hill: University of North Carolina Press, 1996), 12–13.

80. Weinbaum, "Reproducing Racial Globality," 19.

81. Ferguson, "W. E. B. Du Bois," 278.

82. W. E. B. Du Bois, "Forum of Fact and Opinion," *Pittsburgh Courier*, 27 February 1937, in *Newspaper Columns*, 1:174.

83. Ibid.

84. Ibid.

85. W. E. B. Du Bois, "Forum of Fact and Opinion," *Pittsburgh Courier*, 25 September 1937, in *Newspaper Columns*, 1:241. Also see W. E. B. Du Bois, "Forum of Fact and Opinion," *Pittsburgh Courier*, 4 November 1939, in *Newspaper Columns*, 1:267.

86. W. E. B. Du Bois, "Forum of Fact and Opinion," *Pittsburgh Courier*, 23 October 1937, in *Newspaper Columns*, 1:245.

87. Horne, *Race War!*, 111.

88. W. E. B. Du Bois, "As the Crow Flies," *Amsterdam News*, 11 October 1941, in *Newspaper Columns*, 1:388.

89. Henry L. Stimson to W. E. B. Du Bois, 24 January 1940, in *The Correspondence of W. E. B. Du Bois*, 2:205.

90. W. E. B. Du Bois, "As the Crow Flies," *Amsterdam News*, 24 February 1940, in *Newspaper Columns*, 1:287.

91. W. E. B. Du Bois, "Forum of Fact and Opinion," 23 October 1937, 1:245.

92. Toni Morrison, "Home," in *The House That Race Built: Black Americans, U.S. Terrain*, ed. and introd. Wahneema Lubiano (New York: Pantheon Books, 1997), 9.

93. Scott, *Conscripts of Modernity*, 8–9.

94. W. E. B. Du Bois, "The Winds of Time," *Chicago Defender*, 25 August 1945, in *Newspaper Columns*, 2:650; Singh, *Black Is a Country*, 129.

NOTES TO CHAPTER 3

1. *Kokujin Kenkyu* 22 (June 1964): 21; Furukawa Hiromi and Furukawa Tetsushi, *Nihonjin to Afurikakei Amerikajin: Nichibeikankeishi niokeru sono Shoso* (Tokyo: Akashi Shoten, 2004), 132–133; Nukina Yoshitaka, "1808-nen to 1960-nen: Kindaika to Hishisoka no dento," *Kokujin Kenkyu no Kai: Kaiho* 18 (1960): 3.

2. Sterling Stuckey, *Slave Culture: Nationalist Theory and the Foundations of Black America* (New York: Oxford University Press, 1987), 265; on the notion of Black worldliness, see Nikhil Pal Singh, *Black Is a Country: Race and the Unfinished Struggle for Democracy* (Cambridge: Harvard University Press, 2004).

3. Shinoda Toru, "'Kigyobetsu Kumiai wo Chushin to shita Minshu Kumiai' to wa, Part II," *Ohara Shakai Mondai Kenkyujo Zatshi* 565 (December 2005): 16–25; Nukina Yoshitaka to Robert F. Williams, 7 May 1964, Box 1, Robert F. Williams Papers, Bentley Historical Library, University of Michigan (hereafter cited as RFWP).

4. Nukina Yoshitaka, "Kokujin Kenkyu no koto," *Kobe Shimbun*, 23 March 1966; Nukina Yoshitaka, "'Kokujin kenkyu no kai' no koto," *Gendai to Shiso* 25 (September 1976): 102–108; *Kokujin Kenkyu* 22 (June 1964): 21.

5. Furukawa Hiromi, "Soritsu yonjushunen ni mukete: Kaigan to kadai," *Kokujin Kenkyu* 63 (1993): 1–2.

6. *Kokujin Kenkyu* 1 (October 1956); Konishi Tomoshichi, "Kokujin eigo no kenkyu he," *Kokujin Kenkyu* 54 (December 1984): 5; Nukina Yoshitaka, "Abolitionist wo megute (1)," *Kobe Gaidai Ronso* 1 (December 1949): 1–15; Nukina Yoshitaka, "Abolitionist wo megute (2)," *Kobe Gaidai Ronso* 2 (March 1951): 31–38.

7. *Kokujin Kenkyu* 1 (October 1956); Mark Solomon, *The Cry Was Unity: Communists and African Americans, 1917–1936* (Jackson: University Press of Mississippi, 1998), 68–91.

8. *Kokujin Kenkyu* 4 (August 1958); *Kokujin Kenkyu* 10 (December 1959); *Kokujin Kenkyu* 16 (September 1961); *Kokujin Kenkyu* 20 (December 1963); *Kokujin Kenkyu* 29 (March 1966); William L. Patterson, "'Demagogic' Democracy and Racist Practices (1)," *Kokujin Kenkyu* 6 (December 1958): 4–9; William L. Patterson, "'Demagogic' Democracy and Racist Practices (2)," *Kokujin Kenkyu* 7 (February 1959): 11–16; Gerald Horne, *Communist Front? The Civil Rights Congress, 1946–1956* (Rutherford, NJ: Fairleigh Dickinson University Press, 1988), 29–51, 53–54, 155–181; Gerald Horne, *Black Liberation/Red Scare: Ben Davis and the Communist Party* (Newark: University of Delaware Press, 1994), 13; Penny M. Von Eschen, *Race against Empire: Black Americans and Anticolonialism, 1937–1957* (Ithaca: Cornell University Press, 1997).

9. Robin D. G. Kelley, *Freedom Dreams: The Black Radical Imagination* (Boston: Beacon, 2002), 57–59; Von Eschen, *Race against Empire*.

10. Kelley, *Freedom Dreams*, 36–59.

11. Nukina, "'Kokujin kenkyu no kai' no koto."
12. John W. Dower, *Embracing Defeat: Japan in the Wake of World War II* (New York: Norton, 1999), 54.
13. *Kokujin Kenkyu* 56 (1986): 1; Dower, *Embracing Defeat*, 33.
14. Dower, *Embracing Defeat*, 33–64.
15. Ibid., 235.
16. Ibid., 82–84, 346–373.
17. Ibid., 233–244, 254–273.
18. Shiso no Kagaku Kenkyu Kai, ed., *Kyodo Kenkyu Shudan: Sakuru no Sengo Shiso-shi* (Tokyo: Heibonsha, 1976).
19. George M. Beckmann and Okubo Genji, *The Japanese Communist Party, 1922–1945* (Stanford: Stanford University Press, 1969), 213–214; Osawa Shinichiro, "Sakuru no Sengo-shi," in Shiso no Kagaku Kenkyu Kai, *Kyodo Kenkyu Shudan*, 72–74; Michael Denning, *The Cultural Front: The Laboring of American Culture in the Twentieth Century* (New York: Verso, 1996), 63–64; Oguma Eiji, *"Minsyu" to "Aikoku": Sengo Nihon no Nationalism to Kokyosei* (Tokyo: Shinyosha, 2002), 211.
20. *Kokujin Kenkyu* 56 (1986): 1; Oshima Yoshio and Miyamoto Masao, *Hantaisei Esperanto Undo-shi* (Tokyo: Sanseido, 1974), 2–9; 135–137; 157–179.
21. Oshima and Miyamoto, *Hantaisei Esperanto Undo-shi*, 2–9, 135–137, 157–179.
22. Ibid., 24–27.
23. Ibid., 137–146.
24. Nukina, "'Kokujin kenkyu no kai' no koto"; Oshima and Miyamoto, *Hantaisei Esperanto Undo-shi*, 299–307.
25. Nukina, "'Kokujin kenkyu no kai' no koto."
26. Dower, *Embracing Defeat*, 254–273; Christopher Gerteis, "Subjectivity Lost: Labor and the Cold War in Occupied Japan," in *Labor's Cold War: Labor Politics in a Global Context*, ed. Shelton Stromquist (Urbana: University of Illinois Press, 2008), 258–290.
27. Komashaku Kimi, "Kyoto Jinbun Gakuen," in Shiso no Kagaku Kenkyu Kai, *Kyodo Kenkyu Shudan*, 105–111; Oshima and Miyamoto, *Hantaisei Esperanto Undo-shi*, 306–307.
28. Oshima and Miyamoto, *Hantaisei Esperanto Undo-shi*, 336–352; Dower, *Embracing Defeat*, 195–200.
29. Dower, *Embracing Defeat*, 199.
30. Ibid., 488, 501–503.
31. Mari Yamamoto, *Grassroots Pacifism in Post-war Japan: The Rebirth of a Nation* (London: RoutledgeCurzon, 2004), 52.
32. Shinoda Toru, "'Kigyobetsu Kumiai wo Chushin to shita Minshu Kumiai' to wa, Part I," *Ohara Shakai Mondai Kenkyujo Zatshi* 564 (November 2005): 1–16; Shinoda, "'Kigyobetsu Kumiai wo Chushin to shita Minshu Kumiai' to wa, Part II"; Yamamoto, *Grassroots Pacifism in Post-war Japan*, 60–76; Denning, *The Cultural Front*, 64.
33. Shinoda, "'Kigyobetsu Kumiai wo Chushin to shita Minshu Kumiai' to wa, Part

II," 13–25; Miwa Yasushi, "1950-nendai no sakuru undo to rodosha ishiki," in *Sengo Shakai Undo-shi Ron*, ed. Hirokawa Tadahide and Yamada Tako (Tokyo: Otsuki Shoten, 2006); Narita Ryuichi, "1950-nendai: 'Sakuru undo' no jidai heno danpen," *Bungaku* 5:6 (2004): 114–115; Kelley, *Freedom Dreams*, 191–194.

34. Nukina Yoshitaka, "Concord no Thoreau, Part I," *Albion* 7:4 (December 1940): 299–313; Nukina Yoshitaka, "Concord no Thoreau, Part II," *Albion* 7:5 (July 1941): 391–400; Richard Francis, *Transcendental Utopias: Individual and Community at Brook Farm, Fruitlands, and Walden* (Ithaca: Cornell University Press, 1997).

35. Furukawa Hiromi, "Watashino uchi naru amerika" (1986), in *Buratku he no tabiji* (Osaka: Seseragi Shuppan, 1995), 1:93–101; Furukawa Hiromi, "Wagashi, Nukina sensei" (1986), in ibid., 1:154–159; *Kokujin Kenkyu* 1 (October 1956).

36. Furukawa Hiromi, "How I Came to Be a Founding Member of the Japan Black Studies Association (JBSA)," speech delivered at the 54th Annual Meeting of the Japan Black Studies Association, Hiroshima Jogakuin University, Japan, 28 June 2008 (transcript in author's possession); David W. Noble, *Death of a Nation: American Culture and the End of Exceptionalism* (Minneapolis: University of Minnesota Press, 2002), xxix–xxxii.

37. Noble, *Death of a Nation*, xxiii–xlvi; 79–128; Furukawa, "Wagashi, Nukina sensei"; Nukina, " 'Kokujin kenkyu no kai' no koto."

38. Brent Hayes Edwards, *The Practice of Diaspora: Literature, Translation, and the Rise of Black Internationalism* (Cambridge: Harvard University Press, 2003), 68.

39. Furukawa Hiromi, "Langston Hughes: *The Weary Blues* ni miru Negro Folks no 'warai' to 'namida' no so ni tsuite (1)," *Kokujin Kenkyu* 10 (December 1959): 1–14; Furukawa Hiromi, "Langston Hughes: *The Weary Blues* ni miru Negro Folks no 'warai' to 'namida' no so ni tsuite (2)," *Kokujin Kenkyu* 11 (February 1960): 1–12; Furukawa Hiromi, "Langston Hughes: *The Weary Blues* ni miru Negro Folks no 'warai' to 'namida' no so ni tsuite (3)," *Kokujin Kenkyu* 12 (May 1960): 16–22; Edwards, *The Practice of Diaspora*, 68.

40. Furukawa Hiromi, "Rangston Huzu no Omoide," in *Buraku he no Tabiji* (Osaka: Seseragi Shuppan, 1996), 2:69–77; Brent Hayes Edwards, "The Literary Ellington," in *Uptown Conversation: The New Jazz Studies*, ed. Robert G. O'Meally, Brent Hayes Edwards, and Farah Jasmine Griffin (New York: Columbia University Press, 2004), 327.

41. Walter Benjamin, "The Task of the Translator: An Introduction to the Translation of Baudelaire's *Tableaux Parisiens*," in *Illuminations*, ed. and introd. Hannah Arendt, trans. Harry Zohn (New York: Schocken Books, 1968), 72, 76, 79; also quoted in Edwards, *The Practice of Diaspora*, 282.

42. Furukawa, "Langston Hughes: *The Weary Blues* ni miru Negro Folks no 'warai' to 'namida' no so ni tsuite (1)," 10–11; Furukawa, "Langston Hughes: *The Weary Blues* ni miru Negro Folks no 'warai' to 'namida' no so ni tsuite (2)," 2; Yusef Komunyakaa, "Langston Hughes + Poetry = The Blues," *Callaloo* 25:4 (2002): 1140. On the significance of "detour" in theorizing the African diaspora, see Edwards, *The Practice of Diaspora*, 22–25.

43. Furukawa, "Langston Hughes: *The Weary Blues* ni miru Negro Folks no 'warai' to 'namida' no so ni tsuite (1)," 7; Furukawa, "Rangston Huzu no Omoide," in *Buraku he no Tabiji*, 2:69; Furukawa Hiromi, "Atogaki," in *Buraku he no Tabiji*, 3:245; Edwards, *The Practice of Diaspora*, 68.

44. Benjamin, "The Task of the Translator," 80.

45. Kokujin Kenkyu no Kai, ed., *Amerika Kokujin Kaiho Undo: AtarashiNiguro Gunzo* (Tokyo: Miraisha, 1966).

46. Edwards, *The Practice of Diaspora*, 115–118; Kevin K. Gaines, *American Africans in Ghana: Black Expatriates and the Civil Rights Era* (Chapel Hill: University of North Carolina Press, 2006). On Nakajima Yoriko, see Nakajima Yoriko to Robert F. Williams, 19 December 1961, RFWP; Nakajima Yoriko, "King Bokushi to Malcolm X ni tsuite," *Kokujin Kenkyu* 63 (1993): 18–20. On the dimension of the contributions of Black women radicals in *Freedomways*, see Dayo F. Gore, *Radicalism at the Crossroads: African American Women Activists in the Cold War* (New York: NYU Press, 2011), 130–160.

47. Kokujin Kenkyu no Kai, *Amerika Kokujin Kaiho Undo*, 274–314.

48. Nukina Yoshitaka, "Contemporary Negro-Americans: In Place of a 'Preface,'" in ibid., 7–17.

49. Edwards, *The Practice of Diaspora*, 45; Von Eschen, *Race against Empire*.

50. Edwards, *The Practice of Diaspora*, 14, 118.

51. Nakajima Yoriko to Robert F. William, 26 February 1966, RFWP; emphasis is original.

52. Eric Porter, *What Is This Thing Called Jazz? African American Musicians as Artists, Critics, and Activists* (Berkeley: University of California Press, 2002), 167–169; Scott Saul, *Freedom Is, Freedom Ain't: Jazz and the Making of the Sixties* (Cambridge: Harvard University Press, 2003), 90–96; Ingrid Monson, *Freedom Sounds: Civil Rights Call Out to Jazz and Africa* (New York: Oxford University Press, 2007), 171–181.

53. Ella Baker, "We Need Group-Centered Leadership," in *Let Nobody Turn Us Around: Voices of Resistance, Reform, and Renewal*, ed. Manning Marable and Leith Mullings (Lanham, MD: Rowman and Littlefield, 2000), 399; Peniel E. Joseph, *Waiting 'Til the Midnight Hour: A Narrative History of Black Power in America* (New York: Holt, 2006), 8, 39–44; Monson, *Freedom Sounds*, 174–175.

54. Paul Gilroy, *The Black Atlantic: Modernity and Double Consciousness* (Cambridge: Harvard University Press, 1993), 37, 200; Saul, *Freedom Is, Freedom Ain't*, 93–94; Porter, *What Is This Thing Called Jazz?*, 173.

55. Gaines, *American Africans*, 145; Joseph, *Waiting 'Til the Midnight Hour*, 28–34; Julian Mayfield, "Challenge to Negro Leadership," in *The Nonconformers*, ed. David Evanier and Stanley Silverzweig (New York: Ballantine Books, 1961), 5–20; Robert F. Williams, *Negroes with Guns*, ed. Marc Schleifer, introd. John Henrik Clarke (Chicago: Third World, 1973); Timothy B. Tyson, *Radio Free Dixie: Robert F. Williams and the Roots of Black Power* (Chapel Hill: University of North Carolina Press, 1999), 137–165, 220–243.

56. Julian Mayfield, "The Cuban Challenge," *Freedomways* 1:2 (1961): 188. See Gaines, *American Africans*, 145–146.

57. Gilroy, *The Black Atlantic*, 37; John Henrik Clarke, "The New Afro-American Nationalism," *Freedomways* 1:3 (Fall 1961): 285.

58. Gaines, *American Africans*, 137; Joseph, *Waiting 'Til the Midnight Hour*, 39–44.

59. Clarke, "The New Afro-American Nationalism," 285–295; Joseph, *Waiting 'Til the Midnight Hour*, 41; Gaines, *American Africans*, 205–206.

60. Nakajima Yoriko, "The Cuban Revolution and the American Negro of the South: An Eyewitness Account of the Case of Robert Williams and Thereafter," in Kokujin Kenkyu no Kai, *Amerika Kokujin Kaiho Undo*, 126–146; Nakajima, *Kokujin no Seijisanka to Daisanseiki America no Shupatsu*.

61. Nakajima, "The Cuban Revolution and the American Negro of the South"; Nakajima to Williams, 19 December 1961; Gaines, *American Africans*, 140.

62. Gaines, *American Africans*, 146–147, 151; *Kokujin Kenkyu* 17 (September 1962): 55–56; Nakajima, "The Cuban Revolution and the American Negro of the South," 126, 143; Nakajima, "King Bokushi to Malcolm X ni tsuite," 18–20; Nakajima to Williams, 19 December 1961; Nakajima, *Kokujin no Seijisanka to Daisanseiki America no Shupatsu*, 39–44.

63. Given that Nakajima noted in the tenth-anniversary survey of *Kokujin Kenkyu no Kai* that E. Franklin Frazier's *Black Bourgeoisie* (1957), along with Robert F. Williams's *Negroes with Guns* (1962), was the text that decisively sharpened her political outlook, it would not be unfounded to infer that her processes of translating Mayfield's article and composing her commentary were aided by Frazier's sharp critique of Black middle-class leadership. See *Kokujin Kenkyu* 22 (June 1964): 20.

64. Mayfield, "Challenge to Negro Leadership," 19–20.

65. Ibid., 9, 11.

66. Ibid., 11–12; Nakajima, "The Cuban Revolution and the American Negro of the South," 145–146; Gaines, *American Africans*, 138–140; Mary Dudziak, *Cold War Civil Rights: Race and the Image of American Democracy* (Princeton: Princeton University Press, 2000).

67. Nakajima Yoriko, "'Negro' to 'Seiji,'" *Kokujin Kenkyu* 22 (June 1964): 41–44; Nakajima, "Kingu bokushi to Malcolm X nit suite," 18–20; Nakajima, *Kokujin no Seijisanka to Daisanseiki America no Shupatsu*, 48–50.

68. Nakajima, "'Neguro' to 'Seiji,'" 42–44; Nakajima, "Kingu bokushi to Malcolm X nit suite"; Clyde Woods, *Development Arrested: The Blues and Plantation Power in the Mississippi Delta* (New York: Verso, 1998), 25–39.

69. Mayfield, "Challenge to Negro Leadership," 20.

70. Nakajima Yoriko to Robert and Mabel Williams, 15 June 1964, RFWP.

71. Gaines, *American Africans*, 140–141; *Kokujin Kenkyu* 17 (September 1962): 55–56; Nakajima, "The Cuban Revolution and the American Neguro of the South," 143; Nakajima, "King Bokushi to Malcolm X ni tsuite," 18–20.

72. Edwards, *The Practice of Diaspora*, 242–245; Joseph, *Waiting 'Til the Midnight*

*Hour*, 49; Kelley, *Freedom Dreams*, 60, 84. On the notion of a "theme song," see Joseph, *Waiting 'Til the Midnight Hour*, 49. William Worthy, a radical Black foreign correspondent for the *Baltimore-Washington Afro-American*, wrote, "Robert F. Williams is going to be known to the listening world by a theme song. When he begins his series of broadcasts over Radio Havana, the programs will open and close with a very moving song, 'Look At My Chains.' It describes the pains and emotions of people still in bondage" (October 21, 1961, 6, quoted in ibid.).

73. Nakajima, *Kokujin no Seijisanka to Daisanseiki America no Shupatsu*, 319–367; Tyson, *Radio Free Dixie*, 287–308.

74. Nakajima, "'Negro' to 'Seiji,'" 41–44.

75. *Kokujin Kenkyu* 20 (December 1963): 39; *Kokujin Kenkyu* 21 (March 1964): 17; John Oliver Killens, *And Then We Heard the Thunder* (New York: Knopf, 1963), 79; Lorraine Hansberry, *A Raisin in the Sun: A Drama in Three Acts* (New York: Random House, 1959), 98.

76. Furukawa Hiromi, *Buratku he no tabiji*, vol. 2 (Osaka: Seseragi Shutpan, 1995); Furukawa Hiromi, *Buratku he no tabiji*, vol. 3 (Osaka: Seseragi Shuppan, 1997). Nakajima, "Kingu bokushi to Malcolm X nit suite," 18.

NOTES TO CHAPTER 4

1. Robert D. Eldridge, *The Origins of the Bilateral Okinawa Problem: Okinawa in Postwar U.S.-Japan Relations, 1945–1952* (New York: Garland, 2001); Chalmers Johnson, ed., *Okinawa: Cold War Island* (Cardiff, UK: Japan Policy Research Institute, 1999).

2. See Thomas M. Klein, "The Ryukyu on the Eve of Reversion," *Pacific Affairs* 45 (Spring 1972): 12; John K. Emmerson, "Troubles Ahead for Okinawa," *New York Times*, 9 March 1972.

3. Miyume Tanji, "The Enduring Myth of an Okinawan Struggle: The History and Trajectory of a Diverse Community of Protest" (Ph.D. diss., Murdoch University, 2003), 137–178; Gabe Masao, "Rokujyunendai Fukkikyo Undo no Tenkai," in *Sengo Okinawa no Seiji to Ho, 1945–72*, ed. Seigen Miyazato (Tokyo: Tokyo Daigaku Shupan Kai, 1975), 153–211; Oguma Eiji, <Nihonjin> *no Kyokai: Okinawa, Ainu, Taiwan, Chosen, Shokuminchi Shihai kara Fukki Undo made* (Tokyo: Shinyo-sha, 1998), 556–596.

4. Chalmers Johnson, *Blowback: The Costs and Consequences of American Empire* (New York: Metropolitan Books, 2000), 38–40; Oguma, <Nihonjin> *no Kyokai*, 592–596, 601–609.

5. Koji Taira, "Changing Attitudes on Okinawan Reversion," *New York Times*, 22 April 1972.

6. Tanji, "The Enduring Myth of an Okinawan Struggle," 164; Oguma, <Nihonjin> *no Kyokai*, 609–615.

7. Oguma, <Nihonjin> *no Kyokai*, 615–626; "Sengo Yonjunen no Sokatsu," *Shin Okinawa Bungaku* 66 (Winter 1985): 16–25; Miyume, "The Enduring Myth of an Okinawan Struggle," 164–167; Miyume Tanji, *Myth, Protest and Struggle in*

*Okinawa* (London: RoutledgeCurzon, 2006), 97. Also see Arakawa Akira, *Hankokka no kyoku* (Tokyo: Shakai Hyoron Sha, 1996); Arakawa Akira, *Okinawa: Togo to Hangyaku* (Tokyo: Chikuma Shobo, 2000); Michael Molasky, *The American Occupation of Japan and Okinawa* (London: Routledge, 1999), 93–102; Michael Molasky, "Arakawa Akira: The Thought and Poetry of an Iconoclast," in *Japan and Okinawa: Structure and Subjectivity*, ed. Glenn D. Hook and Richard Siddle (London: RoutledgeCurzon, 2003), 225–239.

8. In the wake of the Nixon-Sato joint communiqué, critic Nakano Yoshio characterized the emergence of opposition to reversion as the new beginning of the Okinawan struggle. See Nakano Yoshio, "Atarashi Tatakai no Hajimari," *Sekai* (December 1969): 48–50; Nikhil Pal Singh, *Black Is a Country: Race and the Unfinished Struggle for Democracy* (Cambridge: Harvard University Press, 2004), 43, 89; Angela Davis, "Reflections on Race, Class, and Gender in the USA," in *The Politics of Culture in the Shadow of Capital*, ed. Lisa Lowe and David Lloyd (Durham: Duke University Press, 1997), 322; Robin D. G. Kelley, *Freedom Dreams: The Black Radical Imagination* (Boston: Beacon, 2002), 10; "From the Editors," *Race/Ethnicity: Multidisciplinary Global Perspectives* 1:2 (Spring 2008): v–viii; Laura Pulido, *Black, Brown, Yellow, and Left: Radical Activism in Los Angeles* (Berkeley: University of California Press, 2006).

9. Davis, "Reflections on Race, Class, and Gender in the USA," 322; Kelley, *Freedom Dreams*, 9–10; "From the Editors"; Pulido, *Black, Brown, Yellow, and Left*; Martin Luther King Jr., *Where Do We Go from Here: Chaos or Community?* (Boston: Beacon, 2010), 47, 130.

10. Johnson, *Blowback*, 36–37; Martin Fackler, "Japan Relents on U.S. Base on Okinawa," *New York Times*, 23 March 2010; Martin Fackler and Hiroko Tabuchi, "Japanese Leader Backtracks on Revising Base Agreement," *New York Times*, 4 May 2010; Hiroko Tabuchi and Martin Fackler, "U.S. and Japan Reach Okinawa Deal," *New York Times*, 27 May 2010; Martin Fackler, "Japan's Premier Will Quit as Approval Plummets," *New York Times*, 1 June 2010. In the end, however, this 2010 compromise went nowhere; the relocation of the U.S. Marine Corps Air Station in Futenma reached a stalemate again. In April 2012, the United States and Japan reached another compromise when the United States agreed to transfer approximately five thousand U.S. Marines stationed in Okinawa to Guam. Still the issue of relocating the Futenma Air Station out of Okinawa remains unresolved. See Thom Shankner, "U.S. Agrees to Reduce Size of Force on Okinawa," *New York Times*, 26 April 2012.

11. Kelley, *Freedom Dreams*, 7–10.

12. Ibid., 1–12; Adrienne Rich, "Social Practice," *XCP: Cross Cultural Poetics* 15–16 (2005): 262.

13. Kelley, *Freedom Dreams*, 9.

14. "Black GI Court-Martialled for Refusing to Stand for Playing of National Anthem," 2 June 1973, Carton 5, Folder 53, Pacific Counseling Service and Military Law Office Records, BANC MSS 86/89c, Bancroft Library, University

of California, Berkeley (hereafter cited as PCSMLOR); Kelley, *Freedom Dreams*, 9–10.

15. "Black GI Court-Martialled"; "Statement by Spec 4 Quinton T. Allen, at His Court-Martial for Refusing to Stand for the Playing of the National Anthem," Carton 5, Folder 53, PCSMLOR.

16. "Black GI Court-Martialled."

17. Robin D. G. Kelley, *Yo' Mama's DisFunktional! Fighting the Culture Wars in Urban America* (Boston: Beacon, 1997), 15–42; Steve Estes, *I Am a Man! Race, Manhood, and the Civil Rights Movement* (Chapel Hill: University of North Carolina, 2004), 107–130.

18. Estes, *I Am a Man!*, 116–117, 126–127, 173; Ward Churchill, " 'To Disrupt, Discredit and Destroy': The FBI's Secret War against the Black Panther Party," in *Liberation, Imagination, and the Black Panther Party*, ed. Kathleen Cleaver and George Katsiaficas (New York: Routledge, 2001), 78–117; Stokely Carmichael, "What We Want," in *Let Nobody Turn Us Around: Voices of Resistance, Reform, and Renewal*, ed. Manning Marable and Leith Mullings (Lanham, MD: Rowman and Littlefield, 2000), 448.

19. Kelley, *Yo' Mama's DisFunktional!*, 25, 41–42; Rich, "Social Practice"; "Statement by Spec 4 Quinton T. Allen"; King, *Where Do We Go from Here*, 190.

20. Kelley, *Yo' Mama's DisFunktional!*, 41; Rich, "Social Practice"; "Black GI Court-Martialled"; "Statement by Spec 4 Quinton T. Allen."

21. George Katsiaficas, *The Imagination of the New Left: A Global Analysis of 1968* (Boston: South End, 1987), 8.

22. The phrase "winged seeds" is taken from the title of a prose poem by Li-Young Lee. Li-Young Lee, *The Winged Seed: A Remembrance* (New York: Simon and Schuster, 1995).

23. Grace Lee Boggs, "The Beloved Community of Martin Luther King," *Yes! A Journal of Positive Futures* 29 (Spring 2004): http://www.yesmagazine.org/issues/a-conspiracy-of-hope/the-beloved-community-of-martin-luther-king; Martin Luther King Jr., "A Time to Break Silence," *Freedomways* 7 (Spring 1967): 114; Grace Lee Boggs, with Scott Kurashige, *The Next American Revolution: Sustainable Activism for the Twenty-First Century* (Berkeley: University of California Press, 2011); Kelley, *Freedom Dreams*, 9–10.

24. Kelley, *Freedom Dreams*, 191.

25. "Bill Schaap's Response to the Iwakuni Response to the Okinawa Letter," 11 November 1972, Carton 5, Folder 36, PCSMLOR.

26. "Report on Legal Work, September 10 (Our Arrival) to Present," 13 October 1972, Carton 5, Folder 36, PCSMLOR.

27. "Another Resignation," 9 November 1972, Carton 5, Folder 53, PCSMLOR.

28. "From a Black Marine in the Brig," Carton 5, Folder 53, PCSMLOR.

29. Pierre Mabille, "The Marvelous—Basis of a Free Society," *Race Traitor* 9 (Summer 1998): 40; David Cortright, *Soldiers in Revolt* (New York: Anchor, 1975); Richard R. Moser, *The New Winter Soldiers: GI and Veteran Dissent during the*

*Vietnam Era* (New Brunswick: Rutgers University Press, 1996); Christian G. Appy, *Working-Class War: American Combat Soldiers and Vietnam* (Chapel Hill: University of North Carolina Press, 1993).

30. Wallace Terry II, "Bringing the War Home," *Black Scholar* 2 (November 1970): 6–18; Gerald Gill, "Black Soldiers' Perspectives on the War," in *The Vietnam Reader*, ed. Walter Capps (New York: Routledge, 1991), 173–185; James Westheider, *Fighting on Two Fronts: African Americans and the Vietnam War* (New York: NYU Press, 1997); Herman Graham III, *The Brothers' Vietnam War: Black Power, Manhood, and the Military Experience* (Gainesville: University Press of Florida, 2003); Herbert Shapiro, "The Vietnam War and the American Civil Rights Movement," *Journal of Ethnic Studies* 16 (Winter 1989): 117–141.

31. Terry, "Bringing the War Home," 7; King, "A Time to Break Silence," 114.

32. King, "A Time to Break Silence," 105; Terry, "Bringing the War Home," 8; James Baldwin, "The War Crimes Tribunal," *Freedomways* 7 (Winter 1967): 243–244.

33. George Lipsitz, *The Possessive Investment in Whiteness: How White People Profit from Identity Politics* (Philadelphia: Temple University Press, 1998), 189–190; Daniel Widener, "Seoul City Sue and the Bugout Blues: Black American Narratives of the Forgotten War," in *Afro Asia: Revolutionary Political and Cultural Connections between African Americans and Asian Americans*, ed. Fred Ho and Bill V. Mullen (Durham: Duke University Press, 2008), 62–64.

34. Staughton Lynd, "The First New Left . . . and the Third," in *Living inside Our Hope: A Steadfast Radical's Thoughts on Rebuilding the Movement* (Ithaca, NY: ILR, 1997), 88.

35. Thomas R. H. Havens, *Fire across the Sea: The Vietnam War and Japan, 1965–1975* (Princeton: Princeton University Press, 1987), 57–67; Ivan Hall, "Hotel Room Is Jail for Bucks Pacifist in Japan," *Philadelphia Bulletin*, 19 November 1970, Box 17, SANE—Greater Philadelphia Council Records, Urban Archives, Manuscript Collections, Temple University.

36. Havens, *Fire across the Sea*, 57–67.

37. Iida Momo, "Report on Anti-war, Peace Movement in Japan (Gist)," in *Report on Japan-U.S. Two Nation Conference for Peace in Vietnam*, October 1966, 23, Box 1, A Quaker Action Group Records, Swarthmore College Peace Collection (hereafter cited as Quaker/SCPC); Lynne Shivers on Beheiren, Box 1, Quaker/SCPC; Kuninaga Hiroko, "'Beheiren' Undo: Ninshiki to Kankei no Tenkai" (senior paper, Tsukuba University, 1996), Yoshikawa Yuichi Papers, Center for the Study of Cooperative Human Relations, Saitama University (hereafter cited as YYP); Sekiya Shigeru and Sakamoto Yoshie, eds., *Tonarini Dasohei ga ita Jidai: JATEC, Aru Shimin Undo no Kiroku* (Tokyo: Shiso no Kagakusha, 1998); Tsurumi Yoshiyuki, "Beheiren: A New Force on the Left," *AMPO: A Report from the Japanese New Left* 1 (1969): 5, 9.

38. Havens, *Fire across the Sea*, 62.

39. Oda Makoto, "Making of Peace," in *Report on Japan-U.S. Two Nation Conference for Peace in Vietnam*, 15; "Actions for the Peace in Vietnam," in ibid., 10; Oda

Makoto, *"Beheiren" Kaikoroku de nai Kaiko* (Tokyo: Daisan Shokan, 1995), 44–48, 55–72, 73–87, 239–256.

40. George Lipsitz, *American Studies in a Moment of Danger* (Minneapolis: University of Minnesota Press, 2001), 171.

41. Oda, "Making of Peace," 17; Hall, "Hotel Room Is Jail for Bucks Pacifist in Japan"; Havens, *Fire across the Sea*, 57–63, 199–204; Oda Makoto, "Washington kara no Houkoku," in *Shiryo: Beheiren Undo*, ed. Beheiren, vol. 2 (Tokyo: Kawade Shobo Shinsha, 1974), 218–222; "Conference: U.S. Imperialism and the Pacific Rim," Box 23, Quaker/SCPC; "U.S. Out of Okinawa and Japan, Protest Nixon-Sato Deal," Box 23, Quaker/SCPC.

42. David Cortright, *Soldiers in Revolt: The American Military Today* (New York: Anchor, 1975), 70.

43. Richard DeCamp, "The GI Movement in Asia," *Bulletin of Concerned Asian Scholars* 4 (Winter 1972): 109–118; Takahashi Takemoto, "Dai-niki ga tachiagaru-made," in Sekiya and Sakamoto, *Tonarini Dasohei ga ita Jidai*, 107–200.

44. Cortright, *Soldiers in Revolt*, 61; Honno Yoshio, "'Hoshin Tenkan' to Beigun Kaitai Undo," in Sekiya and Sakamoto, *Tonarini Dasohei ga ita Jidai*, 141–167. A small collection of PCS's primary documents, including recruiting brochures, letters, and papers, are in CDG-A, Pacific Counseling Service, Swarthmore College Peace Collection. On CCCO, see Bill Lynch, "Some Thoughts about CCCO," Box 3, CCCO/An Agency for Military and Draft Counseling, Swarthmore College Peace Collection; "Guide to Good Counseling," Box 4, CCCO/An Agency for Military and Draft Counseling, Swarthmore College Peace Collection.

45. Kenneth Cloke, *Military Counseling Manual: A Guide to Military Law and Procedures for GIs, Counselors and Lawyers*, published by the National Lawyers Guild, Los Angeles Regional Office, Subject File: Conscription, Swarthmore College Peace Collection; Honno Yoshio, "'Hoko Tenkai' to Beigun Kaitai Undo," in Sekiya and Sakamoto, *Tonarini Dasohei ga ita Jidai*, 141–160; Jan Eakes, *Senso no Kikai wo Tomero! Hansen Beihei to Nihonjin*, trans. and ed. Tsurumi Shunsuke (Tokyo: Sanichi Shobo, 1972), 58–60.

46. Alice Lynd, a draft counselor during the Vietnam War era, described that there always existed the danger of perpetuating the power relations between the counselor and the counselee. She described the imperative to avoid such a trapping of power in this way: "The counselor knows about the regulations and steps to take once the counselee has chose a particular course of action, but the counselee knows more than the counselor can ever know about the counselee: what he thinks, his family situation, and what he is prepared to do." Staughton Lynd, with Alice Lynd, "Liberation Theology for Quakers," in *Living inside Our Hope*, 53.

47. Singh, *Black Is a Country*, 185.

48. Hall, "Hotel Room Is Jail for Bucks Pacifist in Japan"; Kakega Kyoko, "Iwakuni no Ninen," in Sekiya and Sakamoto, *Tonarini Dasohei ga ita Jidai*, 168–177.

49. Hall, "Hotel Room Is Jail for Bucks Pacifist in Japan"; "And This Is Being Done," CDG-A, Pacific Counseling Service, Swarthmore College Peace Collection.

50. Prior to returning to Okinawa from mainland Japan in February 1971, Bye was placed under arrest at the Haneda airport hotel for four months. She was denied entry for violating tourist visa provisions because she worked in Japan under false pretenses (which meant that she participated in "political" activities). Beheiren groups organized a transnational "Free Barbara" campaign. In the end, she lost the case and returned to Okinawa. A small collection of "Free Barbara" campaign documents, which include letters, fact sheets, and clippings, are in Box 17, SANE—Greater Philadelphia Council Records, Urban Archives, Manuscript Collections, Temple University.

51. Takamine Tomokazu, *Shirarezaru Okinawa no Beihei* (Tokyo: Kobunken, 1984), 67–68. On the Koza rebellion, see ibid., 45–84; Wesley Iwao Ueunten, "Rising Up from a Sea of Discontent: The 1970 Koza Uprising in U.S.-Occupied Okinawa," in *Militarized Currents: Toward a Decolonized Future in Asia and the Pacific*, ed. Setsu Shigematsu and Keith L. Camacho (Minneapolis: University of Minnesota Press, 2010), 91–124; Fukugi Akira, "Koza: Gekihatsu suru Okinawa no Kokoro," *Sekai* (February 1970): 42–51; *Asahi Shimbun*, 19 July 2000; Isa Chihiro, *Enjo* (Tokyo: Bungei Shunju, 1986); "Koza Uprising," *AMPO: A Report from the Japanese New Left* 7–8 (1971): 1–5; Okinawa-shi Heiwa Bunka Shikou Ka, ed., *Beikoku ga mita Koza bodo* (Okinawa: Okinawa City Hall, 1999).

52. *Demand for Freedom* 3 (25 December 1975): 3, GI News Periodical, Swarthmore College Peace Collection (hereafter cited as GI News/SCPC).

53. Jan Eakes, *Senso no Kikai wo Tomero! Hansen Beihei to Nihonjin*, trans. and ed. Tsurumi Shunsuke (Tokyo: Sanichi Shobo, 1972), 35–40; "Jan Eakes to tomoni," published by Beheiren, 15 February 1971, YYP; "Jan Eakes to tomoni, Part II," published by Beheiren, 4 March 1971, YYP; Natalye Smith, "I Still Sing We Shall Overcome," *State Hornet*, 17 October 2007, http://www.statehornet.com/2.4409/i-still-sing-we-shall-overcome-1.562132 (accessed on June 9, 2010). On Dianne Durst Eakes, see *Fujin Minshu Shimbun*, 12 February 1971, YYP.

54. Eakes, *Senso no Kikai wo Tomero!*, 42–43; "Jan Eakes to tomoni, Part II." On race and coalition, see Stokely Carmichael and Charles V. Hamilton, *Black Power: The Politics of Liberation* (New York: Vintage Books, 1992).

55. Eakes, *Senso no Kikai wo Tomero!*, 117–119.

56. Ibid., 120–121, 166–167; Takamine, *Shirarezaru Okinawa no Beihei*, 211–214.

57. Eakes, *Senso no Kikai wo Tomero!*, 138–158; *Demand for Freedom* 1 (7 October 1970), GI News/SCPC.

58. Takamine, *Shirarezaru Okinawa no Beihei*, 214–215; Inafuku Masatoshi, "Okinawa ni okeru 'Beihei Aite Tokuingai' no Shakaigaku Teki Kosatsu" (unpublished senior thesis, Okinawa International University, 1992), 43–44.

59. Takamine, *Shirarezaru Okinawa no Beihei*, 216–218.

60. "Okinawa to Nyukan," in *Beheiren News Shuksatsu Ban, 1964–1974*, ed. Beheiren (Tokyo: Beheiren <Betonamu ni heiwa wo!> shimin rengo, 1974), 379.

61. *Demand for Freedom* 2 (16 November 1970), GI News/SCPC.

62. Rose M. Brewer, "Black Radical Theory and Practice: Gender, Race, and

Class," *Socialism and Democracy* 17:1 (2003), http://www.sdonline.org/33/ rose_m_brewer.htm (accessed 10 March 2011); Cynthia Enloe, *Maneuvers: The International Politics of Militarizing Women's Lives* (Berkeley: University of California Press, 2000), 67, 89–99; Molasky, *The American Occupation of Japan and Okinawa*, 53–56; Ji-Yeon Yuh, *Beyond the Shadow of Camptown: Korean Military Brides in America* (New York: NYU Press, 2002), 9–41; Saundra Pollock Sturdevant and Brenda Stoltzfus, *Let the Good Times Roll: Prostitution and the U.S. Military in Asia* (New York: New Press, 1992); Katherine H. S. Moon, *Sex among Allies: Military Prostitution in U.S.-Korea Relations* (New York: Columbia University Press, 1997).

63. Koji Taira, "Ryukyu Islands Today: Political Economy of a U.S. Colony," *Science & Society* 22:2 (Spring 1958): 115–116; Takamine, *Shirarezaru Okinawa no Beihei*, 215.

64. Isa Chihiro, *Gyakuten* (Tokyo: Shinchosha, 1977), 31–32.

65. Molasky, *The American Occupation of Japan and Okinawa*, 56–63; Isa, *Gyakuten*, 31–32.

66. Takamine, *Shirarezaru Okinawa no Beihei*, 204–207; Cortright, *Soldiers in Revolt*, 205–206.

67. Takamine, *Shirarezaru Okinawa no Beihei*, 204–214; Touma Kensuke, "Okinawa no Kuroi Chikara," *Datsohei Tsushin* 4 (15 October 1969), in Beheiren, *Beheiren News Shuksatsu Ban*, 696. Also see *Beheiren News*, 1 February 1971, in ibid., 396, 400; Milton White, "Malcolm X in the Military," *Black Scholar* 1 (May 1970): 31–35.

68. Takamine, *Shirarezaru Okinawa no Beihei*, 259–260.

69. Ibid., 199.

70. Ibid., 161–164, 210; Appy, *Working-Class War*, 17–37; Terry, "Bringing the War Home."

71. *Demand for Freedom* 2 (16 November 1970), GI News/SCPC; Maria Damon, "Micropoetries," *XCP: Cross-Cultural Poetics* 15–16 (2005): 235.

72. Kelley, *Yo' Mama's DisFunktional!*, 25–26.

73. *Demand for Freedom* 2 (16 November 1970).

74. *Okinawa Times*, 7 February 1971 (my translation).

75. bell hooks, *Yearning: Race, Gender, and Cultural Politics* (Boston: South End, 1990), 76.

76. Devon W. Carbado, "Introduction: When and Where Black Men Enter," in Carbado, *Black Men on Race, Gender, and Sexuality*, 10. For key Black feminist texts that explore the intersection of race and gender, see, especially, Combahee River Collective, "The Combahee River Collective Statement," in Marable and Mullings, *Let Nobody Turn Us Around*, 524–529; Angela Davis, *Women, Race, and Class* (New York: Random House, 1981); bell hooks, *Feminist Theory: From Margin to Center* (Boston: South End, 1984); Patricia Hill Collins, *Black Feminist Thought: Knowledge, Consciousness, and the Politics of Empowerment* (New York: Routledge, 1990); Kimberlé Williams Crenshaw, "Mapping the Margins:

Intersectionality, Identity Politics, and Violence against Women of Color," in *Critical Race Theory: The Key Writings That Formed the Movement*, ed. Kimberlé Williams Crenshaw et al. (New York: New Press, 1995), 357–383; Brewer, "Black Radical Theory and Practice"; Rose M. Brewer, "Theorizing Race, Gender, and Class: The New Black Feminist Scholarship," in *Theorizing Black Feminisms: The Visionary Pragmatism of Black Women*, ed. Stanlie M. James and Abena P. A. Busia (New York: Routledge, 1993).

77. Enloe, *Maneuvers*, 49–152; Linda Isako Angst, "The Rape of a Schoolgirl: Discourses of Power and Gendered National Identity in Okinawa," in *Islands of Discontent: Okinawan Responses to Japanese and American Power*, ed. Laura Hein and Mark Selden (Lanham, MD: Rowman and Littlefield, 2003), 135–157; Huibin Amee Chew, "Why the War Is Sexist," *Z Magazine* 19:1 (January 2006), http://www.zcommunications.org/why-the-war-is-sexist-by-huibin-amee-chew; George Lipsitz, "Whiteness and War," in *The Possessive Investment in Whiteness* (Philadelphia: Temple University Press, 1998), 69–98.

78. Brewer, "Black Radical Theory and Practice."

79. Takamine, *Shirarezaru Okinawa no Beihei*, 215.

80. *Demand for Freedom* 2 (16 November 1970), GI News/SCPC.

81. Ibid.

82. Ibid.

83. Enloe, *Maneuvers*, 114.

84. Takamine, *Shirarezaru Okinawa no Beihei*, 220–222.

85. "Project Report," 19 September 1973, Carton 5, Folder 45, PCSMLOR.

86. Combahee River Collective, "The Combahee River Collective Statement," 525; Kelley, *Freedom Dreams*, 148–150.

87. "Funding Proposal for the Okinawa Women's House," 6 March 1973, Carton 5, Folder 23, PCSMLOR.

88. Sharon Danaan to Mark Amsterdam and Sheila Watson, 18 March 1974, Carton 5, Folder 22, PCSMLOR; for a brief biography of Sharon Danaan, see Takamine, *Shirarezaru Okinawa no Beihei*, 153–155.

89. Sharon Danaan to Sisters, 3 December (no year listed), Carton 5, Folder 3, PCSMLOR.

90. "Images of Women in Okinawa," Carton 5, Folder 45, PCSMLOR; Danaan to Sisters.

91. Combahee River Collective, "The Combahee River Collective Statement," 524.

92. Sharon Danaan, Lois, and Ellen to the National Lawyer's Guild and the Pacific Counseling Service, 16 October 1972, Carton 5, Folder 22, PCSMLOR.

93. Enloe, *Maneuvers*, 114.

94. Kelley, *Freedom Dreams*, 136.

95. Brewer, "Black Radical Theory and Practice."

96. Anne Shultes, "Still an Activist," *Intelligence*, 12 November 1992, Mary Bye Papers, Friends Historical Library, Swarthmore College; Takamine, *Shirarezaru Okinawa no Beihei*, 234–237.

97. U.S. Senate, Committee on Foreign Relations, *Okinawa Reversion Treaty*, 92nd Congress, 1st sess., on Ex. J. 92-1, 27–29 October 1971 (Washington, DC: U.S. Government Printing Office, 1971), 14.

98. Ibid., 1.

99. Damon, "Micropoetries"; Ralph Ellison, *Shadow and Act* (New York: Quality Paperback Club, 1994), 263; Franklin Rosemont, "Revolution by Night—Preface to *The Morning of the Machine Gun*," in *The Forecast Is Hot! Tracts and Other Collective Declarations of the Surrealist Movement in the United States, 1966–1976*, ed. Franklin Rosemont, Penelope Rosemont, and Paul Garon (Evanston, IL: Black Swan, 1997), 34.

NOTES TO THE CONCLUSION

1. Paul Gilroy, "Living Memory: A Meeting with Toni Morrison," in *Small Acts: Thoughts on the Politics of Black Cultures* (New York: Serpent's Tail, 1993), 181.

2. Stuart Hall, "Subjects in History: Making Diasporic Identities," in *The House That Race Built: Black Americans, U.S. Terrain*, ed. and introd. Wahneema Lubiano (New York: Pantheon Books, 1997), 299.

3. Ibid., 291, 299.

4. Saidiya Hartman, *Lose Your Mother: A Journey along the Atlantic Slave Route* (New York: Farrar, Straus and Giroux, 2007), 231.

# BIBLIOGRAPHY

## MANUSCRIPT COLLECTIONS

Bancroft Library, University of California, Berkeley
   Pacific Counseling Service and Military Law Office Records
Bentley Historical Library, University of Michigan
   Robert F. Williams Papers
Center for the Study of Cooperative Human Relations, Saitama University, Japan
   Yoshikawa Yuichi Papers
Friends Historical Library, Swarthmore College
   Mary Bye Papers
Swarthmore College Peace Collection, Swarthmore College
   CCCO/An Agency for Military and Draft Counseling
   GI News Periodical
   Pacific Counseling Service
   A Quaker Action Group Records
   Subject File: Conscription
Urban Archives, Temple University
   SANE—Greater Philadelphia Council Records

## NEWSPAPERS AND PERIODICALS

*Albion* (Kyoto, Japan)
*AMPO: A Report from the Japanese New Left*
*Asahi Shimbun*
*Black Scholar*
*Bulletin of Concerned Asian Scholars*
*Crisis*
*Crusader*
*Freedomways*
*Gendai to Shiso*
*Journal of Negro Education*
*Kobe Gaidai Ronso*
*Kobe Shimbun*
*Kokujin Kenkyu*

*Kokujin Kenkyu no Kai Kaiho*
*Manchuria Daily News*
*Messenger*
*New York Times*
*Okinawa Times*
*Osaka Mainichi Shimbun*
*Pacific Affairs*
*Race/Ethnicity: Multidisciplinary Global Perspectives*
*Sekai*
*Shin Okinawa Bungaku*
*Socialism and Democracy*
*State Hornet*
*Survey*
*Tokyo Nichi-Nichi Shimbun*
*Yes! A Journal of Positive Futures*
*Z Magazine*

BOOKS AND ARTICLES

Allen, Ernest, Jr. "The New Negro: Explorations in Identity and Social Consciousness, 1910–1922." In *1915, The Cultural Moment: The New Politics, the New Women,
the New Psychology, the New Art and the New Theatre in America*, edited by Adele
Heller and Lois Rudnick. New Brunswick: Rutgers University Press, 1991.

———. "Waiting for Tojo: The Pro-Japan Vigil of Black Missourians, 1932–1943." *Gateway Heritage* 15 (Fall 1995): 38–55.

———. "When Japan Was 'Champion of the Darker Races': Satokata Takahashi and the
Flowering of Black Messianic Nationalism." *Black Scholar* 24 (Winter 1994): 23–46.

Allen, Theodore W. *The Invention of the White Race*, vol. 1, *Racial Oppression and Social
Control*. New York: Verso, 1994.

———. *The Invention of the White Race*, vol. 2, *The Origin of Racial Oppression in Anglo-
America*. New York: Verso, 1997.

Angst, Linda Isako. "The Rape of a Schoolgirl: Discourses of Power and Gendered
National Identity in Okinawa." In *Islands of Discontent: Okinawan Responses to
Japanese and American Power*, edited by Laura Hein and Mark Selden. Lanham,
MD: Rowman and Littlefield, 2003.

Appiah, Anthony. "The Uncompleted Argument." In *W. E. B. Du Bois on Race and
Culture*, edited by Bernard W. Bell, Emily R. Grosholz, and James B. Stewart. New
York: Routledge, 1996.

Appy, Christian G. *Working-Class War: American Combat Soldiers and Vietnam*. Chapel Hill: University of North Carolina Press, 1993.

Aptheker, Herbert, ed. *A Documentary History of the Negro People in the United States,
1933–1945*. Secaucus, NJ: Citadel, 1974.

Arakawa Akira. *Han-kokka no kyoku*. Tokyo: Shakai Hyoron Sha, 1996.

———. *Okinawa: Togo to Hangyaku*. Tokyo: Chikuma Shobo, 2000.

Aydin, Cemil. *The Politics of Anti-Westernism in Asia: Visions of World Order in Pan-Islamic and Pan-Asian Thought*. New York: Columbia University Press, 2007.

Baker, Ella. "We Need Group-Centered Leadership." In *Let Nobody Turn Us Around: Voices of Resistance, Reform, and Renewal*, edited by Manning Marable and Leith Mullings. Lanham, MD: Rowman and Littlefield, 2000.

Baldwin, James. "The War Crimes Tribunal." *Freedomways* 7 (Winter 1967): 242–244.

Barnes, Kenneth C. "Inspiration from the East: Black Arkansans Look to Japan." *Arkansas Historical Quarterly* 69:3 (Autumn 2010): 203–217.

Beckmann George M., and Okubo Genji. *The Japanese Communist Party, 1922–1945*. Stanford: Stanford University Press, 1969.

Beheiren, ed. *Beheiren News Shuksatsu Ban, 1964–1974*. Tokyo: Beheiren <Betonamu ni heiwa wo!> Shimin Rengo, 1974.

———. *Shiryo: Beheiren Undo*. Vol. 2. Tokyo: Kawade Shobo Shinsha, 1974.

Benjamin, Walter. "The Task of the Translator: An Introduction to the Translation of Baudelaire's *Tableaux Parisiens*." In *Illuminations*, edited and with an introduction by Hannah Arendt and translated by Harry Zohn. New York: Schocken Books, 1968.

Boggs, Grace Lee. "The Beloved Community of Martin Luther King." *Yes! A Journal of Positive Futures* 29 (Spring 2004). http://www.yesmagazine.org/issues/a-conspiracy -of-hope/the-beloved-community-of-martin-luther-king (accessed 4 June 2010).

———. *Living for Change: An Autobiography*. Minneapolis: University of Minnesota Press, 1998.

Boggs, Grace Lee, with Scott Kurashige. *The Next American Revolution: Sustainable Activism for the Twenty-First Century*. Foreword by Danny Glober. Berkeley: University of California Press, 2011.

Bogues, Anthony. *Caliban's Freedom: The Early Political Thought of C. L. R. James*. London: Pluto, 1997.

Brewer, Rose M. "Black Radical Theory and Practice: Gender, Race, and Class." *Socialism and Democracy* 17:1 (2003). http://www.sdonline.org/33/ rose_m_brewer.htm (accessed 10 March 2011).

———. "Theorizing Race, Gender, and Class: The New Black Feminist Scholarship." In *Theorizing Black Feminisms: The Visionary Pragmatism of Black Women*, edited by Stanlie M. James and Abena P. A. Busia. New York: Routledge, 1993.

Buhle, Paul. *C. L. R. James: The Artist as Revolutionary*. New York: Verso, 1988.

Bunche, Ralph J. "The Programs of Organizations Devoted to the Improvement of the Status of the American Negro." *Journal of Negro Education* 8 (July 1939): 539–550.

Bundles, A'Lelia. *On Her Own Ground: The Life and Times of Madam C. J. Walker*. New York: Scribner, 2002.

Carbado, Devon W. "The Construction of O. J. Simpson as a Racial Victim." In *Black Men on Race, Gender, and Sexuality: A Critical Reader*, edited by Devon W. Carbado. New York: NYU Press, 1999.

———. "Introduction: When and Where Black Men Enter." In *Black Men on Race, Gender, and Sexuality: A Critical Reader*, edited by Devon W. Carbado. New York: NYU Press, 1999.

Carmichael, Stokely. "What We Want." In *Let Nobody Turn Us Around: Voices of Resistance, Reform, and Renewal*, edited by Manning Marable and Leith Mullings. Lanham, MD: Rowman and Littlefield, 2000.

Carmichael, Stokely, and Charles V. Hamilton. *Black Power: The Politics of Liberation*. New York: Vintage Books, 1992.

Césaire, Aimé. "Poetry and Knowledge." In *Refusal of the Shadow: Surrealism and the Caribbean*, translated by Michael Richardson and Krzysztof Fijalkowski. London: Verso, 1996.

Cha-Jua, Sundiata Keita. "C. L. R. James, Blackness, and the Making of a Neo-Marxist Diasporan Historiography." *Nature, Society & Thought* 11 (Spring 1998): 53–89.

Chew, Huibin Amee. "Why the War Is Sexist." *Z Magazine* 19:1 (January 2006). http://www.zcommunications.org/why-the-war-is-sexist-by-huibin-amee-chew.

Churchill, Ward. "'To Disrupt, Discredit and Destroy': The FBI's Secret War against the Black Panther Party." In *Liberation, Imagination, and the Black Panther Party*, edited by Kathleen Cleaver and George Katsiaficas. New York: Routledge, 2001.

Clarke, John Henrik. "The New Afro-American Nationalism." *Freedomways* 1:3 (Fall 1961): 285–289.

Collins, Patricia Hill. *Black Feminist Thought: Knowledge, Consciousness, and the Politics of Empowerment*. New York: Routledge, 1990.

Combahee River Collective. "The Combahee River Collective Statement." In *Let Nobody Turn Us Around: Voices of Resistance, Reform, and Renewal*, edited by Manning Marable and Leith Mullings. Lanham, MD: Rowman and Littlefield, 2000.

Contee, Clarence G. "Du Bois, the NAACP, and the Pan-African Congress of 1919." *Journal of Negro History* 57 (January 1972): 13–28.

Cortright, David. *Soldiers in Revolt: The American Military Today*. New York: Anchor, 1975.

Cox, Alvin D. "The Pacific War." In *The Cambridge History of Japan: The Twentieth Century*, vol. 6, edited by Peter Duus. New York: Cambridge University Press, 1999.

Crenshaw, Kimberlé Williams. "Mapping the Margins: Intersectionality, Identity Politics, and Violence against Women of Color." In *Critical Race Theory: The Key Writings That Formed the Movement*, edited by Kimberlé Williams Crenshaw et al. New York: New Press, 1995.

Damon, Maria. "Micropoetries." *XCP: Cross-Cultural Poetics* 15–16 (2005): 235.

Davis, Angela. "Reflections on Race, Class, and Gender in the USA." In *The Politics of Culture in the Shadow of Capital*, edited by Lisa Lowe and David Lloyd. Durham: Duke University Press, 1997.

———. *Women, Race, and Class*. New York: Random House, 1981.

DeCamp, Richard. "The GI Movement in Asia," *Bulletin of Concerned Asian Scholars* 4 (Winter 1972): 109–118.

Denning, Michael. *The Cultural Front: The Laboring of American Culture in the Twentieth Century*. New York: Verso, 1996.

Dower, John W. *Embracing Defeat: Japan in the Wake of World War II*. New York: Norton, 1999.

——. *War without Mercy: Race and Power in the Pacific War*. New York: Pantheon Books, 1986.

Duara, Prasenjit. *Sovereignty and Authenticity: Manchukuo and the East Asian Modern*. Lanham, MD: Rowman and Littlefield, 2003.

Du Bois, W. E. B. "Atlanta University." In *From Servitude to Service*. Boston: American Unitarian Association, 1905.

——. *Black Reconstruction: An Essay toward a History of the Part Which Black Folk Played in the Attempt to Reconstruct Democracy, 1860–1880*. New York: Atheneum, 1935.

——. "The Conservation of Races." In *W. E. B. Du Bois: A Reader*, edited by David Levering Lewis. New York: Holt, 1995.

——. *The Correspondence of W. E. B. Du Bois*. Edited by Herbert Aptheker. 3 vols. Amherst: University of Massachusetts Press, 1976.

——. *Dark Princess: A Romance*. 1928. Reprinted with introduction by Claudia Tate. Jackson: University of Mississippi Press, 1995.

——. *Darkwater: Voices from within the Veil*. New York: Harcourt, Brace, 1920. Reprint, New York: Dover, 1999.

——. *Dusk of Dawn: An Essay toward an Autobiography of a Race Concept*. In *Writings*. New York: Library of America, 1986.

——. *John Brown*. Edited and with an introduction by David Roediger. Philadelphia: G. W. Jacobs, 1909. Reprint, New York: Modern Library, 2001.

——. *The Negro*. New York: Holt, 1915. Reprint, Millwood, NY: Kraus-Thompson, 1975.

——. *Newspaper Columns by W. E. B. Du Bois*. Edited by Herbert Aptheker. 2 vols. White Plains, NY: Kraus-Thompson, 1986.

——. *The Souls of Black Folk*. In *Writings*. New York: Library of America, 1986.

——. "The Souls of White Folk." In *Black on White: Black Writers on What It Means to Be White*, edited with an introduction by David R. Roediger. New York: Schocken Books, 1998.

——. *W. E. B. Du Bois on Asia: Crossing the World Color Line*. Edited by Bill V. Mullen and Cathryn Watson. Jackson: University Press of Mississippi, 2005.

——. *The World and Africa: An Inquiry into the Part Which Africa Has Played in World History*. Enlarged edition. 1945. New York: International, 1996.

——. *Writings by W. E. B. Du Bois in Periodicals Edited by Others*. Edited by Herbert Aptheker. Millwood, NY: Kraus-Thompson, 1982.

Dudziak, Mary L. *Cold War Civil Rights: Race and the Image of American Democracy*. Princeton: Princeton University Press, 2000.

Eakes, Jan. *Senso no Kikai wo Tomero! Hansen Beihei to Nihonjin*. Translated and edited by Tsurumi Shunsuke. Tokyo: Sanichi Shobo, 1972.

Edwards, Brent Hayes. "Introduction: The 'Autonomy' of Black Radicalism." *Social Text* 19:2 (Summer 2001): 1–13.

——. "The Literary Ellington." In *Uptown Conversation: The New Jazz Studies*, edited by Robert G. O'Meally, Brent Hayes Edwards, and Farah Jasmine Griffin. New York: Columbia University Press, 2004.

Edwards, Brent Hayes. *The Practice of Diaspora: Literature, Translation, and the Rise of Black Internationalism*. Cambridge: Harvard University Press, 2003.

Eldridge, Robert D. *The Origins of the Bilateral Okinawa Problem: Okinawa in Postwar U.S.-Japan Relations, 1945–1952*. New York: Garland, 2001.

Ellison, Ralph. *Shadow and Act*. New York: Random House, 1964. Reprint, New York: Quality Paperback Book Club, 1994.

Enloe, Cynthia. *Maneuvers: The International Politics of Militarizing Women's Lives*. Berkeley: University of California Press, 2000.

Estes, Steve. *I Am a Man! Race, Manhood, and the Civil Rights Movement*. Chapel Hill: University of North Carolina Press, 2004.

Ferguson, Roderick A. "'W. E. B. Du Bois': Biography of a Discourse." In *Next to the Color Line: Gender, Sexuality, and W. E. B. Du Bois*, edited by Susan Gillman and Alys Eve Weinbaum. Minneapolis: University of Minnesota Press, 2007.

Foley, Barbara. *Spectres of 1919: Class and Nation in the Making of the New Negro*. Urbana: University of Illinois Press, 2003.

Foner, Philip S. *American Socialism and Black Americans: From the Age of Jackson to World War II*. Westport, CT: Greenwood, 1977.

———, ed. *Paul Robeson Speaks: Writings, Speeches, and Interviews, 1918–1974*. New York: Brunner/Mazel, 1978.

Fox, Stephen R. *The Guardian of Boston: William Monroe Trotter*. New York: Atheneum, 1970.

Francis, Richard. *Transcendental Utopias: Individual and Community at Brook Farm, Fruitlands, and Walden*. Ithaca: Cornell University Press, 1997.

Franklin, V. P. *Black Self-Determination: A Cultural History of African-American Resistance*. Foreword by Mary Frances Berry. Brooklyn, NY: Lawrence Hill Books, 1992.

———. *Living Our Stories, Telling Our Truths: Autobiography and the Making of the African-American Intellectual Tradition*. New York: Scribner, 1995.

Frazier, Franklin. *Black Bourgeoisie*. Glencoe, NY: Free Press, 1957.

"From the Editors." *Race/Ethnicity: Multidisciplinary Global Perspectives* 1:2 (Spring 2008): v–viii.

Fukugi Akira. "Koza: Gekihatsu suru Okinawa no Kokoro." *Sekai* (February 1970): 42–51.

Furukawa Hiromi. *Buratku he no Tabiji*. 3 vols. Osaka: Seseragi Shupan, 1995–1997.

———. "How I Came to Be a Founding Member of the Japan Black Studies Association (JBSA)." Speech delivered at the 54th Annual Meeting of the Japan Black Studies Association, Hiroshima Jogakuin University, Japan, 28 June 2008. Transcript in author's possession.

———. "Langston Hughes: *The Weary Blues* ni miru Negro Folks no 'warai' to 'namida' no so ni tsuite (1)." *Kokujin Kenkyu* 10 (December 1959): 1–14.

———. "Langston Hughes: *The Weary Blues* ni miru Negro Folks no 'warai' to 'namida' no so ni tsuite (2)." *Kokujin Kenkyu* 11 (February 1960): 1–12.

———. "Langston Hughes: *The Weary Blues* ni miru Negro Folks no 'warai' to 'namida' no so ni tsuite (3)." *Kokujin Kenkyu* 12 (May 1960): 16–22.

———. "Soritsu yonjushunen ni mukete: Kaigan to kadai." *Kokujin Kenkyu* 63 (1993): 1–2.

Furukawa Hiromi, and Furukawa Tetsushi. *Nihonjin to Afurikakei Amerikajin: Nichibei Kankeishi ni okeru sono Shoso.* Tokyo: Akashi Shoten, 2004.

Gabe Masao. "Rokujyunendai Fukkikyo Undo no Tenkai." In *Sengo Okinawa no Seiji to Ho, 1945–72,* edited by Seigen Miyazato. Tokyo: Tokyo Daigaku Shupan Kai, 1975.

Gaines, Kevin K. *American Africans in Ghana: Black Expatriates and the Civil Rights Era.* Chapel Hill: University of North Carolina Press, 2006.

———. *Uplifting the Race: Black Leadership, Politics, and Culture in the Twentieth Century.* Chapel Hill: University of North Carolina Press, 1996.

Gallicchio, Marc. *The African American Encounter with Japan and China: Black Internationalism in Asia, 1895–1945.* Chapel Hill: University of North Carolina Press, 2000.

Gerteis, Christopher. "Subjectivity Lost: Labor and the Cold War in Occupied Japan." In *Labor's Cold War: Labor Politics in a Global Context,* edited by Shelton Stromquist. Urbana: University of Illinois Press, 2008.

Gill, Gerald. "Black Soldiers' Perspectives on the War." In *The Vietnam Reader,* edited by Walter Capps. New York: Routledge, 1991.

Gilroy, Paul. *The Black Atlantic: Modernity and Double Consciousness.* Cambridge: Harvard University Press, 1993.

———. *Small Acts: Thoughts on the Politics of Black Cultures.* New York: Serpent's Tail, 1993.

Gooding-Williams, Robert. "Outlaw, Appiah, and Du Bois's 'The Conservation of Races.'" In *W. E. B. Du Bois on Race and Culture,* edited by Bernard W. Bell, Emily R. Grosholz, and James B. Stewart. New York: Routledge, 1996.

Gore, Dayo F. *Radicalism at the Crossroads: African American Women Activists in the Cold War.* New York: NYU Press, 2011.

Graham, Herman, III. *The Brothers' Vietnam War: Black Power, Manhood, and the Military Experience.* Gainesville: University Press of Florida, 2003.

Hall, Stuart. "Subjects in History: Making Diasporic Identities." In *The House That Race Built: Black Americans, U.S. Terrain,* edited and with an introduction by Wahneema Lubiano. New York: Pantheon Books, 1997.

Hansberry, Lorraine. *A Raisin in the Sun: A Drama in Three Acts.* New York: Random House, 1959.

Harootunian, Harry. *Overcome by Modernity: History, Culture, and Community in Interwar Japan.* Princeton: Princeton University Press, 2000.

Harris, Cheryl I. "Whiteness as Property." *Harvard Law Review* 106 (June 1993): 1707–1791.

Harris, Joel Chandler. *Uncle Remus.* New York: Schocken Books, 1965. First published 1881.

Harrison, Hubert. *A Hubert Harrison Reader.* Edited by Jeffrey B. Perry. Middletown, CT: Wesleyan University Press, 2001.

Hartigan, Royal, with Fred Ho. "The American Drum Set: Black Musicians and

Chinese Opera along the Mississippi River." In *Afro Asia: Revolutionary Political and Cultural Connections between African Americans and Asian Americans*, edited by Fred Ho and Bill V. Mullen. Durham: Duke University Press, 2008.

Hartman, Saidiya. *Lose Your Mother: A Journey along the Atlantic Slave Route*. New York: Farrar, Straus and Giroux, 2007.

Hata, Ikuhiko. "Continental Expansion, 1905–1941." Translated by Alvin D. Cox. In *The Cambridge History of Japan*, vol. 6, edited by Peter Duus. New York: Cambridge University Press, 1988.

Havens, Thomas R. H. *Fire across the Sea: The Vietnam War and Japan, 1965–1975*. Princeton: Princeton University Press, 1987.

Haywood, Harry. *Black Bolshevik: Autobiography of an Afro-American Communist*. Chicago: Liberator, 1978.

Hill, Robert A., ed. *The Crusader*. 6 vols. New York: Garland, 1987.

———. "Introduction: Racial and Radical: Cyril V. Briggs, The CRUSADER Magazine, and the African Blood Brotherhood, 1918–1922." In *The Crusader*, vol. 1, edited by Robert A. Hill. New York: Garland, 1987.

———, ed. *The Marcus Garvey and Universal Negro Improvement Association Papers*. Vol. 1. Berkeley: University of California Press, 1983.

Ho, Fred, and Bill V. Mullen, eds. *Afro Asia: Revolutionary Political and Cultural Connections between African Americans and Asian Americans*. Durham: Duke University Press, 2008.

Holt, Thomas C. "The Political Uses of Alienation: W. E. B. Du Bois on Politics, Race and Culture, 1903–1940." *American Quarterly* 42:2 (June 1990): 301–323.

hooks, bell. *Feminist Theory: From Margin to Center*. Boston: South End, 1984.

———. *Yearning: Race, Gender, and Cultural Politics*. Boston: South End, 1990.

Horne, Gerald. *Black Liberation/Red Scare: Ben Davis and the Communist Party*. Newark: University of Delaware Press, 1994.

———. *Communist Front? The Civil Rights Congress, 1946–1956*. Rutherford, NJ: Fairleigh Dickinson University Press,1988.

———. *Race War! White Supremacy and the Japanese Attack on the British Empire*. New York: NYU Press, 2004.

Hotta, Eri. *Pan-Asianism and Japan's War, 1931–1945*. New York: Palgrave Macmillan, 2007.

Howard-Pitney, David, ed. *Martin Luther King Jr., Malcolm X, and the Civil Rights Struggle of the 1950s and 1960s: A Brief History with Documents*. Boston: Bedford / St. Martin's, 2004.

Hughes, Langston. *The Weary Blues*. New York: Knopf, 1926.

Inafuku Masatoshi. "Okinawa ni okeru 'Beihei Aite Tokuingai' no Shakaigaku Teki Kosatsu." Unpublished senior thesis, Okinawa International University, 1992.

Iriye, Akira. *After Imperialism: The Search for a New Order in the Far East, 1921–1931*. Cambridge: Harvard University Press, 1965.

Isa Chihiro. *Enjo*. Tokyo: Bungei Shunju, 1986.

———. *Gyakuten*. Tokyo: Shinchosha, 1977.

James, C. L. R. *C. L. R. James on the "Negro Question."* Edited with an introduction by
Scott McLemee. Jackson: University Press of Mississippi, 1996.

———. *A New Notion: Two Works by C. L. R. James.* Edited and with an introduction by
Noel Ignatiev. Oakland, CA: PM Press, 2010.

James, Winston. *Holding Aloft the Banner of Ethiopia: Caribbean Radicalism in Early
Twentieth-Century America.* New York: Verso, 1998.

Johnson, Chalmers. *Blowback: The Costs and Consequences of American Empire.* New
York: Metropolitan Books, 2000.

———, ed. *Okinawa: Cold War Island.* Cardiff, UK: Japan Policy Research Institute,
1999.

Johnson, James Weldon. *The Book of American Negro Poetry.* New York: Harcourt,
Brace, 1958.

Joseph, Peniel E. *Waiting 'Til the Midnight Hour: A Narrative History of Black Power in
America.* New York: Holt, 2006.

Kaplan, Amy. *The Anarchy of Empire in the Making of American Culture.* Cambridge:
Harvard University Press, 2002.

Katsiaficas, George. *The Imagination of the New Left: A Global Analysis of 1968.* Boston:
South End, 1987.

Kearney, Reginald. *African American Views of the Japanese: Solidarity or Sedition?*
Albany: SUNY Press, 1998.

Kelley, Robin D. G. *Freedom Dreams: The Black Radical Imagination.* Boston: Beacon,
2002.

———. Introduction to *A History of Pan-African Revolt,* by C. L. R. James. Chicago:
Kerr, 1995.

———. *Yo' Mama's DisFunktional! Fighting the Culture Wars in Urban America.* Boston:
Beacon, 1997.

Killens, John Oliver. *And Then We Heard the Thunder.* New York: Knopf, 1963.

Kim, David Haekwon. "The Meaning of Her Majesty's Madness: *Dark Princess* and
Afro-Asian Anarchy." Unpublished paper, 2002.

King, Martin Luther, Jr. "A Time to Break Silence." *Freedomways* 7 (Spring 1967):
103–117.

———. *Where Do We Go from Here: Chaos or Community?* Foreword by Coretta Scott
King and introduction by Vincent Harding. Boston: Beacon, 2010.

Klein, Thomas M. "The Ryukyu on the Eve of Reversion." *Pacific Affairs* 45 (Spring
1972): 1–20.

Kokujin Kenkyu no Kai, ed. *Amerika Kokujin Kaiho Undo: AtarashiNiguro Gunzo.*
Tokyo: Miraisha, 1966.

Komunyakaa, Yusef. "Langston Hughes + Poetry = The Blues." *Callaloo* 25:4 (2002):
1140–1143.

Konishi Tomoshichi. "Kokujin eigo no kenkyu he." *Kokujin Kenkyu* 54 (December
1984): 5–6.

Koshiro, Yukiko. "Beyond an Alliance of Color: The African American Impact on
Modern Japan." *positions: east asia cultures critique* 11 (Spring 2003): 183–215.

"Koza Uprising." *AMPO: A Report from the Japanese New Left* 7–8 (1971): 1–5.

Kuenz, Jane. "The Face of America: Performing Race and Nation in Jessie Fauset's *There Is Confusion*." *Yale Journal of Criticism* 12 (Spring 1999): 89–111.

LaFeber, Walter. *The Clash: A History of U.S.-Japan Relations*. New York: Norton, 1997.

Lauren, Paul Gordon. *Power and Prejudice: The Politics and Diplomacy of Racial Discrimination*. Boulder, CO: Westview, 1998.

Lee, Li-Young. *The Winged Seed: A Remembrance*. New York: Simon and Schuster, 1995.

Levine, Lawrence W. *Black Culture and Black Consciousness: Afro-American Folk Thought from Slavery to Freedom*. New York: Oxford University Press, 1977.

Lewis, David Levering. *W. E. B. Du Bois: The Biography of Race, 1868–1919*. New York: Holt, 1993.

———. *W. E. B. Du Bois: The Fight for Equality and the American Century, 1919–1963*. New York: Holt, 2000.

Lipsitz, George. *American Studies in a Moment of Danger*. Minneapolis: University of Minnesota Press, 2001.

———. "'Frantic to Join . . . the Japanese Army': The Asia Pacific War in the Lives of African American Soldiers and Civilians." In *The Politics of Culture in the Shadow of Capital*, edited by Lisa Lowe and David Lloyd. Durham: Duke University Press, 1997.

———. *The Possessive Investment in Whiteness: How White People Profit from Identity Politics*. Philadelphia: Temple University Press, 1998.

Lubiano, Wahneema. "Mapping the Interstices between Afro-American Cultural Discourse and Cultural Studies: A Prolegomenon." *Callaloo* 19:1 (Winter 1996): 68–77.

Lynd, Staughton. "The First New Left . . . and the Third." In *Living inside Our Hope: A Steadfast Radical's Thoughts on Rebuilding the Movement*. Ithaca, NY: ILR, 1997.

Lynd, Staughton, with Alice Lynd. "Liberation Theology for Quakers." In *Living inside Our Hope: A Steadfast Radical's Thoughts on Rebuilding the Movement*. Ithaca, NY: ILR, 1997.

Mabille, Pierre. "The Marvelous—Basis of a Free Society." *Race Traitor* 9 (Summer 1998): 40–41.

Macmillan, Margaret. *Paris 1919: Six Months That Changed the World*. New York: Random House, 2001.

Makalani, Minkah. "For the Liberation of Black People Everywhere: The African Blood Brotherhood, Black Radicalism, and Pan-African Liberation in the New Negro Movement, 1917–1936." Ph.D. dissertation, University of Illinois at Urbana-Champaign, 2004.

———. *In the Cause of Freedom: Radical Black Internationalism from Harlem to London, 1917–1939*. Chapel Hill: University of North Carolina Press, 2011.

Marable, Manning. "The Pan-Africanism of W. E. B. Du Bois." In *W. E. B. Du Bois on Race and Culture: Philosophy, Politics, and Poetics*, edited by Bernard W. Bell, Emily Grosholz, and James B. Stewart. New York: Routledge, 1996.

———. *W. E. B. Du Bois: Black Radical Democrat*. Boston: Twayne, 1986.

Marcuse, Herbert. "The Foundations of Historical Materialism." In *Studies in Critical Philosophy*, translated by J. de Bres. London: New Left Books, 1972.

Marx, Karl. *Economic and Philosophic Manuscripts of 1844*. In *The Marx-Engels Reader*, edited by Robert C. Tucker. New York: Norton, 1978.

Mayfield, Julian. "Challenge to Negro Leadership." In *The Nonconformers*, edited by David Evanier and Stanley Silverzweig. New York: Ballantine Books, 1961.

———. "The Cuban Challenge." *Freedomways* 1:2 (1961): 185–189.

McDowell, Deborah E. "The Neglected Dimension of Jessie Redmond Fauset." *Afro-Americans in New York Life and History* 5 (July 1981): 33–49.

Mills, Charles W. *Blackness Visible: Essays on Philosophy and Race*. Ithaca: Cornell University Press, 1998.

———. *The Racial Contract*. Ithaca: Cornell University Press, 1997.

Miwa Yasushi. "1950-nendai no sakuru undo to rodosha ishiki." In *Sengo Shakai Undo-shi Ron*, edited by Hirokawa Tadahide and Yamada Tako. Tokyo: Otsuki Shoten, 2006.

Molasky, Michael. *The American Occupation of Japan and Okinawa*. London: Routledge, 1999.

———. "Arakawa Akira: The Thought and Poetry of an Iconoclast." In *Japan and Okinawa: Structure and Subjectivity*, edited by Glenn D. Hook and Richard Siddle. London: RoutledgeCurzon, 2003.

Monson, Ingrid. *Freedom Sounds: Civil Rights Call Out to Jazz and Africa*. New York: Oxford University Press, 2007.

Moon, Katherine H. S. *Sex among Allies: Military Prostitution in U.S.-Korea Relations*. New York: Columbia University Press, 1997.

Morrison, Toni. "Home." In *The House That Race Built: Black Americans, U.S. Terrain*, edited and with an introduction by Wahneema Lubiano. New York: Pantheon Books, 1997.

Moser, Richard R. *The New Winter Soldiers: GI and Veteran Dissent during the Vietnam Era*. New Brunswick: Rutgers University Press, 1996.

Mullen, Bill V. *Afro-Orientalism*. Minneapolis: University of Minnesota Press, 2004.

Naison, Mark. *Communists in Harlem during the Depression*. New York: Grove, 1983.

Nakajima Yoriko. "King Bokushi to Malcolm X ni tsuite." *Kokujin Kenkyu* 63 (1993): 18–20.

———. *Kokujin no Seijisanka to Daisanseiki America no Shupatsu*. Tokyo: Chuo Daigaku Shutpan, 1989.

Nakano Yoshio. "Atarashi Tatakai no Hajimari." *Sekai* (December 1969): 48–50.

Narita Ryuichi. "1950-nendai: 'Sakuru undo' no jidai heno danpen." *Bungaku* 5:6 (2004): 114–115.

Nelson, Bruce. *Divided We Stand: American Workers and the Struggle for Black Equality*. Princeton: Princeton University Press, 2001.

Nelson, Dana. *National Manhood: Capitalist Citizenship and the Imagined Fraternity of White Men*. Durham: Duke University Press, 1998.

New York State Legislature. *Revolutionary Radicalism: A Report of the Joint Legislative*

*Committee of New York Investigating Seditious Activities.* Vol. 2. Albany, NY: J. B. Lyon, 1920.

Noble, David W. *Death of a Nation: American Culture and the End of Exceptionalism.* Minneapolis: University of Minnesota Press, 2002.

Nukina Yoshitaka. "1808-nen to 1960-nen: Kindaika to Hishisoka no dento." *Kokujin Kenkyu no Kai: Kaiho* 18 (1960): 1.

———. "Abolitionist wo megute (1)." *Kobe Gaidai Ronso* 1 (December 1949): 1–15.

———. "Abolitionist wo megute (2)." *Kobe Gaidai Ronso* 2 (March 1951): 31–38.

———. "Concord no Thoreau, Part I," *Albion* 7:4 (December 1940): 299–313

———. "Concord no Thoreau, Part II." *Albion* 7:5 (July 1941): 391–400.

———. " 'Kokujin kenkyu no kai' no koto." *Gendai to Shiso* 25 (September 1976): 102–108.

———. " 'Negro' to 'Seiji.' " *Kokujin Kenkyu* 22 (June 1964): 41–44.

Oda Makoto. *"Beheiren" Kaikoroku de nai Kaiko.* Tokyo: Daisan Shokan, 1995.

Oguma Eiji. *"Minsyu" to "Aikoku": Sengo Nihon no Nationalism to Kokyosei.* Tokyo: Shinyosha, 2002.

———. *<Nihonjin> no Kyokai: Okinawa, Ainu, Taiwan, Chosen, Shokuminchi Shihai kara Fukki Undo made.* Tokyo: Shinyosha, 1998.

Okinawa-shi Heiwa Bunka Shikou Ka, ed. *Beikoku ga mita Koza bodo.* Okinawa: Okinawa City Hall, 1999.

Oshima Yoshio, and Miyamoto Masao. *Hantaisei Esperanto Undo-shi.* Tokyo: Sanseido, 1974.

Outlaw, Lucius. " 'Conserve' Races? In Defense of W. E. B. Du Bois." In *W. E. B. Du Bois on Race and Culture,* edited by Bernard W. Bell, Emily R. Grosholz, and James B. Stewart. New York: Routledge, 1996.

Patterson, William L. " 'Demagogic' Democracy and Racist Practices (1)." *Kokujin Kenkyu* 6 (December 1958): 4–9.

———. " 'Demagogic' Democracy and Racist Practices (2)," *Kokujin Kenkyu* 7 (February 1959): 11–16.

Perry, Jeffrey B. *Hubert Harrison: The Voice of Harlem Radicalism, 1883–1918.* New York: Columbia University Press, 2009.

Perry, Matthew C. *The Japan Expedition, 1852–1854: The Personal Journal of Commodore Matthew C. Perry.* Edited by Roger Pineau. Washington, DC: Smithsonian Institute Press, 1968.

Porter, Eric. *What Is This Thing Called Jazz? African American Musicians as Artists, Critics, and Activists.* Berkeley: University of California Press, 2002.

Prashad, Vijay. "Bandung Is Done: Passages in AfroAsian Epistemology." In *AfroAsian Encounters: Culture, History, Politics,* edited by Heike Raphael-Hernandez and Shannon Steen. New York: NYU Press, 2006.

———. *Everybody Was Kung-Fu Fighting: Afro-Asian Connections and the Myth of Cultural Purity.* Boston: Beacon, 2001.

Preble, George Henry. *The Opening of Japan: A Diary of Discovery in the Far East, 1853–1856.* Edited by Boleslaw Szczesniak. Norman: University of Oklahoma Press, 1962.

Pulido, Laura. *Black, Brown, Yellow, and Left: Radical Activism in Los Angeles*. Berkeley: University of California Press, 2006.

Quan, H. L. T. "Geniuses of Resistance: Feminist Consciousness and the Black Radical Tradition." *Race & Class* 47:2 (2005): 39–53.

Rich, Adrienne. "Social Practice." *XCP: Cross Cultural Poetics* 15–16 (2005): 262.

Rief, Michelle. "Thinking Locally, Acting Globally: The International Agenda of Black American Clubwomen, 1880–1940." *Journal of African American History* 89 (Summer 2004): 215–216.

Robinson, Cedric J. *Black Marxism: The Making of the Black Radical Tradition*. Foreword by Robin D. G. Kelley and with a new preface by the author. Chapel Hill: University of North Carolina Press, 2000.

Roediger, David R. "Carry It On: Du Bois's *Black Reconstruction* in the New Millennium." In *History against Misery*. Chicago: Charles H. Kerr, 2006.

———. *Colored White: Transcending the Racial Past*. Berkeley: University of California Press, 2002.

———. "Du Bois, Race, and Italian Americans." In *Are Italians White? How Race Is Made in America*, edited by Jennifer Guglielmo and Salvatore Salerno. New York: Routledge, 2003.

———. "Emancipation: The Biggest Story in U.S. Labor History." In *History against Misery*. Chicago: Charles H. Kerr, 2006.

———. *History against Misery*. Chicago: Charles H. Kerr, 2006.

———. *How Race Survived U.S. History: From Settlement and Slavery to the Obama Phenomenon*. New York: Verso, 2008.

———. "A Reply to Eric Kaufmann." *Ethnicities* 6:2 (2006): 254–262.

———. *Towards the Abolition of Whiteness: Essays on Race, Politics, and Working-Class History*. New York: Verso, 1994.

———. *The Wages of Whiteness: Race and the Making of the American Working Class*. Rev. ed. New York: Verso, 1999.

———. *Working toward Whiteness: How America's Immigrants Became White*. New York: Basic Books, 2005.

Rosemont, Franklin. "Revolution by Night—Preface to *The Morning of the Machine Gun*." In *The Forecast Is Hot! Tracts and Other Collective Declarations of the Surrealist Movement in the United States, 1966–1976*, edited by Franklin Rosemont, Penelope Rosemont, and Paul Garon. Evanston, IL: Black Swan, 1997.

Rubio, Philip F. *A History of Affirmative Action, 1619–2000*. Jackson: University Press of Mississippi, 2001.

Saul, Scott. *Freedom Is, Freedom Ain't: Jazz and the Making of the Sixties*. Cambridge: Harvard University Press, 2003.

Scott, Daryl. " 'Immigrant Indigestion': A. Philip Randolph: Radical and Restrictionist." Center for Immigration Studies. June 1999. http://cis.org/AfricanAmerican AttitudesImmigration-APhilipRandolph.

Scott, David. *Conscripts of Modernity: The Tragedy of Colonial Enlightenment*. Durham: Duke University Press, 2004.

Scott, David. *Refashioning Futures: Criticism after Postcoloniality.* Princeton: Princeton University Press, 1999.

Sekiya Shigeru, and Sakamoto Yoshie, ed. *Tonarini Dasohei ga ita Jidai: JATEC, Aru Shimin Undo no Kiroku.* Tokyo: Shiso no Kagakusha, 1998.

Shapiro, Herbert. "The Vietnam War and the American Civil Rights Movement." *Journal of Ethnic Studies* 16 (Winter 1989): 117–141.

Shimazu, Naoko. *Japan, Race and Equality: The Racial Equality Proposal of 1919.* London: Routledge, 1998.

Shinoda Toru. "'Kigyobetsu Kumiai wo Chushin to shita Minshu Kumiai' to wa, Part I." *Ohara Shakai Mondai Kenkyujo Zatshi* 564 (November 2005): 1–16.

———. "'Kigyobetsu Kumiai wo Chushin to shita Minshu Kumiai' to wa, Part II." *Ohara Shakai Mondai Kenkyujo Zatshi* 565 (December 2005): 13–31.

Shiso no Kagaku Kenkyu Kai, ed. *Kyodo Kenkyu Shudan: Sakuru no Sengo Shiso-shi.* Tokyo: Heibonsha, 1976.

Singh, Nikhil Pal. *Black Is a Country: Race and the Unfinished Struggle for Democracy.* Cambridge: Harvard University Press, 2004.

Sitkoff, Harvard. *A New Deal for Blacks: The Emergence of Civil Rights as a National Issue.* New York: Oxford University Press, 1978.

Smith, Natalye. "I Still Sing We Shall Overcome." *State Hornet,* 17 October 2007. http://www.statehornet.com/2.4409/i-still-sing-we-shall-overcome-1.562132 (accessed on June 9, 2010)

Solomon, Mark. *The Cry Was Unity: Communists and African Americans, 1917–1936.* Jackson: University Press of Mississippi, 1998.

Spence, Jonathan D. *The Gate of Heavenly Peace: The Chinese and Their Revolution, 1895–1980.* New York: Penguin Books, 1981.

Stuckey, Sterling. "'Ironic Tenacity': Frederick Douglass's Seizure of the Dialectic." In *Going through the Storm: The Influence of African Art in History.* New York: Oxford University Press, 1994.

———. "'I Want to Be African': Paul Robeson and the Ends of Nationalist Theory and Practice, 1914–1945." *Massachusetts Review* 17:1 (Spring 1976): 81–137.

———. *Slave Culture: Nationalist Theory and the Foundations of Black America.* New York: Oxford University Press, 1987.

Sturdevant, Saundra Pollock, and Brenda Stoltzfus. *Let the Good Times Roll: Prostitution and the U.S. Military in Asia.* New York: New Press, 1992.

Taira, Koji. "Ryukyu Islands Today: Political Economy of a U.S. Colony." *Science & Society* 22:2 (Spring 1958): 113–128.

Takamine Tomokazu. *Shirarezaru Okinawa no Beihei.* Tokyo: Kobunken, 1984.

Tanji, Miyume. "The Enduring Myth of an Okinawan Struggle: The History and Trajectory of a Diverse Community of Protest." Ph.D. dissertation, Murdoch University, 2003.

———. *Myth, Protest and Struggle in Okinawa.* London: RoutledgeCurzon, 2006.

Taylor, Ula Y. "Intellectual Pan-African Feminists: Amy Ashwood-Garvey and Amy

Jacques-Garvey." In *Time Longer than Rope: A Century of Black American Activism, 1850–1950*, edited by Charles M. Payne and Adam Green. New York: NYU Press, 2003.

———. "'Negro Women Are Great Thinkers as Well as Doers': Amy Jacques-Garvey and Community Feminism in the United States, 1924–1927." *Journal of Women's History* 12 (Summer 2000): 104–126.

———. *The Veiled Garvey: The Life and Times of Amy Jacques-Garvey*. Chapel Hill: University of North Carolina Press, 2002.

Terry, Wallace, II. "Bringing the War Home." *Black Scholar* 2 (November 1970): 6–18.

Trotter, Joe William. "From a Raw Deal to a New Deal." In *To Make Our World Anew: A History of African Americans*, edited by Earl Lewis and Robin D. G. Kelley. New York: Oxford University Press, 2000.

Tsurumi Yoshiyuki. "Beheiren: A New Force on the Left." *AMPO: A Report from the Japanese New Left* 1 (1969): 5, 8.

Tucker, David Vance. "Building 'Our Manchukuo': Japanese City Planning, Architecture, and Nation-Building in Occupied Northeast China, 1931–1945." Ph.D. dissertation, University of Iowa, 1999.

Tyson, Timothy B. *Radio Free Dixie: Robert F. Williams and the Roots of Black Power*. Chapel Hill: University of North Carolina Press, 1999.

Ueunten, Wesley Iwao. "Rising Up from a Sea of Discontent: The 1970 Koza Uprising in U.S.-Occupied Okinawa." In *Militarized Currents: Toward a Decolonized Future in Asia and the Pacific*, edited by Setsu Shigematsu and Keith L. Camacho. Minneapolis: University of Minnesota Press, 2010.

U.S. Department of Labor, Office of Planning and Research. *The Negro Family: The Case for National Action*. Westport, CT: Greenwood, 1981.

U.S. Senate, Committee on Foreign Relations. *Okinawa Reversion Treaty*. 92nd Congress, 1st sess. On Ex. J. 92-1. 27–29 October 1971. Washington, DC: U.S. Government Printing Office, 1971.

Von Eschen, Penny M. *Race against Empire: Black Americans and Anticolonialism, 1937–1957*. Ithaca: Cornell University Press, 1997.

Weinbaum, Alys Eve. "Interracial Romance and Black Internationalism." In *Next to the Color Line: Gender, Sexuality, and W. E. B. Du Bois*, edited by Susan Gillman and Alys Eve Weinbaum. Minneapolis: University of Minnesota Press, 2007.

———. "Reproducing Racial Globality: W. E. B. Du Bois and the Sexual Politics of Black Internationalism." *Social Text* 19 (Summer 2001): 1–41.

Westheider, James. *Fighting on Two Fronts: African Americans and the Vietnam War*. New York: NYU Press, 1997.

White, Milton. "Malcolm X in the Military." *Black Scholar* 1 (May 1970): 31–35.

Widener, Daniel. "Seoul City Sue and the Bugout Blues: Black American Narratives of the Forgotten War." In *Afro Asia: Revolutionary Political and Cultural Connections between African Americans and Asian Americans*, edited by Fred Ho and Bill V. Mullen. Durham: Duke University Press, 2008.

Williams, Chad L. "Vanguards of the New Negro: African American Veterans and Post–World War I Racial Militancy." *Journal of African American History* 92:3 (Summer 2007): 347–370.

Williams, Robert F. *Negroes with Guns*. Edited by Marc Schleifer and introduction by John Henrik Clarke. Chicago: Third World, 1973.

Winant, Howard. *The World Is a Ghetto: Race and Democracy since World War II*. New York: Basic Books, 2001.

Woods, Clyde. *Development Arrested: The Blues and Plantation Power in the Mississippi Delta*. New York: Verso, 1998.

Worcester, Ken. *C. L. R. James: A Political Biography*. Albany: SUNY Press, 1996.

Yamamoto, Mari. *Grassroots Pacifism in Post-war Japan: The Rebirth of a Nation*. London: RoutledgeCurzon, 2004.

Yellin, Victor Fell. "Mrs. Belmont, Matthew Perry, and the 'Japanese Minstrels.'" *American Music* 14:3 (Fall 1996): 257–275.

Yuh, Ji-Yeon. *Beyond the Shadow of Camptown: Korean Military Brides in America*. New York: NYU Press, 2002.

*Page numbers in italics indicate illustrations.*

and, 26–29, 37–40, 45–46, 51, 53; anti-
imperialism and, 23, 28–29, 33, 38–40,
46–47, 50, 53; of Black intellectual-
activists, 6, 20–21, 28, 30, 37, 40–41, 52;
Black women's participation in, 33–37;
coalition work and, 48; core principles
of, 30; culture of liberation and, 21, 30,
49; disarmament dissenters in, 41–53;
Fifteenth Point in, 22–28; First World
War and, 19–21, 24, 34–37, 50; monitor-
ing of, 30–33; Paris Peace Conference
and, 28–41; pro-Japan provocation and,
19–53
*Nihon Minshushugi Bunka Renmei* (Japan
Democratic Culture League; *Bunren*),
109–10
*Nihon Puroretaria Bunka Renmei* (Japan
Proletarian Cultural Federation;
KOPF), 107, 109, 136
Nixon, Richard, 139, 154, *157*, 157–58
Noble, David W., 116
Nordic race, 75, 77–79
Nukina Yoshitaka: in *Amerika Kokujin
Kaiho Undo*, 122–23; in *Kokujin Kenkyu
no Kai*, 97–101, *99*, 105–11, 113–16, 122–
23, 136; "On Abolitionists" by, 101, 116;
in racial groove, 115

Obama, Barack, 143
Oda Makoto, 154–58, *157*
Okinawa: anticolonialism in, 152, 163, 176;
anti-imperialism in, 142, 149–50, 153–
54, 158, 162–63, 174, 176, 182; antiracism
in, 8–9, 149, 153, 165; Black liberation
in, 138–82; coalition work in, 142, 148,
153, 158–59, 161–62, 164, 166, 168, 174,
177, 180; creative process of identification and, 15; culture of liberation in,
9–11, 142–43, 155, 181, 184; Futenma Air
Station in, 143, 209n10; gender and,
174–78; internationalism in, 147, 153,
157; Kadena Air Base in, 139, 163, 166,
168, 173–74; *Kokujin Kenkyu no Kai*
and, 137; reversion of, 138–42, 144, 153,
158, 162, 165, 170–71, 174, 180–82, 184,
209n8; sexual politics in, 174–78; soul
pursued in, 142–53; spirit of insurgency

in, 6–7; U.S. in, 138–82; Vietnam War
and, 8–9, 139, 142, 148–53, 155–58,
*157*, 161, 163–64, 169, 171–72, 175, 181–
82; women in, 169, 174–82. *See also*
Black GIs
"On Abolitionists" (Nukina), 101, 116
Open Door policy, 41–42, 45
*Osaka Mainichi Shimbun* (Osaka Daily
Newspaper), 73–75
Owen, Chandler, 23, 26, 34, 46, 52;
pro-Japan provocation of, 21, 37–40;
race consciousness and, 37–40; Razafinkeriefo contrasted with, 44–45

Pacific Counseling Service (PCS), 159–61,
168, 178
Pacific Rim Coalition, 158
Pan-African Congress, 28
Pan-Africanism: in African Blood Broth-
erhood, 21, 34; pan-Asianism unity
with, 53, 74, 85
Pan-Asianism: of Japan, 2, 7, 52, 57, 73;
pan-Africanism unity with, 53, 74, 85
Paris Peace Conference: Japan's racial-
equality clause at, 24–28, 32, 37–39,
52; New Negro radicalism and, 28–
41; operating principles of, 28–29;
race consciousness at, 28–41; white
supremacy at, 22–28, 38
Passion, 70–71
Patterson, William L., 103–4
PCS. *See* Pacific Counseling Service
People's Educational Forum, 34–35
People's House, 149
Perry, Jeffrey B., 22–23, 29, 43
Perry, Matthew, 1–2, 189n1
Peterman, Sidney, 159–60
Philippine-American War, 152
*Pittsburgh Courier* columns, 3, 54–55, 71
Pogroms, 36–37, 39
Politics: coalition, 164–66; grassroots, 7,
30–31, 126, 141, 161; of identification,
antiracism and, 100; race and, 21, 29, 63,
83, 124. *See also* Gender politics; Sexual
politics
Popular Front, 8, 100, 105, 107, 109, 111,
113

## ABOUT THE AUTHOR

Yuichiro Onishi is Assistant Professor of African American & African Studies and Asian American Studies at the University of Minnesota, Twin Cities.